HOMEOWNER'S LEGAL GUIDE

OTHER RESOURCES FOR HOMEOWNERS FROM
CONSUMER REPORTS BOOKS:

The Mortgage Book
by John R. Dorfman
How to Buy a House, Condo, or Co-op
by Michael C. Thomsett
How to Sell Your House Condo Co-op
by Amy Sprecher Bly and Robert W. Bly

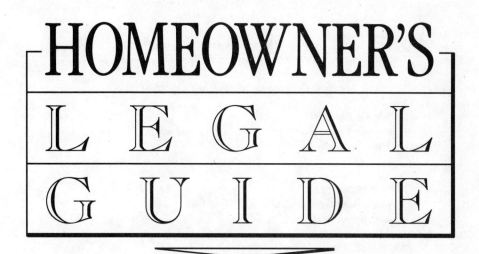

HOMEOWNER'S LEGAL GUIDE

Cynthia L. Cooper
and
the Editors of Consumer Reports Books

CONSUMER REPORTS BOOKS
A DIVISION OF CONSUMERS UNION
Yonkers, New York

MAY 1996

Copyright © 1993 by Cynthia L. Cooper
and Consumers Union of United States, Inc.,
Yonkers, New York 10703.

Published by Consumers Union of United States, Inc.,
Yonkers, New York 10703.

All rights reserved,
including the right of reproduction in whole or in part in any form.

Library of Congress Cataloging-in-Publication Data

Cooper, Cynthia L., 1950–
    Homeowner's legal guide / Cynthia L. Cooper and the editors of
Consumer Reports Books.
    p.   cm.
    Includes index.
    ISBN 0-89043-535-9
    1. Homeowners—Legal status, laws, etc.—United States.
I. Consumer Reports Books.   II. Title.
KF390.H53C66   1993
346.7304′3—dc20
[347.30643]   92-30781
                                                                CIP

Design by Ruth Kolbert
First printing, May 1993
Second printing, March 1994
Printed on recycled paper ♲
Manufactured in the United States of America

Homeowner's Legal Guide is a Consumer Reports Book published by Consumers Union, the nonprofit organization that publishes Consumer Reports, the monthly magazine of test reports, product Ratings, and buying guidance. Established in 1936, Consumers Union is chartered under the Not-For-Profit Corporation Law of the State of New York.

The purposes of Consumers Union, as stated in its charter, are to provide consumers with information and counsel on consumer goods and services, to give information on all matters relating to the expenditure of the family income, and to initiate and to cooperate with individual and group efforts seeking to create and maintain decent living standards.

Consumers Union derives its income solely from the sale of Consumer Reports and other publications. In addition, expenses of occasional public service efforts may be met, in part, by nonrestrictive, noncommercial contributions, grants, and fees. Consumers Union accepts no advertising or product samples and is not beholden in any way to any commercial interest. Its Ratings and reports are solely for the use of the readers of its publications. Neither the Ratings, nor the reports, nor any Consumers Union publication, including this book, may be used in advertising or for any commercial purpose. Consumers Union will take all steps open to it to prevent such uses of its material, its name, or the name of Consumer Reports.

ACKNOWLEDGMENTS

I wish to acknowledge the assistance of Marcus Alpert, Susan Carroll, Jennifer R. Clarke, Lory Frankel, Eric Wollman, and my agent, Carol Mann.

WITHDRAWN

MAY   1996

The information in this book reduces complex and confusing law to practical general strategies for the consumer. These strategies are meant to serve as helpful guidelines when you experience related problems. They are *not* intended to replace the services of an attorney. Laws vary considerably from state to state. In addition, each situation is different, and the particular facts of a case can have a significant bearing on how it should be approached. Homeowners with legal questions should contact a local attorney familiar with the subject matter involved.

CONTENTS

INTRODUCTION   *1*

1   *Documents Related to the Home*   *5*

2   *Defects Discovered After Purchase*   *24*

3   *Property Boundaries, Easements, and Encroachments*   *45*

4   *Zoning and Other Land Use Regulations*   *61*

5   *Repairs, Additions, and Construction*   *78*

6   *Hiring a Contractor*   *85*

7   *Injuries to Third Persons on the Property*   *103*

8   *Water, Air, and Earth Support*   *116*

9   *Trespassers, Unwanted Visitors, Intruders, and Security*   *139*

10   *Private and Public Nuisance*   *153*

11   *Taxes and Abatements*   *164*

12   *Financial Difficulties and the Home*   *181*

13   *Refinancing, Home Equity Loans, Prepayment, and Reversible Mortgage*   *203*

14   *Co-ownership, Personal Relations, and the Home*   *214*

15   *Environmental Contaminants Inside the Home*   *226*

16   *Takings of Private Property for Public Use*   *233*

17   Homeowner's Associations, Condominium Associations,
       and Cooperative Boards   246

18   Working at Home   269

19   Leasing a Portion of a Home   277

20   Selling the Home   296

21   The Legal Process and the Homeowner   307

     INDEX   334

Introduction

The United States has the highest percentage of home ownership of any nation in the world—64 percent of households. This adds up to over 50 million houses, valued at more than $6 trillion.

Buying a house is the largest expense most people will undertake. And the purchase price is only part of the picture—added to it is the cost of maintaining, rehabilitating, landscaping, decorating, and furnishing a residence, to say nothing of insurance, taxes, and assessments.

Protecting this investment requires knowing the rights and responsibilities of home ownership. Understanding the law can prevent problems with property use and management from turning into legal catastrophes. When problems arise, knowledgeable homeowners can often find less costly and stressful solutions than a lawsuit.

Property rights have always had a central place in American history. But the laws have expanded in scope and number. For example, in an effort to preserve community values, safety, health, and welfare, local zoning and private land use regulations define what homeowners can and cannot do to their property. These ordinances touch upon everything from the size of lots to the height of buildings, the type of plumbing pipes to the licensing of contractors.

At the same time, homeowners have traditionally not had the same protection as consumers of other products. Homes—considered unique—were set apart from laws covering mass-produced consumer items. Now, at last, the homeowner is beginning to be treated as a consumer and offered more protection in purchase and ownership. Warranties, required disclosures and inspections, insurance, and other tools can aid the home buyer.

Still, homeowners need to use vigilance and common sense—not only in the initial purchase, but in remodeling, contracting, buying products, and making decisions about their property.

Changes in other areas of the law also affect the homeowner. The cost of personal injuries and an increased awareness of legal responsibility for them have induced homeowners to pay attention to potentially dangerous conditions on their property. A more assertive attitude toward individual rights means that the proverbial fence between neighbors can become the subject of a serious dispute or even a lawsuit. Noises, smells, and intrusions are now a central concern. In some cases, homeowners have banded together in neighborhood associations for mutual benefit and have been able to assert community control over pollution, taxation, or unnecessary government regulation.

Today, homeowners can rarely escape legal issues affecting ownership. Familiarity with the law is no longer a luxury; it is a necessity.

Owning a home allows individuals to shape and control their environment, protect their privacy, and welcome—or eject—visitors. A home can provide comfort and financial security for the present and an investment for the future.

Along with these benefits come responsibilities to the community, taxing agencies, neighbors, the holders of easements, lenders, tenants, and homeowner's associations.

For example, homeowners pay property tax and assessments, including those for water, sewage, and waste removal. The maintenance and repair of sidewalks in front of the property often fall to them, even though the sidewalk is controlled by the city. They may be required to protect and trim trees on their property, cut the grass to a certain height, and eliminate weeds or overgrowth. In many cities, homeowners are required to dispose of garbage by separating cans, bottles, and other recyclables.

In an emergency or when necessity requires, homeowners must give access to fire fighters, emergency medical personnel, or police officers.

Property owners have obligations to neighbors when it comes to shared resources—air, water, and ground support. A homeowner is obligated to prevent mud from sliding onto a neighbor's property by installing grading or fill. In most places, the use of water in a stream is subject to a neighbor's use as well.

Property owners must abide by their property's boundaries. Fences or trees along boundaries must be jointly maintained. A homeowner cannot interfere with a neighbor's property by encroachments or trespass and cannot undertake activities that create annoying smells, noise, or pollution.

Homeowners have an obligation to prevent injuries to visitors on the property from dangerous conditions and even from minor hazards that could have been prevented. Homeowners may even need to ensure that visitors do not engage in activities that would put them or others at risk, such as serving alcohol to a guest who is already obviously intoxicated.

People who buy property in a subdivision, planned unit development, cooperative, condominium, and certain vacation com-

A homeowner has an obligation to prevent injuries to visitors on the property from dangerous conditions—even from minor hazards that could have been prevented.

munities must follow the covenants, conditions, and restrictions in the deed (CC&Rs), which are usually enforced by a homeowner's association. These rules can be extensive.

This book covers a variety of legal matters that affect homeowners—the assertion of rights and fulfillment of responsibilities by a homeowner, potential claims by a homeowner, and homeowners' defenses to the claims of others. It contains key information about the law, providing background and context, practical points, and useful tips.

But the book is *not* meant to replace the services of a lawyer. If a question of law arises, contact a lawyer familiar with the subject matter as soon as possible.

> *The law related to home ownership is not the same in every location. Consult a local lawyer to determine the law in your community.*

The law related to home ownership is not the same in every location. In this regard, the law is like a house. The structure, framework, and major systems of the law have universal similarities, just as each house has a structure, framework, and basic systems of plumbing and electricity. But as the features and trim vary in houses, so do the features of the law differ—whether they are the specific details of laws passed in local communities or the individualistic interpretation of rights and duties by state courts. On some matters, the law on property ownership differs from state to state; in others, from county to county, city to city, and even neighborhood to neighborhood.

This book provides general guidance and pragmatic direction. Homeowners faced with specific legal issues will need to determine the exact law or laws that apply in their locality.

Because homeowners have so much at stake, they need to be informed on legal matters. This book cuts through the thicket of legal issues likely to be encountered, so that you can enjoy your property to the fullest extent possible.

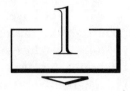

Documents
Related
to the Home

Centuries ago in England, the transfer of land was finalized when a fistful of earth was handed to the new owner. In modern times, that ritual has been replaced by the presentation of several folders full of documents, while a loan officer, lawyers, escrow officers, and other individuals hover in the background.

In amassing these documents—each of which could become important in a future legal dispute—homeowners mark the beginning of record keeping that will be important throughout their ownership of the home. In addition to documents, the homeowner should maintain other information: expenses, fees, financial information, the names and addresses of persons dealt with, and details of problems as they arise. (For tips on buying and financing a home, see *How to Buy a House, Condo, or Co-op* by Michael C. Thomsett, published by Consumer Reports Books.)

Of the many documents that might be involved in the sale of a home, some of the following could become important in a legal dispute:

Contract for Purchase   When the buyer makes a written offer, which is usually accompanied by an earnest money deposit, and the seller accepts it in writing, this document becomes the contract for purchase of the house. A contract to purchase a house must be in writing; an oral agreement is not binding. When the conditions of the purchase are completed—after title inspection, financing, and so on—the seller transfers the deed to the buyer and the terms and conditions of the contract for purchase are incorporated into the deed. Prior to a final contract, the parties often sign a *binder agreement,* which, along with a *deposit,* serves as an interim agreement. Keep copies of preliminary documents— the binder agreement and intermediate contract proposals— along with the final contract.

Escrow Agreement   In many states, after the purchase agreement is signed the buyer and seller engage an escrow agent who holds the earnest money in trust and facilitates the collection and recording of documents. The tasks to be performed by the escrow agent are contained in escrow instructions for both the buyer and the seller.

Deed   This is the written document that shows ownership of the property or the title to the property. It must be signed by the prior owner or owners of official record in order for it to be valid. The deed and claims against the title are recorded, usually at a county recorder's office.

The deed describes the property by its official plan or map (called a *plat*) or recorded description—for example, Jones Corner, Lot 14. It can also be described by boundaries (called *metes and bounds*) or a physical description of the terrain and distances between boundary points. In some cases, the new owner will also have a *legal description of property,* which gives the official property boundaries.

There are two common types of deeds. A *warranty deed* offers the most protection for the purchaser. In it, the seller warrants that the title is good—that the seller is, in fact, the true owner of the property, that there are no claims against the title, and that the seller has the right to sell the property.

A warranty deed does not give any type of warranty or guarantee about the condition of the property or of the house. The warranties pertain only to the legal soundness of the title, which is also verified by a title search and insured by title insurance.

> Without a legally valid deed, another individual could appear later, claim to be a prior owner of the property, and strip the most recent owner of all rights, even though that owner paid for the property. For this reason, a good deal of attention is given at the time of purchase toward verifying the deed.

A *quitclaim* deed does not contain any guarantees. With this type of deed, the seller is merely transferring the ownership interest that is in the seller's power, which could be none. The seller doesn't guarantee that there isn't another owner or that there aren't claims against the property. A quitclaim deed is sometimes used between relatives or is the means for one property owner to acquire the adverse claim of another property owner. It is a risky proposition for a purchase (see chapter 3).

Covenants   Conditions contained in a deed are known as covenants, and the purchaser is bound by them. Covenants can "run with the land" and, once inserted by an original landowner, can be requirements in every future deed. They may restrict the use of the property; for example, stating that the property shall never be used for a business purpose. Covenants that try to accomplish an illegal purpose are not enforceable, such as prohibiting the sale of the property to members of a particular religion or race, a practice forbidden by civil rights laws (see chapter 3).

Extensive covenants (sometimes known as CC&Rs—covenants, conditions, and restrictions) are common in new developments. They lay out rules and regulations that can specify everything from the height of trees to the number of vehicles that may be kept on the property. These covenants are enforceable and, when the deed is transferred, the buyer agrees to follow them (see chapter 17).

Easements and Licenses   Interests of ownership in the property by persons other than the title owner may be contained in formal easements and licenses. These are agreements by which others can use the property for a specified period of time—giving a neighbor the right of access to a lake, permitting a utility company to string wires, selling an oil company the right to dig a well (see chapter 3).

Lien and Lien Releases   A lien is a formal money claim posted against the property, stating that the property owner owes an enforceable debt to the person holding the lien. A *mechanic's lien* can be attached to the property by a contractor or supplier of building materials who has not been paid; a *tax lien,* by revenue authorities; a *judgment lien,* by people who have won a lawsuit against the property owner. Liens are encumbrances to the marketability of the property and must be settled, paid off, or removed before a new owner can receive a clear title. A *lien release* that has been filed on record, on the other hand, indicates that a former lien has been satisfied and discharged, so that the buyer can be protected from unpaid debts of the prior owner (see chapters 6 and 12).

Title Search   The title establishes ownership of the property, much like an automobile title. A title search tracks the deed back through the years to make certain that there have been no flaws in prior transfers of ownership. A title search also reveals whether there are any claims or other encumbrances on the property.

Abstract of Title   This is a written history of the property, listing the owners, easements, lawsuits, and anything else discovered during the title search that affects the title. Often it is accompanied by an *attorney's opinion* about the validity of the title, sometimes known as the *certificate of title.*

Title Insurance   Even after the title is searched, a homeowner will usually pay for title insurance, which guarantees the accuracy of the title search and protects against mistakes in it. The purpose of the title search and title insurance is to give the buyer maximum protection against someone appearing and making an ownership claim against the property. Banks will not generally make home mortgage loans without the purchase of title insurance, but a lender's policy covers only the bank. An owner's policy covers the buyer.

Title insurance can exclude certain areas of coverage, which can be insured by purchasing *endorsements*. In a standard policy, typical exclusions (contained in Schedule A of the title policy) include zoning changes, boundaries, unfiled claims, and inflation value of the property. Physical defects to the property are never covered by title insurance, even with additional policy protection.

Survey A formal survey updates, clarifies, or verifies the property boundaries. Formal surveys are not conducted in all purchases, but in some cases a copy of a prior survey can be obtained from the seller. Surveys are sometimes required by a bank or other lender.

Appraisal A formal review of the market value of the property by a qualified appraiser is sometimes conducted prior to the closing date and may be required by lenders before they will agree to finance the purchase.

Loan Application In order to obtain a mortgage loan, the buyer must usually complete a fairly rigorous loan application. A buyer should keep copies of these documents in case the loan is denied or delayed, or if the buyer later seeks refinancing.

Co-op Board Application The purchaser of a co-op unit has to complete an application and supply loan information to the co-op board (see chapters 17 and 20).

Mortgage The note and mortgage contain the agreement with the bank or other lender by which the house and land are promised as collateral in exchange for a loan from the bank. Technically, the note is the promise of the homeowner to repay the loan. The mortgage is the document that gives the bank the right to collect the money owed on the note and operates as a security agreement. The mortgage gives the bank the right to hold the property as collateral and to foreclose on it if the note falls into default. (For further discussion of the mortgage loan process and default, see chapter 12.)

A mortgage may also have various *riders,* which are additional agreements with the bank. An adjustable-rate rider sets out the terms by which interest on the loan is changed from time to time; a condominium rider defines the different interests involved in that form of ownership (see chapters 12 and 17).

Cooperative owners do not obtain or secure mortgages, but get a share loan by which they sign a loan note and the shares in the cooperative are held as the collateral (see chapter 17). *Share certificates* are usually held by the bank, and the purchaser is provided with copies. The co-op owner also receives a *proprietary lease* from the co-op board, which permits the owner to live in the unit and sets out conditions and responsibilities.

Second Mortgage or Purchase Money Contract   Some homeowners will enter into more than one loan agreement in order to finance the property purchase. These secondary loan instruments—whether from a lender, mortgage broker, or the seller— are documented in instruments separate from the first mortgage.

Mortgage Insurance   A buyer who is unable to make the minimum down payment required by the bank may be allowed to pay a lesser amount if mortgage insurance is also purchased. This protects the lender in the event the buyer defaults on the loan, and it usually lasts until an amount equal to the normal down payment has been paid. The buyer pays for mortgage insurance, and the cost is usually added to the monthly mortgage payments. (*Guide to Single Family Home Mortgage Insurance* is available free from the U.S. Department of Housing and Urban Development, Seventh and D Streets, S.W., Washington, DC 20410-3000.)

Mortgage life insurance is sometimes required by a lender, or is purchased by a homeowner, depending on individual life insurance needs. This insurance pays off the mortgage in event of the homeowner's death.

Special Information Booklet   Under the federal Real Estate Settlement Procedures Act (RESPA), the buyer must be given a copy of the Special Information Booklet, which explains closing practices, lender obligations, and homeowner rights.

Uniform Settlement Statement   The bank or lender is supposed to detail all of the costs of settlement that the buyer will have to pay and put it in a form designed by the federal government. The Uniform Settlement Statement must be available to you before the closing, but only one day in advance.

Loan Disclosure Statement   A statement that explains the mortgage loan—the total amount borrowed, the interest on that amount, the annual percentage rate, the date for payments to start, the amount of monthly payments—must be given to the buyer on a special form. Balloon payments—an agreement to pay off the full amount of the original price and interest on a specific date—must also be noted. This statement is required by the federal Truth-in-Lending Act.

Bank Escrow   The buyer is expected to pay the cost of taxes and homeowner's insurance into an escrow account. Escrow payments are collected with the monthly mortgage payment. The account assures the lender that there will be no default in tax or insurance payments that could jeopardize its loan. The buyer should get a statement about the escrow account, including what charges will be made against it and any interest applied to it.

Property Disclosure Statements   Where required by law, or if offered otherwise, the buyer may get disclosure statements that detail the condition of the property. These include inspection reports from an independent inspector or engineer, a termite inspection report or other pest inspection report; an environmental inspection report or, alternatively, a report on asbestos, radon, or other contaminants. If defects later arise on the property, these documents are essential in defining whether the buyer has a legal claim against the seller (see chapter 2).

Home Warranties and Home Warranty Insurance   Purchasers of a new home and, in some cases, the purchasers of older homes may have home warranties or home warranty insurance. In general, home warranty insurance covers the costs of repair of the house's major systems, usually for a period of one to three years (see chapter 2).

Rules and Restrictions; Proprietary Lease   Homeowners in cooperatives, condominiums, or areas with neighborhood associations will receive a copy of rules and restrictions—sometimes called "the black book"—which, along with deed covenants and other documents, states restrictions that apply to the property. Cooperative owners also receive a proprietary lease, which gives them the exclusive right to inhabit the unit that they are buying and outlines their responsibilities to the co-op (see chapter 17).

Contracts for Nonfixture Purchases   Nonfixtures are items not attached to the property—for example, furniture. A buyer who purchases nonfixtures from the seller should have them documented in a separate contract, in which the items and the amounts paid for them are specifically stated (see chapter 20).

Appliance and Property Warranties   A buyer should get copies of product warranties that apply to products in the home. This precaution is particularly important for new home purchases (see chapter 2). *Remodeling warranties* purchased by the seller may also be passed on to the buyer (see chapter 6). *Service contracts* on appliances or work done on the property, along with service records for major structural systems, should also be obtained from the seller at the closing.

Assessment and Property Tax Reports   Assessments and property tax reports from the local government should be made available to you, along with any history of objections or reductions.

Tax Transfer   Many states and localities require either the purchaser or the seller to pay transfer fees. Receipts should be supplied at the closing.

Lease for Rental Unit   If the property has a rental unit, the buyer should request copies of any leases or agreements between the seller and the tenant. The buyer is not necessarily obligated by the lease in all cases; local law and the language of the lease prevail (see chapter 19).

> *The home buyer who purchases nonfixtures from the seller should have them documented in a separate contract.*

Homestead Exemption A homestead exemption, available in most states, can protect a home from the claims of certain creditors. A document declaring that the property is subject to the homestead exemption is often filed with a county recorder's office at the time of closing.

Independent Agreements Keep copies of any independent agreements signed in conjunction with the property purchase, such as a personal loan for a down payment, a prenuptial agreement, or a cohabitation agreement (see chapter 14).

Homeowner's Insurance Keep copies of current information, even if the payments are part of the escrow paid by the bank.

OTHER INFORMATION TO GATHER

Buyers should keep a record of names and addresses of persons connected to the purchase documents. If a problem develops later, any legal recourse will depend on the ability to find the person or persons responsible.

If the seller has removed blinds that the buyer believes were part of the sale, this may be grounds for a claim against the seller. But such a claim is meaningless if the seller cannot be located. Trying to track someone down after the fact can be difficult, sometimes impossible.

Try to gather a full range of information at or before the closing. If this isn't possible, try to pull it together immediately after the closing. This information should include

- The seller's new address; if not known, the seller's place of employment or a relative who will know how to contact the seller
- The name and address of the seller's attorney

- The names and addresses of all real estate brokers involved in the sale
- The name of the loan officer and mortgage brokers
- The name and address of the escrow agent, the insurance agent, the title insurance agent, the home warranty company
- Names of the individuals, corporate name and address of the developer, contractor, or sponsor of a condominium or cooperative
- The name, license (if any), and address of home inspectors
- The name and address of appraisers
- The name, address, and affiliations of any mortgage provider or purchaser, such as private/public agencies that purchase mortgages from banks or other lenders (such as Federal Home Mortgage Association or a state mortgage association)
- The name, address, and corporate name of any contractors who worked on the property in the prior five years and, if possible, copies of the contracts the seller had with them
- Copies of any advertisements for the home or any promotional materials given to the buyer by a seller, agent, broker, or developer

HOMEOWNER'S INSURANCE

Homeowner's insurance provides two types of coverage. *Liability* insurance pays for injuries to third persons on the property (see chapter 7). *Casualty* insurance covers damage to the house itself and to personal property inside the home.

Homeowner's insurance, on the whole, is not expensive, and it provides much-needed protection. An owner's financial security can be threatened by claims on the property—whether from the injury of a neighbor's child playing in the backyard or a fire that sweeps through the basement. The central question in evaluating homeowner's insurance policies is what is covered if a claim arises.

Lenders require homeowner's insurance, and payments are usually collected by the bank with the monthly mortgage payment, held in escrow, and paid out directly by the bank (see chapter 13).

Liability Insurance In reviewing the liability portion of the homeowner's policy, the homeowner should ask the following questions:

• *Are dollar limits on coverage adequate?* Liability coverage often limits payout for an injury to $25,000 to $100,000. If someone is seriously injured, medical costs can quickly exceed the coverage. A policy of up to $300,000 or more is available with a modest increase in premium and is well worth it.

A homeowner may be able to purchase a supplementary umbrella policy to cover special risks. Umbrella policies can provide for liability of $1 million or more, but they are usually available only to homeowners who already have substantial home and auto insurance. Homeowners with a swimming pool or other "attractive nuisances," pets, or frequent child or elderly visitors should increase their coverage (see chapter 7). Homeowners with a high income or assets that could be attached in an unusual accident should consider an umbrella policy.

Liability insurance does *not* cover an injury to the homeowner or any resident family members, even if the injury arises from a condition on the property. Nor does it cover injuries intentionally inflicted.

• *Are workers on the property or business visitors covered?* Most basic liability policies do not cover gardeners, domestic workers, or contractors. Special protection to cover those individuals can be obtained, and if they are frequent visitors, it will be worthwhile to do so. Some states require homeowners to buy worker's compensation coverage for workers on the property. In addition, if the owner has a business on the property that involves clients, special protection must be purchased (see chapter 18).

• *If the price of the policy is excessive, can costs be cut by raising the deductible?* Increasing the coverage on liability insurance generally doesn't raise the premium cost very much. If the premiums seem too high, consider raising the deductible. For example, if an owner is personally responsible for a deductible of $500, it could be raised to $1,000, while leaving the maximum coverage at $300,000. In that case, the owner is responsible for minor injuries on the property but has protection from catastrophic injuries that could bring financial ruin.

CASUALTY INSURANCE

There are seven standard casualty policies offered by insurance companies. These have varying names, but they are designated by similar symbols, such as HO-1 (HO stands for *homeowner's*).

> **Increasing the coverage on liability insurance generally doesn't raise the premium cost very much.**

Several aspects of the casualty portion of your homeowner's insurance require special attention:

• *What is excluded from coverage?* A key difference in policies is what is *not* covered. Homeowner's insurance may not cover some damages, depending on what causes the damage or the peril. You need to know what "perils" are excluded and what are included in the policy. Floods and earthquakes are never covered; they require special insurance.

• *In setting policy limits, how is the property value calculated?* The goal is neither to be underinsured nor overinsured, but to have adequate coverage in the event of a loss.

A homeowner can be underinsured if the policy is designed to protect only the investment of the lender on the property.

Underinsurance can also occur if the inflation value of the house is not considered. If the property increases in value, the homeowner's policy needs to reflect that increase. A periodic review of the property's value, even with paid reappraisals, may be necessary.

Homeowners can be overinsured if the value of the land is added to the coverage limits. Land is not considered replaceable. If a fire destroys the house, they still own the land on which to rebuild—there is no insurable loss. Land is normally considered to account for 20 percent of a property's value, but this may vary depending on the location.

• *How will the insurance company figure damage to the structure?* It is important that the insurance covers the replacement cost of the property, or what it would cost to rebuild the damaged area, rather than actual value (purchase price less depreciation), which is usually lower. Seek a policy that has "guaranteed replacement value."

Some homeowner's policies pay a percentage of the replacement value in the event of damage or loss. Do not accept anything below 80 percent. Not only is the risk unacceptably high if the replacement percentage goes below 80 percent, but the insurance company can also invoke a rule that permits it to pay only a percentage of partial damage.

> A kitchen destroyed by fire has a replacement tag of $40,000. If the home is insured to 80 percent of the replacement value, the full damage—$40,000—is covered (at policy limits of $100,000). If the home is insured to only 60 percent of the replacement value, the insurance company can invoke a different formula that pays only 60 percent of the $40,000 fire loss, or $24,000.

Replacement cost does not cover special and unique features, such as the Tiffany glass window. Special coverage is needed for custom products and items that are part of the structure.

> **Landscaping is normally covered only up to 5 percent of the level of coverage of the structure.**

Landscaping is normally covered only up to 5 percent of the level of coverage of the structure. A homeowner can purchase more coverage.

Replacement value of a house needs to be calculated by a qualified appraiser and should be periodically updated. Inflation in building costs can raise the replacement value of the house, and, if the insurance policy isn't updated, owners can be left underinsured.

• *How will the insurance company calculate damage to personal property?* Make a full and specific inventory of items in the house and their replacement value. If the total exceeds the payable limits, buy additional insurance. Keep the list somewhere *outside* the home, such as your office or safe-deposit box. Many insurance experts recommend taking pictures or videotapes of your home and your belongings.

Again, aim for replacement value. The limit on personal property claims in homeowner's insurance is 50 percent of the coverage on the structure. If personal property adds up to more than 50 percent of a home's value, the owner is underinsured.

Most policies also have limits on or exclude particular types of items unless they are insured specially under a floater or rider. Coverage is limited on stamp collections, manuscripts, securities, boats, jewelry, furs, precious stones, metals and coins, firearms, and silver or gold housewares. Business property is not normally covered.

TYPES OF HOMEOWNER'S CASUALTY POLICIES

HO-1, the Basic Form   This policy covers damage to the structure or personal property arising from 11 perils: fire or lightning, windstorm or hail, explosion, riots, aircraft, vehicles damaging the structure, smoke, vandalism, theft, breakage of glass, volcanic eruption.

HO-2, the Broad Form   This is a more popular form, covering everything in HO-1 plus damage resulting from five other perils, including weight of snow, ice, or sleet; electrical surges; plumbing, heating, air-conditioning, or appliance malfunction, leak, or freeze; collapse of a building; falling objects.

HO-3, the Special Form   Known as the "all-risk" policy, this includes the perils in HO-1 and HO-2 and all other perils excepting floods, earthquakes, war, or nuclear accidents. HO-3 offers maximum protection for the structure, but personal property coverage is not as thorough as HO-5, unless a special endorsement is written.

HO-4, Renter's Insurance This protects personal property of renters, which is not covered by the homeowner's policy.

HO-5, the Comprehensive Form A step up from HO-3 coverage, this policy is the most expensive. It provides the all-risk coverage of HO-3 for both the structure and personal property. Some companies do not offer HO-5, but can provide a rider to an HO-3 policy.

HO-6, the Condominium Policy This policy covers the interior space and contents owned by the unit owner. A more inclusive all-risk policy is available and an endorsement (HO-33) can cover personal property while the condominium is rented to others. The condominium association provides coverage for the common areas and the structure, the costs of which are part of the unit owner's maintenance fee. Endorsements can cover losses assessed to the unit owner. HO-9 covers cooperative units.

HO-8, Older Homes Policy This policy covers only the perils of an HO-1 policy, but it insures the house for actual cash or market value, as opposed to replacement value. Insurance companies consider replacement value too high on some older homes. The property is supposed to be returned to serviceable condition, if not full value.

In some cases, the homeowner can save money on an insurance policy by adding security and safety devices—burglar alarms, fences, sprinkler systems, and smoke detectors.

Vacation property must have separate coverage from the residence property. In some cases, an owner can combine automobile and homeowner's insurance to save money.

The cost of homeowner's insurance varies depending on the neighborhood and location of the home. High-crime areas and high-market-value neighborhoods may have higher insurance price tags.

Tips on Homeowners' Insurance (Publication 24–197) is available for $1 from the Better Business Bureau, 1515 Wilson Boulevard, Arlington, VA 22209, or from a local Better Business Bureau. The Insurance Information Institute, 110 William Street, New

York, NY 10038, provides a National Insurance Consumer Helpline at 1-800-942-4242, and has several brochures, such as "Tips for Homeowners," "How to File an Insurance Claim," and "Taking Inventory." The National Insurance Consumer Organization, 121 North Payne Street, Alexandria, VA 22314; 703-549-8050, sells for $3 the "Buyer's Guide to Insurance: What the Companies Won't Tell You."

Flood, Earthquake, and High-Crime-Area Insurance

Homeowners who live in earthquake zones must purchase special coverage. Earthquake coverage is available from the homeowner's insurance company for an extra cost. It generally has a deductible of 10 percent.

Flood insurance is not included in standard homeowner's insurance policies. Until the mid-1960s no insurance at all was available for flood damage. In response, Congress set up the National Flood Insurance Program (NFIP) to make insurance available at subsidized rates to people in certain flood-prone communities.

The NFIP insurance is available to homeowners in approved districts, so long as the community takes certain steps to control and reduce flood damage. Approximately 18,000 communities qualify.

Some caveats apply to flood coverage. The homeowner must often take steps to remove personal belongings from the property during a flood alert (but costs of removal will be paid). A standard deductible of $500 applies to damage to the structure and personal belongings. In addition, there is a five-day waiting period between the purchase of flood insurance and its effective date. In other words, homeowners who apply during a flood alert will not be covered. Flood insurance does not cover wind damage from a hurricane or other source. Separate windstorm policies are available.

Local insurance brokers should be familiar with flood insurance, and private insurers can write the coverage. (Information can be obtained from the Federal Emergency Management Agency, Washington, DC 60472; 202-646-2781 or 1-800-638-

6620. *In the Event of a Flood* is available free from the Consumer Information Center, Pueblo, CO 81009.)

After a flood or earthquake, the Federal Emergency Management Agency (FEMA) may be able to step in if the event is declared a disaster. FEMA can arrange low-cost loans or other assistance as disaster relief.

Homeowners in some high-crime areas may be unable to obtain adequate insurance. Federal crime insurance is available to cover burglary or robbery in certain areas. High-crime areas have been declared in portions of 14 states and the District of Columbia. Federal crime insurance has a deductible and limits on the value per item that will be paid. (Information can be obtained from the Federal Crime Insurance Program, P.O. Box 6301, Rockville, MD 20850; 1-800-638-8780.)

Property Claims

Claims on homeowner's insurance must usually be made within 60 days of the accident or damage. Filing a claim requires completing a substantial amount of paperwork.

Claims on homeowner's insurance must usually be made within 60 days of the accident or damage.

To speed up processing of the claim, it will help to document what, when, and how an incident occurred. Obtain copies of police and fire reports and get the names of any officers who come to the premises. If there were witnesses, try to gather a list of names, addresses, phone numbers, and what the people saw.

Damage may need to be documented, as well. Take photographs of the damage before cleanup. A videotape is also a good idea.

If the claim is substantial, it may be wise to speak to an attorney before submitting a form to the insurance company. This can prevent the homeowner from inadvertently using language that would permit the insurance company to deny the claim. For example, if the insurance does not cover casualties caused intentionally, and the owner uses language that does not explain how an accident occurred, the wrong conclusion could be reached.

In some cases when the damage is great, it may be desirable to contact a public claims adjuster. Public adjusters know how to prepare the forms so that homeowners get the maximum benefits to which they are entitled. Public adjusters are listed in the telephone book and are licensed in several states. Public adjusters often charge a percentage of the settlement obtained from the insurance company. If that percentage is large, a homeowner could lose in the end. In order to avoid being victimized, it is best to consult with more than one adjuster and check references.

Insurance companies are regulated by state insurance agencies. If the insurance company denies a claim, pays an amount that seems unfair, delays payment, or acts in other egregious ways, a homeowner may be able to appeal within the insurance agency. If this isn't effective, the next step would be to contact the state insurance agency (see chapter 21).

In addition, if an insurance salesperson misrepresents the coverage for property damage and it turns out to be inadequate, homeowners could sue to seek compensation for losses to the full amount of the coverage they thought they had.

It is important to note, however, that a claimant cannot accept the settlement or cash a settlement check and also hope to get fuller compensation later, even through a valid complaint process. Acceptance of the settlement indicates agreement with the insurance company's estimate of the damage. Usually the check is accompanied by a statement that it is "payment in full" or by settlement papers that have similar statements. Unless the company agrees in writing to allow the homeowner to accept a check as partial payment, the homeowner is without further recourse.

If any doubts arise about the payment offered or about the settlement process, it would be prudent to consult a lawyer.

RECORD KEEPING

Throughout the period of home ownership, the owner needs to keep exceptionally good records as protection from future claims.

Financial information All information relevant to the purchase, loan, fees, appraisals, and taxes

Insurance information Details of insurance policies and an inventory of property

Condition information Reports by inspectors or appraisers, contractors, and value assessors

Improvement information Full documentation of costs and materials of home improvements, building permit, certificate of occupancy, licenses of contractors, contracts entered with contractors, liens or lien releases

Ownership information Deeds, easements, licenses, leases, property conditions, legal description, survey, plat, and any other documentation of ownership, and notices relating to zoning or neighborhood association decisions

Product information Warranties related to product purchases, inventory of products, and service contracts

Correspondence Any correspondence with government officials, agencies, lawyers, or neighbors, and especially any legal documents served on or sent to you

Contacts The names of attorneys, appraisers, agents, brokers, contractors, government agencies or officials, and others who can provide assistance when a problem arises

In addition, begin a property diary. Among other things, keep track of payments, assessments, improvements, problems, or changes in the property condition. Whenever a dispute arises that involves the property, document all phone calls, contacts, and details. This information will be especially useful if the problem grows into a legal dispute (see chapter 21).

PROTECTING THE INVESTMENT

If all the documents and record keeping make owning a home seem like a business, that's just what it is. An owner can best protect the investment and be prepared to handle any type of legal situation that arises by using good business sense. Understanding the documents that apply to the home and undertaking solid record keeping are the foundation of smart home property management.

Defects
Discovered
After Purchase

After homeowners move in, they may discover problems and defects they didn't know existed before signing the final contract.

In order to avoid unpleasant surprises before purchasing a house, home buyers should inspect the property personally and ask the seller or broker questions about all of the major structural systems, as well as the history of the property. A clause in the contract for purchase should permit the buyer to back out of the deal if a home inspection uncovers significant problems that were not disclosed.

An experienced home inspector should be engaged to conduct a thorough inspection. (The American Society of Home Inspectors, Inc., which maintains lists of qualified inspectors, is located at 1735 North Lynn Street, Suite 950, Arlington, VA 22209-2022; 703-524-2303.) In addition, the buyer will need a termite inspection and may want asbestos, radon, and environmental inspections. A complete title search should be conducted by a title company. Before closing, the buyer can negotiate with the seller to lower the price or repair the property if poor conditions are found.

In some circumstances, buyers can insulate themselves from having to pay the costs of repair for defects in major structural systems by purchasing home warranty insurance. Some buyers have successfully negotiated indemnity clauses in the contract, in which the seller agrees to pay for the costs of major repairs that arise soon after the sale. (A free publication that provides guidelines for prepurchase inspections, *A Guide for Veterans Planning to Buy or Build Homes,* is available from the Department of Veterans Affairs, 252 Seventh Avenue at Twenty-fourth Street, New York, NY 10001.)

Despite these efforts, major property defects may not be detected until after the homeowner has moved in. In some cases, the defects may have been concealed by the seller; in others, they may not have been noticed or were latent and impossible to find, even by the best inspector. Some of these defects may be minor— chipped plaster or paint in a closet. Other defects may demand a major investment in repair—leaky roof or contaminated water.

WHEN RECOVERY MAY BE POSSIBLE

In recent years courts have begun to recognize legal recourse for buyers when defects are discovered after the property is purchased. This is a change from the past, in which the standard of *caveat emptor*—let the buyer beware—applied to all real estate purchases. Legal recourse is still limited and differs from state to state. In addition, these laws will be helpful only in instances in which large sums of money are involved in correcting the defect, or when the defect will seriously ruin enjoyment of the property for the owners. But the trend indicates that the rights of home buyers to recover for defects discovered after purchase will continue to grow.

Whether or not the buyer has a possibility of legal recourse for a defect discovered after the purchase will depend on a number of factors:

1. How far the laws of the state have gone in following the trend of a consumer movement to protect homeowners

2. Whether the house is new or old
3. The seriousness and type of the defect—whether material or latent
4. Whether the defect was concealed or misrepresented in any way
5. The exact language in the contract and deed

Trend Toward Recognizing Purchaser Expectations Under the Law

Some courts and legislatures have recognized that home buyers are legitimately entitled to certain expectations in the purchase of a home. Where recognized, these expectations can be implied in a contract, whether or not they are written in the contract, and are known as *implied warranties.*

Two implied warranties are relevant to home purchases: an *implied warranty of habitability* and an *implied warranty of fitness.* These warranties were first found to exist in home purchases by courts reviewing the sale of new homes. The courts held that a home purchase involved more than the sale of land; it also involved the sale of a structure. The courts determined that the purchase of a new home should be treated like the purchase of any other product and that the home buyer was entitled to some protection from flawed products or unscrupulous sellers.

When implied warranties are found, the purchaser is recognized as having the right to expect that a home will be free from unexpected material defects. In some cases, the same concepts of implied warranties have now been extended to the purchase of old homes.

Under the implied warranty of habitability, the person buying residential property is entitled to expect that the home will be fit for people to live in, unless the contract states otherwise—just as the purchaser of an automobile is entitled to believe that the car is fit to drive. Not all states recognize an implied warranty of habitability.

In some cases, a second implied warranty of fitness for a particular purpose has also been applied to a home purchase. An implied warranty of fitness arises when the purchaser makes it clear to the seller that the property will have some special use.

> If an accountant is interested only in a house that can also be used as an office, and makes this fact known to the seller, the seller could breach the warranty of fitness by failing to disclose that zoning laws do not allow a home office. If, after the purchase, the accountant discovers that the home office is not permitted, the seller could be liable for breaching the implied warranty.

A small number of states have passed consumer protection laws that specifically apply to real estate sales. For example, Texas has a "deceptive trade practices" act that makes it illegal for the seller of a home to fail to disclose relevant information about the property to a prospective buyer. Other states have passed laws requiring a seller to provide disclosure to a buyer about specific conditions on the property (see chapter 20).

PURCHASERS OF NEW HOMES

Buyers of new homes have additional special protection. Court decisions or laws in most states require builders or developers of new homes to provide and honor specific warranties on the property.

SERIOUSNESS OF DEFECT

Real estate that is not newly built will not be perfect. Even though property is well maintained, there will be inevitable wear and tear. If defects are readily visible or observable, the purchaser is expected to know about them, and a purchaser will not be permitted to make a claim against the seller after the sale.

But the purchaser may have legal recourse for a defect discovered after the purchase when the condition involves major problems, or *material defects*. Buyers of old homes who discover small defects that would be expected in any old home will rarely succeed in pursuing a claim for damages.

Of course, there can be significant disagreement about what

constitutes a material defect. In general, a material defect is one that would have prevented a reasonable person from buying the property had it been known, or that significantly reduces the value of the property.

Material defects can fall into several categories:

1. dangerous conditions, such as a rotten stairwell on which someone is injured
2. faulty conditions with the structure or on the land itself that would require repair, such as a heating system that does not work or decaying trees that would require removal
3. conditions that make living on the property impossible or undesirable, such as bad water quality or toxins in the ground
4. conditions that ruin the likelihood of enjoying the property, such as pending construction that would obstruct a scenic view
5. rules or regulations not related to the structure itself that would prevent the homeowner from using the land as anticipated, such as a building code that does not permit the upper floor of a house to be rented as a separate apartment

Following are examples of material defects for which purchasers were permitted legal recourse:

- a persistent flooding condition on the property
- failure to disclose a foreclosure proceeding
- a severe problem with termites
- a multiple murder on the site
- insufficient water supply in a well

Whether or not a claim for an undiscovered material defect will be successful varies greatly from state to state.

LATENT DEFECTS

Latent defects create another category of problems for which a homeowner may have legal recourse.

A latent defect is a lingering problem that *could not* have been discovered for a long time. For example, the purchaser of a home may not discover until several years after moving in that the house was actually built on a toxic waste dump.

In some cases, a purchaser may have legal recourse because of a serious latent defect, provided the action is taken soon after the defect is discovered.

MISREPRESENTATION OR CONCEALMENT BY SELLER

When the seller or broker hides a serious defect or misrepresents the property to the buyer, the buyer has suffered an injustice. In these cases, the law will probably give the buyer an opportunity to seek legal recourse against the seller for defects discovered after the purchase. Misrepresentation occurs when the buyer is deceived in order to complete the sale. If a material or latent defect is discovered after the purchase, and misrepresentation about it has occurred, the buyer may have legal recourse.

A misrepresentation can occur in several ways, such as when the seller

- omits to tell a buyer about a defect known to the seller, such as a leaky roof
- hides evidence of a known defect, such as painting over any stain marks from a leaky roof

A home buyer may have legal recourse even if the seller unintentionally makes a misrepresentation about the property. In one case, a seller stated that the property was part of a community water arrangement that provided adequate water supply to the property. After the purchase, the buyer learned that a neighbor owned the well and had decided not to supply water any longer. Even though the seller did not purposely mislead the buyer, the buyer might have legal recourse against the seller.

- inaccurately describes a condition to the buyer, such as telling the buyer that the roof has no problems, even though
  it has been leaky
- provides information about a defect in writing, but contra-
  dicts it orally, such as listing the roof under an itemization
  of problems on the contract for purchase, but telling the
  buyer that the roof is in great shape

LANGUAGE OF THE CONTRACT

The contract signed by the purchaser bears directly on the outcome if a defect is discovered. Some contracts include an inspector's report that lists defects; others may name specific defects on
the property. A clause in the contract may then disclaim any seller
liability for those conditions. In this case, the law would assume
that a purchaser has been adequately warned of those defects and
will not have cause to complain later.

Some contracts state that the property is being purchased "as
is" or "with all faults." If a purchaser has signed a contract with
this language, the purchaser will be expected to live with the
property, flaws and all. For example, purchasers in one case were
not allowed to collect damages for a brick retaining wall that collapsed, because the real estate contract said the purchase was
"as is."

> A purchaser was not allowed to get out of a contract
> when it was discovered that a septic tank was defective.
> The contract said that the buyer had "examined the
> property and agreed to accept it" in its condition.

Some states now require that an "as is" clause in a contract
must be conspicuous and noticeable. When the "as is" wording
is obscured in legalistic language—such as within a paragraph
that disclaims any implied warranties—the purchaser cannot be
expected to understand it. In those cases, the purchaser might
have a valid legal claim if the defects are discovered after the
purchase.

There are, however, always exceptions for unusual circumstances. Even if a contract says "as is," a home buyer might be allowed to make a claim for the costs of material defects discovered after the purchase if the seller has deliberately engaged in misrepresentation.

TIMELINESS

Normally a homeowner who wants to pursue a legal claim for a defect discovered on the property must do so as quickly as possible after it is discovered.

The time period in which a lawsuit must be brought is generally the same as for any contract action in the state—which can be up to six years, but often claims are limited to a year or some specific time period after purchase.

If the defect is a major one but was not discovered immediately, the homeowner may still have a claim by acting as soon as possible after the defect is discovered. This is particularly true with latent defects, which do not become known until many years after the purchase.

LIABILITY FOR DEFECTS DISCOVERED AFTER THE PURCHASE

In addition to the seller, a real estate broker can be liable for misrepresentation. The National Association of Realtors has adopted a code of conduct for its broker members that states that brokers cannot misrepresent, conceal, or misconstrue the property.

In some situations, lenders (banks or others) can be liable for misrepresentation, too. For example, if a bank provides a loan to a homeowner knowing that the seller has lied or that there are serious problems on the property or that the property is not really valued at the amount of the loan, it could be found liable.

An inspector or appraiser could also become liable for a faulty report that misses a material defect and upon which the purchaser relied.

In some cases, a title search company could be liable for defects discovered after the purchase if, for example, the title search failed to locate an encumbrance on the property.

Damages or Recovery from a Defective Condition

If a defect is discovered, the homeowner will need to decide what kind of recovery or compensation would be most satisfactory.

If the problem is so serious that the homeowner no longer wants the property, the buyer may want to cancel the sale altogether and give the house back to the prior owner in exchange for a refund of monies paid. This is known as rescinding the contract.

If the condition is one that can be repaired, the purchaser may want to be compensated for the costs of the repair. If personal injuries have resulted from the defect, such as burns caused when a damaged hot water pipe burst, or furniture and clothing were ruined because of water seeping through a roof, compensation for these costs may be sought. When the damages are great, concepts of fairness pressure courts to provide legal recourse to the purchaser of a home.

What to Do When a Defect Is Discovered After the Purchase

As soon as the full scope of a defect is known, the purchaser may want to consider legal recourse. Since acting in a timely fashion can be a factor, there should be no delays.

Purchasers should check to see if a home warranty is in effect. Home warranty plans are insurance plans purchased by the buyer or seller at the time of closing (and are distinct from implied warranties). The home warranties insure major systems—plumbing, electrical, central heating, air-conditioning—and typically cover problems that arise within a year after the sale. The insurance usually does not cover structural defects—cracks in the foundation, for example. Most policies also have a deductible of several hundred dollars, costs that must be paid before the insurance coverage begins.

In some cases, title insurance might cover the discovered defect. This is true when the homeowner finds out that the property boundaries or limitations are not as stated in the deed (see chapter 3). For example, a neighbor might claim an easement to use a certain portion of the property, or a fence may be improperly posted. The homeowner might argue that a title search should have discovered this problem and that the title insurer was negligent. In such a case a letter to the title insurance company and possible legal claim should be considered.

In the majority of cases, though, the homeowner will not have insurance that covers the defect. The homeowner will need to contact the seller and the seller's representatives, or other potentially responsible parties, by letter, stating the nature of the problem, the damages sought, and why the purchaser believes that the seller (or other responsible party) should pay for the damages. If the defect is a major one, an attorney should be consulted.

In the case of newly discovered defects, it may be especially important for the purchaser to try to resolve the problem without filing a lawsuit. The law on physical defects discovered after the purchase is still changing, and results of a lawsuit can be uncertain. A certain settlement may be better than an uncertain lawsuit.

THE PROBLEM OF REMOVAL OF FIXTURES DISCOVERED AFTER PURCHASE

Upon moving into a home, a purchaser may discover that the seller has removed fixtures that the purchaser considered part of the sale. Resolving this problem is not as complicated legally as the newly discovered defect, but the homeowner can encounter significant practical difficulties.

A real estate contract includes the property and all of the structures or items that are permanently affixed to the property. The seller is not permitted to remove any fixtures after the contract is signed. But it is not always clear whether or not some items are fixtures. All major systems of the house—plumbing, electricity, and so on—are fixtures. Most appliances are not fixtures. Lights attached to the ceiling are fixtures, but lamps are not. A laundry tub is a fixture; a washer is not. Central air-conditioning is a fixture; a window air conditioner is not.

If the item is classified as a fixture, the purchaser has the right to collect damages from the seller for improper removal. If the item is not a fixture—even though the purchaser expected that it was part of the sale—the seller has a right to remove it.

In many cases, a separate contract is signed between buyer and

seller in which the seller agrees to transfer or sell certain nonfixtures, such as a refrigerator or drapes. On the other hand, the
seller may have a particular attachment to a certain fixture—an
antique chandelier, for example—and include a clause in the
house contract excluding it from the sale.

The buyer has a right to be compensated for missing fixtures
that were not excluded from the contract. If the buyer has a complaint about missing fixtures, the seller should be contacted by
letter at once. A copy of the letter should also be sent to the real
estate brokers involved in the deal.

If the seller will not voluntarily pay for the missing fixtures, the
homeowner will need to go to court. This can present practical
difficulties if the seller has moved out of town, or if the seller's
address is unknown to the buyer (see chapter 21).

SPECIAL PROTECTION FOR NEW HOMES

Special rules have developed concerning the sales of new homes.
Defects in the construction resulting from contractor error or
negligence have been treated much like defects in a car resulting
from manufacturer error or negligence—the builder, like the
manufacturer, is expected to be responsible for repairs or injuries caused by its errors. Builders and developers are considered
to be in a better position than a home buyer to bear the costs of
damage or repair.

Warranties—express and implied—are applied to the sales of
new homes. A few states have applied the same standards of warranty to home remodelers, as well (see chapter 6).

When buying a new home, homeowners buy more than four
walls and a door. Many products are contained in the home—
whether air-conditioning or carpeting, heating pipes or faucet
valves. The laws of product warranty and product liability have
been applied to all of these items, providing other avenues of
recovery for the disappointed purchaser of a new home.

WARRANTIES

There are two types of warranties that apply to new homes:
express warranties and implied warranties.

Express warranties are those specifically written out by the builder or developer or those provided by product manufacturers. Unfortunately, unless there are laws that state exactly what type of warranty must be offered, many builders limit the express warranties by time (for example, to a year), by potential claimant (for example, to only the original purchaser), or by what is covered (for example, repair, instead of replacement and costs of consequential damages).

Implied warranties are not written anywhere. But they are such basic concepts that they will be implied to exist, whether stated or not.

The courts in all states but Georgia (and to a lesser extent, Ohio) have said that two warranties for new homes will be implied: the *implied warranty of habitability,* which means that the house must be reasonably fit to occupy comfortably, and the *implied warranty of workmanship,* which means that the house was constructed safely, with attention to good building standards.

EXPRESS WARRANTIES

The terms of express warranties are spelled out in the contract with the seller. The warranties state both the specific items and the length and type of coverage.

Express warranties can also be created by an express statement. For example, a builder selling a new home made express warranties in a purchase agreement that a well was in good operating condition and available for household use. The court found that the builder was liable for a breach of express warranty when that turned out not to be true.

When sales agents make statements about the quality of the workmanship, an express warranty is created. Some states require express warranty coverage in the sales of new homes.

IMPLIED WARRANTIES

Implied warranties were first applied to mass-developed homes, but have been extended to even small builders of new homes or solo units. Implied warranties still may not apply when the homeowner buys the land and then hires a builder who builds to the purchaser's design and specifications.

In practical terms, when a homeowner has a problem with a new home, the claim will state a breach of both the implied warranty of habitability and the implied warranty of workmanship. Judges reviewing problems often consider both warranties to be the responsibility of the builder.

IMPLIED WARRANTY OF HABITABILITY

There are no exact guidelines on what habitability means. Failure to meet the "standard of habitability" does not mean that the property must be completely unusable or unlivable. Habitability means that the house is suitable for ordinary purposes, that the basic systems will function safely and readily.

> In one case, an implied warranty was applied when the water to a new home was rusty, smelly, caused stains, and was undrinkable. Since good running water is a reasonable expectation of any homeowner, the builder's failure to provide it was considered a breach of the implied warranty of habitability.

Breaches of the implied warranty of habitability in new homes were found in cases in which there were some of the following defects: the overpowering smell of formaldehyde from a carpet, water that periodically flooded the basement, defects in a well, and problems with a sewage disposal system. An implied warranty of habitability was applied in one case even though there was an attempted disclaimer in the contract.

An implied warranty of habitability was *not* found in cases in which there were cracks in exterior bricks years later, a swimming pool had problems, soil erosion caused trees to die, and the home was legally sold "as is."

IMPLIED WARRANTY OF WORKMANLIKE QUALITY

Above and beyond "habitability," courts began to impose an obligation on builders to complete the work in a good and workmanlike manner. Although there is no precise definition of work-manlike manner, builders can be held to the standards of the building profession, trade associations, and prevailing standards of quality in the region. The warranty of workmanship means that the construction and the products are free from defects. It is broader than the implied warranty of habitability because it applies to all aspects of the construction, not just those that affect "livability."

The warranty of workmanlike quality has been applied to a sinking patio, defective air-conditioning, a floor that collapsed nine years after purchase, a leaky roof, settling caused by water in the soil under the home.

The warranty of workmanlike quality does not apply to unimproved land in most cases. But in one case, the builder was held liable for selling land with poor drainage when the builder knew that the property owner intended to build a home on it.

Contracts for home remodeling usually state that construction must be completed in a workmanlike manner (see chapter 6).

CLAIMING A BREACH OF IMPLIED WARRANTY

An important element of the implied warranties for new homes is that no negligence has to be proved. The court will ask, Does an implied warranty exist? If so, was it broken? The *reason* that the implied warranty is broken is irrelevant. The implied warranty becomes an unwritten clause in the contract, and failure to meet it is a breach of the agreement between builder and buyer.

This attitude bodes well for homeowners. If the homeowner had to prove that the builder acted improperly or with negligence, the case would be much more difficult. Of course, if the builder did act negligently, the case for the homeowner is even stronger.

A breach of implied warranties does not have a specific time limitation (or *statute of limitations*). The homeowner is expected to raise the claim within a reasonable period and as soon as it is discovered. In some cases, though, the defect may be latent and may not become apparent for years.

Many states have held that implied warranties can also be extended to the second (or even later) purchaser of a newly constructed home. In the past, warranties were often valid only when pressed by the original purchaser.

HOMEOWNER RIGHTS
UNDER BREACH OF WARRANTY

The exact remedies a buyer can obtain under an express warranty are written into the contract. In general, however, when express or implied warranties are breached, the homeowner is entitled at least to have the problem corrected at no cost. The builder will be required to repair or replace the defective item.

In some cases, the homeowner may suffer other damages. For example, furniture may be damaged by a leaky roof. A flood may force the homeowner to vacate the premises for a period and rent temporary living space. The builder is responsible for paying the cost of those *consequential* damages that are a direct result of the breach of warranties (unless the contract states otherwise).

LIABILITY FOR NEGLIGENCE
BY BUILDERS OF NEW HOMES

Builders of new homes are also liable to homeowners for negligence in construction. When a person is injured because of a defect in the construction, the builder/developer can be held liable. A builder can also be liable for negligence in supervising workers or in using a poor design.

> When scalding water was released from a bathroom sink because of a defective valve, the builder was held liable for damages.

Under theories of strict liability in personal injury law, the builder of a new home may be held to an even higher standard if injuries result. Under theories of strict liability, the builder need not have intended to harm the purchaser. Liability is incurred merely for having sold a house with preventable defects that resulted in a personal injury.

Actions for which a builder could be strictly liable include designing the home defectively, causing a dangerous defect, installing a dangerous product, installing an undangerous product in a dangerous manner, failing to discover a defect, or failing to warn the homeowner about the defect adequately.

Oftentimes when an injury occurs, a home buyer will raise claims both of breach of implied warranties (a contract claim) and negligence or strict liability (tort claims).

State Legislation Establishing Express Warranties

A limited number of states—for instance Connecticut, Indiana, Louisiana, Maryland, Minnesota, New Jersey, West Virginia— have passed laws requiring new-home sellers to provide certain warranties. These laws make the implied warranties of good workmanship and habitability a part of every sales contract for a new home.

New Jersey has gone even further and sets standards that must be met by the builder for all common systems and components of the new home. Under the law, if problems arise the homeowner notifies the builder and the builder is required to make repairs. If the matter is not resolved, the homeowner can initiate a claims procedure. The state program also established a new-home security fund. In 1991, the fund agreed to release $50 million to repair or replace roofs on new homes that were built with fire-resistant treated plywood (FRTP) that was deteriorating prematurely.

Builders of new homes in some states can either register in a state warranty program or select from a private warranty plan approved by the state. The state attorney general's office usually handles these claims.

Private Warranty Programs

Some insurers and private associations have developed their own warranty programs for new homes. One is the Home Owners Warranty (H.O.W.) program, an independent program begun by the National Association of Home Builders (see chapter 6 for warranties on remodeling).

The H.O.W. program covers registered H.O.W. builders who

pay for insurance. The program warrants the home and all major structural systems against defects in workmanship and materials in the first two years, and in major structural defects for another eight years.

Under the H.O.W. program, the builder agrees to perform repairs at no cost to the homeowner. If the builder fails to make repairs, H.O.W. insurance will cover it. The program extends to any owners of the property during the first ten years, not just the first owner.

The program also offers dispute resolution if the builder and homeowner disagree about responsibility for repairs. Information on the H.O.W. program is available by writing: Home Warranty Program, P.O. Box 152087, Irving, TX 75015-2087.

CLAIMS FOR PRODUCT DEFECTS AND FAILURES

In building a new home, the builder uses hundreds of products, as is also true in home remodeling (see chapter 6). The new home itself is one giant product, and many of the theories applied to home builders also apply to the manufacturers of products used in constructing and equipping the home.

Problems with products fall into two broad categories: The product fails to perform as it should, causing a breach of an express or implied warranty; the product performs so badly or defectively that it injures someone and the manufacturer can be held strictly liable for the damages under theories of product liability.

PRODUCT WARRANTIES

When the product itself fails, the purchaser of a new home will have an avenue of recourse against the builder who installed the product. The new homeowner may also have a breach of warranty claim against the manufacturer of the product. In those cases, the homeowner is usually seeking repair or replacement of the defective product.

A lawsuit based on product warranties will rely upon the contract, the Uniform Commercial Code, state warranty laws, and certain federal laws, such as the Magnuson-Moss Warranty Act of 1975.

The Magnuson-Moss Act does not require that products have

warranties or specify what a warranty must offer, but only that when companies do offer warranties, the information must be written and available to the consumer. Coverage under a warranty can be "full" or "limited." A limited warranty may limit the services that the company offers, so long as the exclusions are explicit. For example, coverage may include parts but not labor charges, may require that the product be shipped to the factory, may exclude "consequential" damages for other problems caused by the product failure—for example, a countertop burned by faulty wiring in a toaster. A company may decline to honor a warranty if warranty conditions were not followed—for example, the product was not used as intended or was not installed according to company specifications.

In every state new products also have certain implied warranties. One implied warranty is of "merchantability"—that the product does what it is supposed to do. For example, a toaster is supposed to make toast.

There may also be an implied warranty of "fitness for a particular purpose." If the purchaser (who in this case may be the builder) has made known the particular use for the product, the seller will be held to that purpose.

The home purchaser should keep copies of all product warranties. If a product in the new home is defective, the homeowner should contact both the manufacturer and the builder. If the manufacturer's warranty is insufficient or the company will not honor it, the homeowner should consider seeking reimbursement from the builder.

CLAIMS FOR PRODUCT FAILURES THAT CAUSE INJURY

More serious than the failure of a product to perform is an injury caused by a dangerous or defective one. For example, a boiler might blow up because of a defective thermostat, a door might shatter because it is made of low-grade glass, a fire might spread rapidly because of the use of flammable materials, or a child might become ill from ingesting lead paint or other toxins.

When something is designed or manufactured defectively, without adequate testing, or with disregard for safety features, or when a dangerous product is sold without adequate warnings to the purchaser, causing the innocent user to be injured, the manufacturer, distributor, or seller can be held strictly liable for damages.

The law can become quite technical, but the general policy is that the manufacturer or seller is in the best position to prevent injuries. Courts have ruled that when an innocent consumer is hurt, the manufacturer—who is, after all, making money on the sale of the product—should bear the cost, rather than the injured party. The injured party would not have to show that the manufacturer made a mistake or was negligent or intended to cause an injury. The injured claimant only needs to show that the manufacture was deficient in some way—design, engineering, or warnings. This is usually accomplished through the testimony of experts. If a deficiency in the product is proven, the injured person could then recover damages for injuries. In serious cases of product failure, the manufacturer may have to pay punitive damages as well.

In defending against a product liability case in a new home situation, the manufacturer will inevitably say that the builder installed the product defectively. The homeowner, who only knows that *someone* should be responsible, generally has to sue all the parties who could potentially be liable, including the manufacturer, builder, and distributor.

Sophisticated personal injury lawyers handle product liability claims. If a client is accepted, the lawyer usually provides representation on a contingency basis—taking a percentage of the amount that is recovered from the claim. In some instances, class actions have been initiated when one defective product causes injuries to a large number of persons.

LEGAL STRATEGIES FOR NEW-HOME PURCHASERS

The purchaser of a new home or a home that was built or manufactured in the preceding ten years will have a strong and valid legal position if problems develop in or on the property.

Here are some legal strategies that a new-home owner should pursue to deal with problems that develop on the property:

1. Keep copies of all forms, warranties, reports, and promises made by the builder.
2. Notify the builder as soon as a problem is apparent; if the

problem is not corrected immediately, be sure to write to the builder explaining the difficulty.

3. Take photographs or make a videotape of any problems that develop for later reference; keep records of visits by repair persons, including date, time spent on the property, names, and purported action taken.

4. If the problem remains uncorrected, contact the state attorney general's office to see what state laws might apply, and notify any private warranty programs that have been purchased to cover the property.

5. Initiate any claims procedures, including arbitration or mediation efforts that may be available through warranty programs, state laws, or nearby business associations. Treat any meeting or hearing as seriously and professionally as a trial in court.

6. Contact other homeowners who have homes built by the same builder to see if they are experiencing the same problem. If so, consider joining forces to press claims.

7. If the home is in a subdivision, or is in a cooperative or condominium, contact the homeowner's association about taking action on behalf of the homeowners whose units are affected by the problem.

8. Consider notifying the lender, Better Business Bureau, and home builders associations if the builder will not respond to the complaints.

9. If defects persist, consider bringing legal action against the home builder (and possibly any product manufacturers) for breaches of express or implied warranties.

10. If the problem has resulted in an injury to someone, a product liability action or negligence case might be the appropriate response, and the homeowner should contact an attorney.

MOBILE OR MANUFACTURED HOMES

Mobile and manufactured homes, whether purchased for a primary residence or for a retirement or vacation home, are treated by the law more like products than like real estate. Rules of product warranty and product liability are more liberally applied to mobile and manufactured homes than to other housing.

A mobile home—properly called a manufactured home—

comes complete from the factory with kitchen appliances, built-in furniture, and basic features such as plumbing, a heating system, a water heater, and electricity. Federal laws specify that the homeowner should receive information explaining all the systems in the home and providing warranties for all products.

Manufactured homes built after 1976 must comply with specifications set by the U.S. Department of Housing and Urban Development (HUD). In addition, many states have established special laws to protect the owners of manufactured homes.

Modular homes, which are delivered to a site 80 percent complete and then finished on location, also must comply with building code requirements in the locality. (For more information about modular homes, contact the National Association of Home Builders' Building Systems Councils, Fifteenth and M streets, N.W., Washington, DC 20005.)

Local laws also affect the siting of mobile homes with regard to skirting the foundation, anchoring to the ground, adding steps with handrails, and various fire prevention measures. In many communities, mobile homes are restricted by zoning laws. (For more information on mobile and manufactured homes, *Tips on Buying a Manufactured Home* is available for $1 from the Council of Better Business Bureaus, Inc., 4200 Wilson Boulevard, Arlington, VA 22203, 703-276-0100.)

Federal laws require the manufacturers of mobile homes to provide warranties for quality and workmanship. If defects are uncovered in a mobile or manufactured home, the homeowner can contact the manufacturer, the retailer who sold the product, the state attorney general's office, HUD (Manufactured Housing and Construction Standards Division, Room 9158, Washington, DC 20410, 202-708-2210), or the Federal Trade Commission (Washington, DC 20480; for general FTC information, call 202-326-2222 or a local federal information center).

CHANGING LAWS ON DEFECTS

The laws protecting homeowners against defects discovered after the purchase are in great flux and are unpredictable. Buyers of new homes have greater legal remedies, but if a serious problem arises with the property after purchase, consult a local attorney as soon as possible.

3

Property Boundaries, Easements, and Encroachments

Boundaries indicate how much land legally belongs to each property owner. Boundaries also imply rights—property owners can claim the right to do whatever they want within the property's boundaries (so long as it is also within the boundaries of the law).

The property's boundaries are stated in the contract and deed, often in a long description that by its very length makes it seem irrefutable. But boundaries are not always as exact as they may appear. In years past, boundary descriptions used landmarks—a tree, a body of water, even a neighbor's fence. But all of those things can change. In addition, land is three-dimensional. Property descriptions on paper are poor substitutes for the real thing. Technical transcriptions lend themselves to error. On the other hand, the exact line of a boundary—whether one foot to the east or two to the west—is often not terribly important. Most property owners get along just fine with slight uncertainty about the exact boundaries of their land.

The original boundaries may have been altered by use, whether or not official permission was granted. The overhanging roof of a neighbor's shed may cross another's boundary, or a neighbor may have gained the legal right to use a shortcut through another's property by actual longtime use. If no objection has been made, this is known as *adverse possession.*

> *If a boundary question arises, take corrective action quickly. At risk is the loss of some use of the land.*

In addition, right to a property is rarely total. Utility companies and municipalities may have a right-of-way, or an *easement,* for lines, poles, and streets. Tree roots may stretch from one lot to another, without regard to who owns the property, sometimes creating an intrusion or *encroachment* onto another's land.

Some rights are formalized by recordings in the deed or county recording system. Others are not, yet they are perfectly valid.

Legal questions about boundaries fall into three basic categories:

1.   an error in boundary locations or the failure to record boundaries or adjustments in the title, deed, or contract
2.   use of the property by an easement, covenant, encroachment, license, or adverse possession, in which someone gains rights to use another's land
3.   the maintenance of property that lies on a boundary—a fence, a tree, or an underground cable

If a boundary question arises, take corrective action quickly. At risk is the loss of some use of the land.

> If neighbor A builds a driveway partially on neighbor B's land and B does nothing to object, that driveway may become a permanent pathway on the property, which could ultimately lower B's property value.

FIXING BOUNDARIES

Boundaries must be written into the deed or contract. At times, the boundaries may be described by reference to an official map or to a *plat,* a document that describes lot size, street width, and other defining property features. Plats are prepared privately and filed with a government office. Most states have a government survey system. Property descriptions are filed in the county recorder's office.

Ownership extends from the land into the airspace above the property for at least 50 feet, and up to 500 feet, depending on the state. Ownership also extends below ground, so that someone who wishes to mine below the surface or plant cable would need to get a special agreement or license.

The title search and resulting abstract of title, protected by title insurance, is intended to guarantee that the purchaser gets all the property stated in the deed. The title search company is obliged to double-check all records and affirm the title's accuracy.

An error-free warranty deed, in particular, is intended to contain the proper description of the property and its boundaries, be properly recorded, and grant property that is not subject to undisclosed covenants, easements, encroachments, adverse claims, or other encumbrances (see chapter 1).

BOUNDARY ERRORS

Fixing the dimensions of the boundary line on paper is complex and errors can result. The homeowner is protected from an error in recording the boundaries by title insurance. Few home purchasers want to pay for a survey to double-check the boundaries, although a bank might require it in some cases. At a minimum, a buyer is expected to conduct a visual inspection.

If the boundaries are misrepresented to the buyer in any significant way, the homeowner would have a legal claim against the seller for failing to deliver a marketable title—a breach of the guarantee that the property is accurately described in the title. Alternatively, a homeowner might have a claim against the seller for a defect discovered after the purchase (see chapter 2).

In modern subdivisions, the lots are generally divided by a developer who owns the entire parcel of land and creates smaller lots. These boundaries are often more concise and less susceptible to recording error, although situations do arise in which even these boundaries are misrecorded.

A homeowner who discovers an error in the stated boundaries should bring an action to correct the recorded title, sometimes known as an action to *quiet title*. The homeowner is not seeking damages or financial compensation but is merely making certain that the record is accurate so that neighbors, builders, and subsequent owners are officially notified about the property boundaries. An action to quiet title goes before a judge and the judge's decision is recorded. These cases are procedurally technical and an attorney is usually necessary.

In addition, if an error was made in the title search or if the title search failed to discover an encumbrance, encroachment, easement, or competing claims to the land, the homeowner could consider making a claim to the title insurance company.

UNCERTAIN BOUNDARIES

At times, neighbors are legitimately uncertain about the exact boundaries of their properties. The original marker—stream, tree, or well—may have been removed or altered.

Particularly when one person wants to build or construct on land that is in question, neighbors may decide it is time to enter into a voluntary agreement fixing the boundaries.

An agreement to fix the practical locations will be acknowledged only if (1) the owners are genuinely uncertain about the boundary, (2) they agree on a new boundary, and (3) they recognize the new boundary in practice by marking it on the ground in some way. A ground marker, such as a fence, will serve as a notice to other people.

Once these boundaries are agreed on, they should be described in a written document that includes the formal property descriptions from the deed, statements that the boundary is uncertain and what the new boundary will be, and signatures of both parties. The homeowner should keep a copy with the deed to the property and file a copy with the county recorder.

A voluntary agreement on boundary lines also can be handled by each neighbor signing a *quitclaim deed* to the other. By this document, A assigns to B any possible ownership interests that neighbor A might have in B's property, with a full description of neighbor B's property. In a similar document, B signs over any possible interest in A's property. Both deeds are then filed.

If you have a mortgage or other loan from a bank, you may have to check with the lender before a voluntary adjustment in property lines can be effective.

A homeowner can also hire a surveyor to set the boundary lines. That relieves the neighbors from having to wrangle over exact placement of the boundary.

If neighbors simply cannot agree informally, an action to correct the title, or quiet title, can be brought in court.

Water Boundaries

Many boundaries are formed by streams, lakes, or oceans. Water boundaries are somewhat trickier than land boundaries, since water can readily shift course. The ownership of water is rarely total, except for a lake entirely contained within the property. Water rights are subject to the use of people up and down the stream and often to the superior ownership of the government (see chapter 8).

The basic rule of ownership of the land under the water is that the same right that was acquired by the prior owner, by deed or by changes over time, belongs to the new owner. The flexibility of this rule reflects the difficulty of marking water-covered land accurately.

A homeowner is generally considered to own the land under a lake or stream to the center, or the "meander," of the stream. If the stream shifts, so does the land ownership. There is a major exception to this rule: The government has ownership of navigable streams, tidal streams, and certain other watercourses. If a stream belongs to the government, private property ends at the water's edge. The difference could be important if an owner wanted to erect a dock or deck overhanging the water.

Property surrounding lakes is also usually owned to the water's edge. In some cases, by state law or title, the individual's property interest can extend to the center of the lake. Some lake communities may have covenants granting or prohibiting the building of structures in the water or granting access to the water that covers land owned by another person.

Property along the ocean or on a bay is considered to extend to the high-tide line. The land under the ocean is owned by the federal government. Access to oceanfront property may also be subject to government control, specific covenants and grants in deeds, or special determinations in land-use regulations.

In addition to traditional restrictions on zoning and building, recent environmental and conservation regulations limit construction on waterfront property.

FORMAL RIGHTS OF OTHERS

Other people or entities can gain rights to use the land within a property owner's boundaries. Many of these uses are formal and will be recorded in the deed and filed at the county recorder's office. These can include formal restrictions on property use, known as *covenants;* rights-of-way through the property, known as *easements;* and permits to use the property for some other purpose (such as mining), known as *licenses.*

Some easements are informal and are not stated on any title, but they can still be valid (see following sections). In order to know for certain if an informal easement exists, a property buyer should talk to neighbors and inquire about habits of property usage, informal trails, and access to streets and natural sites that cross the property.

COVENANTS

An ancient rule of property allowed the original owner of a plot of land to put restrictions onto the use of the land when it was sold or passed on. These covenants, unless illegal or outrageous, are valid and limit the homeowner's use of the property.

A covenant might state, for example, that a homeowner agrees not to use certain material in a fence or operate a business or build more than one residence on the property. A covenant might permit all owners in an oceanfront community to have access to one set of stairs to the beach. These covenants are legal and binding.

Covenants today are often used in subdivisions and planned communities. Homeowner's associations and condominium or cooperative boards may also have extensive covenants (known as covenants, conditions, and restrictions, or CC&Rs), which are part of the deed or other ownership documents.

Illegal covenants try to do privately something that is otherwise prohibited by law. Covenants that try to restrict the future sale of property to people of a particular race or religion are illegal under civil rights law and are unenforceable.

> *Covenants that try to restrict the future sale of property to people of a particular race or religion are illegal.*

There is no real mechanism to enforce a covenant other than a lawsuit asserting that a covenant has been violated. In general, the only persons who can sue to enforce the covenant are those who made the covenant or others who are subject to a similar covenant or who might benefit or be injured by the covenant.

CC&Rs created in subdivision, condominium, and cooperative housing are subject to different treatment, because when the covenants are created, enforcement mechanisms are built in. A homeowner's association might have the right to fine or eject a homeowner who violates a covenant (see chapter 17).

Covenants that no longer have any modern purpose can be invalidated. A covenant inserted in an eighteenth-century deed, prohibiting a business use of property that is now in the core of a city, might be invalidated as irrelevant.

FORMAL EASEMENTS

Easements are the most common type of restriction on property usage. An easement allows someone else to use a portion or strip of another's property. Public streets are often easements through private property. Individual deeds will show that the homeowners own land to the center of the street, but the municipality has an easement over part of the land to create a street. An *express easement* is contained in a written document. The formal grant of an easement is similar to the sale of property in that it must be in writing in order to be valid (see following).

An easement creates a property right in the easement holder. The easement holder is permitted to use the portion of the property described for the purposes set out in the easement. Using more property or using it for other purposes exceeds the scope of the easement and can be stopped by an injunction.

Otherwise, the owner of the land upon which the easement is located may not interfere with the rights of the easement holder. An easement holder whose rights are disrupted would have a claim for damages against the property owner, and could get an injunction to stop the interference.

Easement rights exist whether or not the actual easement is used. A municipality can have an effective roadway easement, even though the plans for the street are on paper and it has not been built. In some cases, an easement that is not used for a long time can be considered abandoned. A determination of abandonment would be made by a court through an action to quiet title.

Easements can exist underground or above ground, as well as on the ground. A driveway over a neighbor's property is a common easement. Railroad companies have easements through private property for tracks and track maintenance. Utility companies have easements to string wires above a property owner's land. Landowners have easements for water pipes to run under a neighbor's land.

Some easements are established under rules of eminent domain, by which the government takes over a portion of the property. Railroad, street, and power-line easements are usually acquired in this way (see chapter 16).

Easements by necessity are permitted in most states. Property that is without access to public streets has an easement by necessity through land owned by another to prevent any property from being blocked in.

The exact location and dimension of the boundaries of an easement must be described specifically. Doing this creates the same difficulties that arise in establishing boundaries in general.

INFORMAL EASEMENTS

Some easements are not written into the deed or recorded—they exist simply because they have existed. Even when an easement has not been recorded, the user of the easement can gain a legal right to use it. These are known as *easements by prescription.*

If the easement user has used the easement openly, plainly, and without objection for a number of years (5 to 20), the property owner cannot cut off that right.

If neighbor B has openly used a shortcut through neighbor A's property for 20 years, A cannot put up barriers to keep out B. Neighbor B has an easement by prescription. Neighbor A has lost the right to complete control over this portion of the property; it is now subject to the right of B to use the shortcut. Neighbor A could ask B to sign a release of the easement or could arrange to buy back the easement.

In the above example, neighbor B's stake in the property remains valid, even if A sells to C. Once an easement right is acquired, the land is subject to the easement regardless of the owner. On the other hand, if B's use of the land is not open or does not meet other conditions for an easement by prescription, A has the right to stop B's use.

NONPERMITTED USES

Because the right to use property can be lost by merely acquiescing in someone else's use, homeowners should be cautious if their property is being used by another. A use that is not agreed upon is an encroachment (see below). A property owner can object to an encroachment and should do so by letter, stating that such use has come to the owner's attention and it is not a permitted use. Posting signs can be effective as well.

Because the right to use property can be lost by merely acquiescing in someone else's use, homeowners should be cautious if their property is being used by another.

If necessary, the homeowner can seek a court injunction to prevent unauthorized use of the property.

Granting or Getting an Easement

The sale or grant of an easement must be in writing, preferably in a deed that grants the easement holder the right-of-way or other usage. It must provide the following information:

1.   the identity of the parties
2.   the exact use (for example, a footpath to the beach)
3.   the location of the easement (on the northeast corner of Jones's property, plat 3, lot 5, starting at the southern tip of the redwood fence)
4.   the dimensions of the easement (3 feet wide by 41 feet long)
5.   any uses that are not permitted (no motorized vehicles)
6.   any conditions attached to the easement or special uses allowed (landowner also has the right to use the footpath; easement holder agrees to be responsible for clearing trees along the path)
7.   the price paid to the landowner (for consideration of $250 paid by B to A)
8.   the length of time for which the use is being permitted (for five years from June 30, 1993)
9.   signature of both parties, but, at a minimum, the signature of the person who owns the property and is granting the easement.

This document must be filed at the county recorder's office along with the deed of the land on which the easement is located. Both parties should keep copies as well.

The homeowner with a mortgage will need to contact the bank before agreeing to sell an easement. In most states, the person granted the easement right is responsible for paying property taxes on the easement.

In some cases property is subject to an easement but the original property owner wants to build on the easement portion of the land. One approach for the property owner is to seek a written release from the easement holder. Without such an agreement, the property owner can be held liable for infringing on an easement owner's rights.

Sometimes an easement user exceeds the scope of the easement. If the property owner fails to take steps to limit the easement holder to the agreed-on uses, the easement holder can gain *by prescription* a greater right to use the property than originally intended.

A homeowner may also want to acquire an easement on a neighbor's property. For example, the homeowner wants the right to use a road for access to a fishing stream or wants to lay an underground pipe for better plumbing. An easement could significantly increase the value of the homeowner's property. In order to obtain an easement, the homeowner should contact the other property owner and suggest the easement use. If the neighbor agrees, put the agreement in writing, and pay him or her some amount of money, however small, to create a valid contract.

LICENSES

Homeowners can license the use of property. Unlike an easement, a license is revocable and can be terminated. A right-of-way can be licensed. Oil companies may license property to drill for oil. Air rights and underground-water rights may also be licensed. If the homeowner wishes to grant a neighbor the right to take shortcuts over the property, a revocable license may offer the most flexibility. A revocable license will prohibit the neighbor from claiming a greater right to use the shortcut than the owner intends, and the license can be revoked at a later time if desired.

Licenses should be in writing and recorded at the county recorder's office and noted in the deed.

OTHER LEGAL RESTRICTIONS ON BOUNDARIES

There may also be other official limitations that affect property boundaries. Municipalities may require a certain setback from the street for fences. Fences, for that matter, may be limited in height and material by various local building and zoning ordinances (see chapter 4).

Encroachments and Adverse Possession

An *encroachment* is an intrusion into the property rights of another—a fence that is built over a property line, a tree branch that dangles dangerously over someone's roof, a change in landscaping resulting in a water runoff, or the nonpermitted use of a right-of-way.

As stated previously, someone who trespasses or encroaches on another's property may ultimately gain an interest in the property (called adverse possession). After permitting the conditions for establishing adverse possession to exist (open, visible, continuous use that is inconsistent with the rights of the owner for a substantial amount of time), a property owner may not suddenly complain about the activities or take away the use of the adverse possessor.

Adverse possession is well established in the law. As protection, the homeowner should take action against an encroachment when it first occurs. At times the encroachment can be unintentional, and the first step should be to contact the neighbor informally and ask that the situation be corrected.

In some cases, the encroachment is not objectionable. The homeowner still needs to make an agreement in writing with the neighbor to sell an easement, grant a license, or rent the property for a particular use. Then exactly what is being permitted can be acknowledged and limited, without surprising future owners with a claim of adverse possession that could create a doubt about the property title.

A serious encroachment may require further action. If a neighbor begins to cut trees on the property or builds a new patio that crosses a boundary, the owner should contact the neighbor in writing, and, if necessary, go to court to stop the encroachment by an injunction. Doing nothing indicates acquiescence and could result in a permanent loss of property rights.

Trees: A Common Encroachment

A tree is considered to belong to the property in which its trunk is located. A tree owner is charged with preventing damage to neighbors from roots and branches that extend onto their property. Likewise, a neighbor may not harm a tree on another person's property.

If a neighbor's tree branches threaten a homeowner's property, the homeowner should notify the owner of the tree by letter, explaining the danger. If the tree owner does not take corrective action, a local government agency should be notified. In some cases, the homeowner may be permitted to cut dangerous limbs that overhang the land. Before cutting dangerous tree overhangs, the homeowner should write to the owner again, explaining the intention and seeking permission.

If damage occurs from an unsound tree belonging to a neighbor, the homeowner may seek compensation from his or her homeowner's insurance or that of the tree owner. The tree owner could also be sued for the cost of the repair by pursuing the case in small claims court (see chapter 21).

Sometimes a homeowner who does nothing when the danger from a neighbor's tree becomes apparent is said to acquiesce to the situation. The cautious route is to notify the neighbor and take corrective steps before a crisis occurs.

Tree overhangs are often the subject of local private nuisance laws (see chapter 10). Some communities also have specific ordinances that apply to the planting or trimming of trees.

In addition, covenants in deeds, particularly in subdivisions, may apply to tree planting, maintenance, and trimming. Homeowners may be prohibited from removing trees because the developers wanted the community to have a "forested look."

Easements granted to utility companies generally permit the company to trim trees that endanger wires or poles.

TREES ON A BOUNDARY

If a tree is right on the boundary of two properties, both owners are responsible for it. Neither party is supposed to trim the tree or spend money for its care without the approval of the other.

If reaching an agreement with the neighbor isn't possible and maintenance is necessary to deal with a dangerous condition, the property owner should notify the neighbor, spend the money, and then write to the neighbor again with a copy of the receipt, requesting payment for half the cost. If the neighbor is unwilling to pay, the case will have to be pursued in small claims court.

BOUNDARY FENCES

Like boundary trees, boundary fences belong to both of the neighboring property owners. These co-owners are jointly responsible for the maintenance and care of the fence, including compliance with local laws on height, color, and materials. One homeowner may not remove the fence without the permission of the other.

If one property owner has erected the fence, it belongs to that person. But if a neighbor uses that fence, the neighbor becomes a co-owner and can be asked to pay for part of the cost of the fence. "Using the fence" means treating it as one side of an enclosure for one's own property.

Neighbors are supposed to agree on the maintenance of a boundary fence and share in the costs. If one wants to make repairs, the other can be asked to share the costs. If the neighbor is unwilling or thinks the repairs are unnecessary, the homeowner should evaluate the reasonableness of the need. If the fence looks truly ragged, and the homeowner makes the repairs, the neighbor can be asked to pay half the costs. If the neighbor refuses, the matter can be taken to small claims court or a neighborhood dispute resolution center.

Some subdivisions state in covenants which neighbor owns the fence and how maintenance costs are to be divided. Homeowners can also make an agreement about the care of the fence. One homeowner may be willing to handle all the maintenance.

In some cases, a line of trees acts like a "boundary fence." Again, maintenance is a joint responsibility.

If a property owner builds a truly obnoxious or ugly fence that serves no purpose other than to annoy, it could constitute a *spite fence*. In several states, neighbors can stop the building of such an eyesore by going to court. Sometimes a spite fence is also treated as a private nuisance (see chapter 10).

LEGAL STRATEGIES IN BOUNDARY DISPUTES

Boundary questions are particularly sensitive because they involve someone who lives right next door, often a friend.

When faced with a boundary dispute, take these steps:

1. *Communication.* Try to settle the dispute informally by contacting the neighbor with a friendly letter setting out the prob-

lem—the fence needs mending, and as co-owners the cost should be shared; a sculpture in the backyard has crossed the boundary line.

2. *Agreement.* Try to reach an agreement about the matter. Agreements made to fix boundaries should be in writing, following some of the specifics described earlier, and signed by both parties, then filed at the county recorder's office.

3. *Agency help.* If an informal agreement cannot be reached, a homeowner might have recourse to a government agency, such as a building department, or to a homeowner's association. Disputes between neighbors are so sensitive that some communities have established mediation or neighborhood resolution centers to hear cases informally. Informal does not mean unprepared, though, and if mediation is used, bring a clear and concise explanation of the problem, property descriptions, photographs, bills, receipts, copies of letters, and desired resolution.

4. *Title insurance claim.* The homeowner may have a claim against a title insurance company that was paid at the time of purchase to guarantee the validity and accuracy of the title. An error could occur in failing to note a prior use of the property, whether formal or informal. Send a notice of claim to the title insurance company.

5. *Legal action.* If a problem is not easily resolvable, consider taking legal action. A formal letter from a lawyer may bring the desired result. The matter can be taken to small claims court if the amount of money needed to pay for the damage is small— for example, a neighbor's tree fell and damaged the house.

A lawsuit will need to be pursued in district court if the homeowner is concerned with correcting the boundary lines, quieting title, enforcing a covenant, stopping an encroachment, obtaining an injunction, or recovering substantial damages (see chapter 21).

PREVENTING THE LOSS OF PROPERTY RIGHTS

Total rights to the property can be reduced if the boundaries are not fixed properly or if they are ignored by someone who encroached on the property without permission. Property rights are also limited by licenses, covenants, and easements that give another person the rights to use the property and limit what can be done with it.

Loss of full rights to the property can be temporary, such as an easement granted for a period of years. Or the loss can be permanent, such as a neighbor building a garden kiosk that crosses the boundary line and the homeowner does nothing to object.

Failing to object to a serious encroachment or other use that extends onto a homeowner's property can have significant long-term effects on the property and its value. Whenever a property owner suspects that someone is crossing a boundary, encroaching, or making an adverse claim to the property, the owner should not hesitate to take appropriate action.

Zoning
and Other
Land Use Regulations

The majority of property in the United States is affected by zoning ordinances. Zoning is a way of classifying land and limiting its use. In broadest terms, land was first classified as residential, commercial, or industrial. But most communities now also incorporate extensive designs for land-use control, which describe size of lots, size of structures, bulk, height, esthetic considerations, setbacks, and even such specifics as the shape of structures, architectural review, protection of forestry, limitation on home business use, definitions of family groupings, and parking space regulation.

Zoning is established by local planning boards and applied to local parcels of land. In this regard, zoning is uniquely localized and community-linked.

Zoning is one of several types of land use controls. Others include landmark preservation and environmental regulation. In addition, planned communities, subdivisions, cooperatives, and condominiums may incorporate their own regulations in the form of covenants, conditions, and restrictions (see chapter 17). These are a kind of "private" zoning that places restrictions on the use and design of the property in the same way that zoning regulations do, but they are regulated and enforced by a home-owner's association or developer instead of local government.

The use of zoning is fairly universal. So is the legal framework for adoption and appeal of zoning laws. Communities differ, though, in the exact zoning rules and land-use limitations. The differences are important because they affect individual decisions to build, modify, redesign, or use property in a new way.

Zoning will most directly affect an individual when (1) the community decides to undertake a rezoning plan; (2) a neighbor or someone else in the community seeks a zoning variance or new use that has an impact on the property (a developer seeks a variance for a multiple-family dwelling in a single-residence neighborhood, a doctor's office is sold to a business that intends to open a taxi garage, a community group plans to build a residential shelter); or (3) the homeowner wishes to use the property in a way that is not included in the zoning regulations (to add an apartment on the property for a parent to occupy, to raise the roof for loft space above the allocated heights in the zoning law, to rent a room to a student, to build a basketball court in the front yard, to open a woodworking business in the garage).

How Zoning Affects Property Owners

Zoning directly affects any homeowner who wants to use the property in a particular way or change the use of the property. Since zoning changes can affect the value of property, home-owners will want to be aware of them and know how to use the zoning laws to their advantage. Consider these examples:

- *Adding an extension to the house.* Will the addition comply with zoning requirements on bulk, open space, ratio of property used for the structure, and for the land, setbacks, esthetics, and any number of other possible restrictions?
- *Using the property for a business.* Does the zoning permit business use in general and this specific business use in particular, and can regulations on parking, signs, and so on, be met (see chapter 18)?

Before making any major changes to the property, learn what the current zoning laws permit.

- *Renting a basement apartment.* Does the zoning permit rentals, and does the space meet specifications for entrances and exits or other requirements (see chapter 19)?
- *Paving over the front lawn and turning it into a rock garden.* Do zoning regulations require certain landscaping?
- *Converting a manufacturing loft into an apartment for residential living.* Does the manufacturing zone permit residences, and if not, how can a zoning change be effectuated?
- *A nearby corner grocery store is converting into a drive-in fast-food franchise.* Do zoning laws permit this change of business plan, when traffic, noise, safety, pollution, and hours of operation will be affected?
- *A house in a mostly residential area is operating a private club for college students.* Are zoning requirements being met?
- *A car-parts yard in the neighborhood is now collecting medical waste.* Will this create an adverse impact on property values and does this new use comply with zoning regulations?

Before making any major changes to the property, the homeowner should learn what current zoning laws permit. But this is only the beginning. Zoning laws can be modified. If the change in use or structure is important to the homeowner, the homeowner may want to take further steps to obtain a variance or rezoning or take advantage of a special exception in the zoning law.

At times, a zoning change is sought by a property owner or local business. Other property owners in the area will want to be assured that any zoning change is appropriate and that regulations designed to protect community health and welfare are being followed.

ESTABLISHING ZONING REGULATIONS

Zoning is an exercise of governmental power to promote health, safety, and welfare permissible under interpretations of the U.S. Constitution, so long as the zoning laws are fairly enacted. Zoning laws are under the control of state and local governments. No zoning regulations are enacted by the federal government. Most zoning decisions are made by local planning boards. Recently, states have exercised more control over local boards by specifying the terms and background of the members of zoning boards as well as the standards they must apply in making decisions.

Some states also apply broad restrictions or use permission to blocks of land—designating certain land exclusively for rural, forest, or park use; applying environmental regulations; preventing local zoning boards from overruling certain uses, such as residences for the mentally disabled; or restricting the use of property bordering a highway.

Zoning and planning are probably two of the most powerful tasks of local government, and abuses can occur. If local authorities abuse zoning power, the regulations they make may be subject to challenge.

THE AGENCIES OF ZONING

A zoning board usually consists of professional planners and appointed citizens who adopt a plan for the area. This plan is approved by the city council or other local legislative body.

This plan creates zones of specified use, designated neighborhood by neighborhood, and maps streets, parks, utilities, waste disposal, and other public needs. Planning commissions hold public hearings about the comprehensive plan.

Many cities have a zoning administrator who handles day-to-day zoning functions. A zoning board of adjustment, sometimes known as a zoning board of appeals, is empowered to grant variances and make exceptions in special cases (see below).

Zoning decisions and variances can be appealed in court, but as long as the regulations are not abusive or oppressive, they will be upheld. The court's main considerations are whether the *process* was fair and whether the decision of the zoning board was *reasonable,* even if it was not perfect.

HOW ZONING IS DONE

Zoning is geographically based. The community is divided into physical zones—business, industrial, residential, mixed use, single-family residential, apartment, and so on.

These zones are often given a code designation, such as "Zone R2." Commonly, letters of the alphabet describe the type of zone—R for residential, C for commercial, I or M for industrial or manufacturing. Within each zone, numbers may indicate levels of use. R1 might be a single-family residential district, R2 might be a two-family residential district, and R10 a zone for apartment complexes. The exact designation depends on the scheme in the community.

The zones are drawn on a zoning map in each community. The maps and regulations are on file at city hall, the zoning board, or some other public agency and open to the public to review.

Restrictions differ from zone to zone. A commercial zone might permit buildings to be 10 stories high and require each building to have 10 parking spaces for each commercial tenant. A residential zone might limit buildings to 2 stories and require that a house fill no more than two-thirds of the lot. Within each zone with the same designation, the regulations must be the same for each piece of property.

Because zoning is a neighborhood-by-neighborhood regulation, zoning rules that apply in one part of a community may be different in another part of the town. Homeowners must know the exact zoning of their property and are entitled to receive notices of any intent to change the zoning of property nearby.

Regulations within a zone commonly define

- *Lot* size and shape, including minimum size and minimum frontage
- *Building,* including height, bulk, or area of the property to be covered with a building, open space, minimum floor space, floor-area ratio (FAR), and design control of new buildings
- *Use,* including limits on business and commercial activity

USE ZONING

Lot and building regulations make specific physical demands on the property. Use zoning is more controversial because it limits what an owner can do on the property.

Under most zoning schemes, industrial zones have the lowest use, and residential zones have the highest use. A low-use zone may include higher uses, such as permitting residences to be built in an industrial zone. But unless special exceptions are made, a high-use zone such as a residential area excludes lower uses—for example, a factory cannot open in a residential zone.

Zoning regulations can require compliance with the regulations of other agencies of government—for example, board of health regulations or environmental rules. Zoning regulations usually incorporate these rules only by a general reference, and specifics need to be obtained from the other agency. Board of health regulations, for example, might specify the size of sewer pipes; environmental regulations might require the removal of asbestos during any new construction.

Zoning can be very specific. *Commercial zoning* might be divided into small stores, shopping malls, office buildings, gas stations, restaurants, drive-in facilities, adult-entertainment districts, and so on. An *industrial zone* might be described by the type of industries allowed, as well as details such as the permitted level of air pollutants that can be released. *Residential zoning* can be divided into single-family, multiple-dwelling, hotels, boardinghouses, mobile homes, dorms, and institutional housing.

Some communities have tried to limit the types of people who may live in residences—for example, by prohibiting more than two persons not related by marriage or blood from living in a single-family residence. One such regulation, aimed at college students, was upheld by the U.S. Supreme Court in 1974 as a valid way to apply health and safety regulations. But a regulation that defined family in a way that excluded a grandmother from living with her son and two nephews was struck down by the Court in 1977.

Zoning has limited the number of pets a homeowner may have. Some communities restrict the number of dogs or cats to three. Other communities specify that certain animals may not be kept in a residential zone—live farm animals such as chickens, rabbits, sheep, or horses.

Zoning is not permitted if it excludes particular uses from every zone in the municipality. Zoning rules that prohibit stores or apartment buildings from being built anywhere in a community have not been upheld.

Contemporary Zoning Issues

In addition to concerns about types of families and general limits on the use of property, communities are grappling with the fine details of various zoning issues.

Affordable Housing   One concern is raised when communities exclude families with lower incomes by requiring exceptionally large lot sizes and floor area ratios for houses in every part of the town or city. Zoning regulations that required one-acre lot sizes and floor space of 1,600 square feet were found invalid in one case. Some states are actively requiring communities to adopt zoning regulations that permit the development of affordable housing.

Group Residences   Housing for unrelated adults with specific characteristics, such as housing for seniors, for persons with disabilities, or for the previously homeless, is often hotly contested. Neighborhood issues are pitted against overall community needs, and state rulings have varied widely. Some states are under court order to establish group residences for certain populations and must open them *somewhere,* resulting in the passage of laws that prohibit municipalities from rejecting group residences.

Dumps   The not in my backyard (NIMBY) questions often land in the lap of zoning boards, which have the power to make land-use decisions. The locations of dumps and less safe environmental uses are controversial. Overburdening of some neighborhoods—often those with low-income families or those populated more heavily by minorities—is causing many communities to review these decisions.

Pornography   Disagreement invariably arises over pornography zoning. Communities have attempted to restrict adult movie houses or establishments that cater to adult entertainment. Some communities have established a porn district, a geographical area in which all adult entertainment is located. Others have set regulations that prohibit adult entertainment from being within a certain distance of schools, churches, or even another adult entertainment establishment.

Home Business   The number of people who work at home has grown, and many home businesses are small and don't increase traffic or congestion. On the other hand, the need for certain home businesses has expanded, such as day care for children or seniors, even though they may increase noise and activity in the neighborhood. Home business regulations are being challenged or reevaluated in many communities.

ESTHETIC ZONING

In suburban and high-income areas especially, communities have adopted esthetic zoning, which establishes community standards for building and architectural decisions by individual homeowners. Esthetic zoning may require that home building plans be approved by an architectural review committee.

Architectural review often includes look-alike ordinances that restrict buildings from imitating other buildings in the community to prevent monotonous neighborhoods, and compatibility ordinances that require buildings to fit in with other structures to prevent jarring single lots that can lower property values and disturb continuity. Although these ordinances can seem inconsistent, many communities have both.

> Under esthetic zoning, communities can prohibit billboards and advertisements. In one recent case, a homeowner was prohibited from planting religious symbols on the lawn fewer than 30 feet from the roadway. In that case, not even powerful First Amendment claims to religious freedom or freedom of expression could overcome what was seen as a reasonable zoning ordinance.

Esthetic zoning has also been used to describe permissible landscaping, fences, lawn objects, solar panels, decks, antennae, satellite dishes, trees, colors of paint, types of materials, shapes of roofs, and recreational additions such as pools or ballfields.

EXISTING USES

Zoning was enacted in many communities after a significant portion of the community was already built. Under "grandfather" clauses, zoning ordinances do not affect property that was already standing and had a certain use, unless that use is abandoned.

Existing uses that are allowed as exceptions to the zoning plan are known as *nonconforming uses*. A store that existed in a residential neighborhood prior to the enactment of zoning regulations may remain a store. If the store is closed for a period of time, for example, five years, the use is abandoned, and the nonconforming property is subject to current zoning regulations.

Nonconforming uses may also be limited by preventing an expansion or enlargement of the use. A store that is nonconforming may be prohibited from adding another room or opening an outdoor sales lot.

SPOT ZONING

For zoning regulations to be fair and effective, the same regulations must apply to every parcel in the same zone. Some planning boards have sought to single out one parcel within a block of property for zoning or rezoning, known as spot zoning. Spot zoning defies the logic of a *plan* for zoning regulations by making exceptions to the overall concept. It often stems from favoritism and manipulation, and can lead to an abuse of power. The courts have generally found spot zoning improper.

VARIANCES

A variance is permission to depart from some portion of the zoning regulation. As a kind of safety valve from a rigid application of zoning laws, a variance may be granted by the zoning board of appeals. Variances are supposed to be granted only if the zoning regulation can be demonstrated to cause "unnecessary hardship" or "practical difficulty."

The thinking behind the grant of variances is that property is necessarily unique. Some property—perhaps because of the curve of the land—may conform to certain zoning requirements more easily than other properties. A neighborhood might have height restrictions on buildings in order to maintain a view, keep open space and light, and to prevent overbuilding in a neighborhood. This is an acceptable zoning plan. But one property might be in a valley, so that sticking to the strict height limitation would make the property difficult to build on and not particularly attractive. By seeking a variance, a property owner might be relieved of the duty to follow the strict letter of the zoning ordinance.

In granting a variance, the zoning board might apply other requirements to the property. The property owner might be allowed to build higher than other property but be required to use a smaller land area for the foundation, in this way keeping the same floor-area ratio as other property in the same zone.

A zoning board is entitled to consider the impact of the variance on the community as a whole and on the neighboring property. Variances that will have a slight impact are, of course, more readily granted than those that seek dramatic changes. Variances can also be granted if the zoning laws will cause an "unnecessary hardship" to an individual owner. Zoning boards differ considerably in the standards used to grant or reject variances.

Variances can be appealed by an aggrieved party, which might be a neighbor or other citizen, although appeals are rare.

SPECIAL EXCEPTIONS

Special exceptions are like variances or spot zoning. They permit an individual property owner to make an adjustment to the zoning for a parcel of land. These are also known as *special uses* or *conditional uses.*

But special exceptions differ from variances and spot zoning in one important way. Special exceptions are specifically listed in the planning scheme as uses that *can* be allowed in that zone if an application is approved by the local zoning board. A church or temple might be a special exception to a residential zone—that is, a property owner can build a church or temple in a residential zone if the circumstances are right and an application is approved.

Similar to special exceptions are *floating zones.* These zones and the uses they allow are not designated to any particular land on the zoning map. If property owners apply to use their property for a specified floating-zone purpose, the matter is presented to the zoning board or city council for a determination.

REZONING

Rezoning or the adoption of zoning amendments is an effort to change the entire scheme of zoning in an area. Rezoning is at times undertaken for practical reasons—for instance, the original zoning ordinances are outdated and the needs of the community have changed. Rezoning cannot be done solely by the zoning board; it must be passed by the local legislative body, such as a city council. A zoning amendment permanently readjusts the classification of the property on the zoning map.

Rezoning, like zoning, is supposed to accomplish the underlying goals of promoting health, safety, welfare, and morals. It is meant to be undertaken in conjunction with a comprehensive plan and to benefit the community as a whole.

Rezoning has also been attempted to treat particular parcels of land favorably, almost like a giant variance or illegal spot zoning. If rezoning is considered to be spot zoning that merely benefits a particular property, a court may find it to be illegal.

Some property has been reclassified as open space, preventing building. Large areas are often subject to limited development. Open-space provisions are frequently challenged as amounting to a "taking" of property for which the property owner should receive compensation from the government (see chapter 16). Few property owners have successfully challenged open-space provisions, but it is a subject that is likely to continue to be tested in court.

Communities have attempted to declare moratoriums on development by restricting zoning variances, special exceptions, or rezoning. Courts are beginning to view moratoriums as temporary measures that a community can adopt while it plans rezoning or makes a new overall development plan. Moratoriums that turn into stonewalling may be considered an abuse of power.

ZONING AND PROCEDURAL FAIRNESS

Zoning enactments must be adopted according to a comprehensive plan. The laws must be a rational means of achieving a legitimate end. They cannot be arbitrary or capricious.

The zoning regulations must follow rules of procedural fairness. Homeowners are entitled to be notified about zoning decisions affecting their property. The ordinances must allow property owners to seek relief from the law, often through the variance process.

> *Homeowners are entitled to be notified about zoning decisions affecting their property.*

A property owner must be able to appeal zoning decisions. An administrator's decision can be appealed to a zoning board, and a zoning board's decision to a city council or court.

FAILURE TO COMPLY

The ramifications of violating the zoning laws can be severe. The city or neighbors may seek an injunction to stop the new building or construction. In the harshest cases, buildings that are constructed in violation of zoning laws can be torn down and removed. On the other hand, it is not uncommon for zoning violations to be ignored.

The city is primarily responsible for enforcing zoning regulations. If violations occur, a homeowner will get a notice of violation and it can be contested. If the homeowner fails to comply with a final zoning decision, the city could take further enforcement action, such as denying a building permit or ordering that the violation be removed.

Citizens can bring violations to the attention of city officials. If the city does not act to enforce the law, the citizens could bring a lawsuit against the zoning organization for failing to uphold its duty. Political and organized community pressure may get action from a zoning board.

Similarly, if the citizens feel that zoning board decisions are arbitrary, they can sue and seek to have the decision reversed.

Many zoning violations are undetected by city authorities and go uncorrected. Nevertheless, it is risky to ignore zoning requirements. If the homeowner makes a permanent change to the property that violates zoning laws, a problem can arise at the time of a future sale: The seller will not be able to guarantee that the property complies with all existing zoning laws, a common requirement in a sale. The seller may be forced to correct the violation, withdraw the property from sale, or accept a reduced price. Worse, the seller could face a lawsuit if the property is sold and the zoning violations are discovered later (see chapter 2).

Seeking a Modification in Zoning

A property owner who wants to make a change in the property or the use of the property that is not consistent with zoning ordinances can seek a variance.

Since zoning laws are locally governed, the difficulty in obtaining a variance changes enormously from place to place. In large cities with complex zoning laws, an attorney will be necessary.

To make a change on or in the use of the property, take these steps:

1. *Research property zoning.* Check out the zoning laws and see if the planned new use of the property complies.

2. *Check zoning laws for special exceptions or floating zones.* If the use is not permitted in the property zone, research whether there is a special exception clause or floating-zone provision. If so, apply to the zoning board or city council to qualify for those provisions.

3. *Modify planned use.* If the use intended does not comply with the zoning, consider whether the use can be modified. For example, perhaps a planned extension could be altered in width to fit within existing zoning requirements. If modification is not possible, consider dropping the plan. A real estate attorney familiar with the community can evaluate your chances of winning a zoning challenge.

4. *Seek a variance.* If the change in structure or use of the property is not major, or if the zoning rule seems unfair as applied to the property, apply for a variance. The request for a variance will be heard by the local zoning administrator.

5. *Appeal the denial of a variance.* If the request for a variance is denied by a zoning administrator, an appeal can be made to a local zoning board, and then to a court. At this stage a review by an attorney would be wise.

6. *Seek a rezoning amendment.* If a variance is denied, and the

property owner is ambitious, trying to change the entire zoning plan for the city—or state, for that matter—is an option. When real estate developments involve large sums of money, this step is not unrealistic. For the individual homeowner, it probably is. At times community groups feel so strongly about zoning changes that they can act as a whole. In some states, community groups have sought to change zoning by initiative or referendum votes, though the constitutionality of these actions is still being debated.

STANDARDS USED IN GRANTING VARIANCES

The standards for granting variances differ enormously from community to community. Many cities grant "area" variances more easily than they grant "use" variances.

For a variance in the *use* of the property, a homeowner ordinarily needs to show that

- The zoning ordinance poses an unnecessary hardship in the use of the property. Unnecessary hardship includes practical difficulty in using the property. It might also extend to a financial burden by depriving the owner of the property's value, as shown by appraisal evidence.
- The hardship is unique and is a consequence of owning this particular piece of property, and does not apply to the majority of the zone. Also, the hardship was not brought on by the owner.
- The variance requested will not affect the basic character of the neighborhood.

The standards for granting an *area* variance are often less stringent. In general, an area variance is balanced against community needs. A slight area variance that has little impact on the community's health or welfare is usually granted. A large variance in area requirements that has a major impact on the community's health and welfare is likely to be denied.

In seeking an area variance in the size of the structure the homeowner needs to show that

- the variance will not have an undesirable effect on the character, environment, or esthetics of the neighborhood

- the benefit sought cannot be readily achieved by some other method
- the variance is not large (smaller variances are more likely to be granted)
- if the variance is not granted, the property owner will suffer an economic burden

In requesting a variance, a property owner should be as well prepared as if the matter were a case in court (see chapter 21). Decisions by the zoning administrator or the zoning board of appeals are unlikely to be overturned in court, unless they are shown to be unreasonable, arbitrary, or capricious. The zoning board has extensive power, and the best strategy is to try to persuade the board that the variance should be granted.

In the hearing on the zoning variance, present as much information as possible. The property owner or an attorney should state clearly what zoning variance is sought and why, and should supply evidence—drawings, survey, architectural design, the testimony of an architect or builder, financial information, and appraisal—to support the case.

In granting a variance, the zoning board can impose certain conditions. A greater setback might be approved if the homeowner agrees to plant more trees. Variances can also be limited to a certain period of time.

Objecting to Zoning Variance

A homeowner who objects to a neighbor building a new structure—whether a skateboard park for the children, a hothouse for a small vegetable business, or a major industrial plant for construction of computer parts—will want to show that

- the use is inconsistent with the neighborhood
- it will have an adverse impact on the neighborhood by decreasing property values
- it was not intended in the original zoning ordinance
- it will affect the health and safety of neighbors, for example, by increasing traffic, pollutants, noise, posing a threat, or causing other disruptions to tranquillity
- it will change the character and physical environment of the neighborhood

- existing regulations do not pose an unnecessary hardship or inordinate economic burden on the property owner seeking the variance
- the property owner could make modifications in the property in a less intrusive manner

Those who object to a zoning change must do so at the earliest possible opportunity, such as at a hearing before a zoning administrator or zoning board of appeals.

In some cases, homeowners do not find out about or understand the ramifications of a zoning change until after it has been granted. In order to challenge the zoning at this point, the homeowner will probably need to file a lawsuit and seek an injunction.

LANDMARK AND HISTORIC DISTRICTS

Some communities have established landmark or historic zones. The French Quarter in New Orleans is a historic zone and certain blocks of property in Boston, Raleigh, New York City, Dallas, and elsewhere have landmark designations.

Historic and landmark areas are regulated by a preservation or landmark commission, which restricts the demolition, alteration, or development of property in the area. To preserve the character of the district, emphasis is placed on the building exteriors.

In these areas, a property owner must make a specific request to a preservation commission before making any change or alteration to the property. In order to prevent the landmark designation from becoming burdensome, the landmark commission is empowered to grant significant variances. The process is similar to that for granting zoning variances.

In some cases, the historic designation can add to a property's value. Tax deductions may be available for rehabilitation of landmark properties (see chapter 11).

ENVIRONMENTAL LAWS

Environmental laws prohibit the development of property in certain areas.

These laws generally affect rural property owners, large developers, and businesses rather than individual homeowners in cities and suburbs. The owners of property that has been subject to environmental land-use regulation claim that their property has been made unusable to them and economically inviable. They have pressed for compensation, arguing that the environmental laws are a government taking of property (see chapter 16).

OTHER LAWS THAT AFFECT HOMEOWNER USE

Noise abatement laws may restrict activities on private property, such as loud music or drilling, that exceeds decibel restrictions. Health codes may prohibit the accumulation of garbage and junk. Nuisance laws may halt an activity if it is offensive because of its smell or dangerous to public health, such as keeping chemicals on the property (see chapter 10). Sanitation codes may require the separation of garbage for recycling or require specific installation of septic-tank disposal systems and maintenance of leaching fields. Water boards may limit the household use of water, particularly in times of drought.

Laws may prohibit cutting trees or require trimming of them. Some communities require homeowners to cut their grass, and outlaw weeds or overgrowth. Animal control laws may place limitations on pet ownership. Building codes may make specific provisions for construction, including materials that can be used, and design limitations (see chapter 5).

As with zoning and land-use regulations, when challenged, these laws have been considered valid, falling within the power of local governments to secure the health, welfare, and safety of the community as a whole. Despite the inconveniences to private-property owners, only local laws that are unreasonable, discriminatory, capricious, fail to provide fair procedures, or contravene state or federal laws are cast aside.

Repairs,
Additions,
and Construction

An advantage of home ownership is being able to tailor the property to fit individual taste. Remodeling, improvements, and repairs—whether adding a fireplace or a room—can enhance the property enormously. Americans spend over $100 billion a year on home renovations.

Extensive home remodeling is governed by various city codes. In most communities, a building permit is required for major structural repairs, and zoning restrictions, covenants in property deeds, and housing codes may restrict remodeling choices.

STANDARD MAINTENANCE AS PREVENTION

Neglecting basic maintenance can have legal ramifications. If a neighbor's property is damaged by a limb that crashes from a homeowner's tree, the homeowner can be liable (see chapter 7).

While homeowner's insurance covers most damages or injuries

to other people or property, the insurance company is not obligated to pay for damages caused by the homeowner's failure to maintain the property in keeping with building, zoning, or other codes and laws. An insurance company also might refuse to pay for damages that resulted from dangers of which a homeowner was aware but failed to correct. Nor does homeowner's insurance cover injuries suffered by the owners or members of their family. Regular home maintenance is a basic legal protection.

Remodeling and Taxes

Home repairs are distinguished from major home improvements in property tax appraisals and federal income tax calculations (see chapter 11).

Repairs include patching the roof, painting the exterior, and plastering walls. Home remodeling includes adding a room; converting a room for a new use; or installing a major structural system, such as a new roof, plumbing, central air-conditioning, or wiring.

In terms of property taxes, major home remodeling can result in a reappraisal of the property to a new, higher fair market value, and a consequent rise in property taxes. But repairs that are necessary maintenance do not result in an increase in fair market value. In many locations, property tax appraisers follow up on building permits and visit property for reevaluation.

> *Home repairs are distinguished from major home improvements in property tax appraisals and federal income tax calculations.*

Home improvement can lower the federal taxes homeowners may owe if they sell their property. The costs of improvements (but not repairs) can be added to the adjusted base value of the house, lowering the homeowner's profit, or capital gain. It is capital gain on which federal income tax must be paid (except if the money is reinvested or subject to exclusion—see chapter 11). A homeowner should keep complete records of home improvement expenditures during ownership of the property.

If the property is used as a work space or part of it is rented to a tenant, the prorated cost of home repairs can be deducted from the income received.

If the property is used as a work space or part of it is rented to a tenant, the prorated cost of home repairs can be deducted from the income received. The costs of the repairs are deducted in the year in which they are made (see chapters 18 and 19).

Also, some types of renovations may entitle a homeowner either to federal or state tax breaks. These deductions change from time to time and from state to state. Homeowners have been permitted to deduct a portion of the cost of repairs that increased the energy efficiency of a house or that introduced alternative energy uses. Property with historic or landmark designation is sometimes entitled to favorable tax treatment when rehabilitation is undertaken.

BUILDING PERMITS

Building codes exist virtually everywhere, and they can be extensive. Before undertaking any major new construction or renovation, a homeowner may be required to get a building permit.

In practice, some single-family homeowners can undertake building projects without getting a permit, depending on the level of scrutiny by local authorities. The problem with not getting a permit is that some code requirement might be overlooked and the entire renovation might have to be redone. Upon sale, the contract generally guarantees that the house complies with all code requirements. The discovery of violations can result in having to make those corrections or, in the worst case, the buyer backing out of a contract to purchase, or even suing. Getting a permit can prevent later problems.

If the construction is being undertaken on a multiple-family dwelling, condominium, or cooperative, a building permit is necessary. If a contractor is hired, a permit is a must for the homeowner. Exterior renovations will obviously alert city officials to construction, and failure to have a building permit could bring the project to a halt. Homeowners have been slapped with stop orders, fines, and, in the rare case, arrest. The city can deny a certificate of occupancy when the construction is done, making it illegal for anyone to live on the property.

To receive a permit, homeowners pay a fee and fill out an application that describes the changes they plan to make. Architectural drawings, plans, and specifications are attached. Homeowners must comply with regulations on the pickup and disposal of construction material, such as making arrangements for a Dumpster to be on-site.

The city department reviews the plans to make certain that they comply with building and other codes, such as fire and health. The building department also considers the zoning laws. But the homeowner can't rely on the building department's interpretation and must make an independent evaluation of zoning laws.

After the city or town grants a permit, an inspector usually makes periodic on-site inspections to check on the progress of the work, and on completion signs off on the project. A building permit can expire if not used within a specified time after it is issued, for example, 180 days.

Getting a building permit is not always easy. The process is so difficult in some cities, such as New York, that property owners regularly hire trained expediters to navigate the process. Architects, engineers, free-lance building inspectors, and contractors can handle the building permit process for a homeowner in many cities.

If the building permit is denied, the homeowner can make adjustments to the application or appeal the denial. An appeal will be heard by a board of appeals, not unlike the process described in zoning appeals (see chapter 4). In making an appeal, retaining an attorney familiar with the process is helpful.

If the board of appeals rejects the application, the homeowner can go to court, but the standards applied will be strict, and unless the decision by the board of appeals was unreasonable, a court will uphold it.

THE CODES

Building codes were enacted to promote health, welfare, safety, and morals. A standard building code touches on zoning ordinances as well as fire code regulations, health regulations, electrical codes, and environmental laws.

Building codes are available for public inspection in the city buildings department and in most public libraries. Since building codes are updated frequently in many communities, review the most recent version.

Building codes define minimum requirements in

- height, setback, bulk, yard space, and building lines, including the location of auxiliary buildings such as sheds, garages, greenhouses, or any prefab or modular housing
- structure—walls, roofs, ceilings, floors, windows, and foundation, including regulations about adequate light and ventilation, such as requiring a window in every room
- materials—setting standards for fireproofing, lumber grade, and durability; prohibiting the use of asbestos or lead paint and requiring removal when construction is undertaken; specific requirements such as covered drains or metallic leaders to the roof
- fire regulations—exit doors, fire walls between adjoining houses, fireproof construction, and special treatment in certain types of buildings (sprinklers in nursing homes)
- sanitation—specifications on plumbing, connections to sewers, size of pipes, prohibition or regulation of septic tanks, rat proofing, and disposal of garbage
- electrical—materials and wiring, usually contained in an electrical code and requiring a licensed electrician to complete
- miscellaneous systems—elevators in condominium buildings, incinerators, fireplaces, and chimneys

One area of particular concern is converting a one-family dwelling to a multifamily residence, which involves a good deal of additional building code requirements concerning fire exits, entrances, ventilation, permitted occupancy per room, plumbing, and cooking facilities.

Another renovation that touches off crucial building permit questions is when a new structure or expansion of the house is being built. Because additions involve multiple areas of the building code—structural, electrical, and safety—the homeowner or architect needs to make certain that each code is consulted and that all systems are in compliance with the current requirements. If excavation is involved, a special permit must be secured and all neighbors notified in advance.

ZONING

Building alterations must comply with zoning ordinances. These may prohibit two-family dwellings and may have limitations on height, curb setback, percent of land space that can be covered with structures, and many other requirements (see chapter 4). Since the particular requirements of a zone vary from zone to zone and in some cases from neighborhood to neighborhood, consult zoning ordinances directly before making major structural alterations.

Be particularly careful to double-check zoning laws if neighbors are likely to object to major remodeling.

> In one case neighbors challenged the building permit for a new house, claiming that the height of the home violated zoning laws. The objections were raised after the construction was well under way, and the homeowner was forced to halt the project while the matter was decided by a zoning board.

BUILDING RESTRICTIONS IN COVENANTS, DEEDS, AND RULES

Many neighborhood developments, planned unit developments (PUDs), subdivisions, condominiums, and cooperatives have restrictions on the type of remodeling that can be done on the property. These covenants are generally contained in the deed or bylaws of the homeowner's or condominium owner's association (see chapter 17).

Covenants and association restrictions are not considered in the building permit review, since these are private rules about the property. Deed restrictions can limit home remodeling. Esthetic considerations are rigorously enforced in many communities through an architectural review committee. The covenants may limit secondary structures such as sheds, require certain materials and even colors to be used in the construction, and even demand extensive nightly cleanup.

In addition, some condominium or cooperative buildings limit the hours or days during which construction can take place. Some buildings prohibit renovation during certain months—limiting work to summertime when more people are on vacation.

Before undertaking major remodeling or exterior renovation, make certain that the plans are consistent with the rules and regulations of homeowner's associations and all covenants or deed restrictions.

HEADING OFF PROBLEMS BY EXTENSIVE RECORD KEEPING

Record keeping should include *all* receipts, information that accompanies products, warranties, contracts, names and addresses of suppliers, attorneys, and building inspectors, along with a diary of work undertaken and completed.

As recommended previously, keep records during the entire period of home ownership; problems and issues may not arise for years. Tax implications of home repairs, for example, can be both short term and long term. In the short term, a homeowner might want to challenge a property tax reassessment by showing the board of equalization that the remodeling was not extensive and that an increase in the fair market value was unwarranted. Long-range tax benefits might accrue only upon the sale of the property, by using the costs of home improvements to reduce income tax owed on the profit (see chapter 11).

Product information must also be kept, from Sheetrock to stoves. If the product causes an injury and a question of seller or manufacturer liability arises, complete information about the manufacturer, retailer, installer, and product warnings supplied may be needed for a product liability claim (see chapter 2).

In addition, every homeowner who works with a contractor should keep a diary containing contracts, products ordered, names of subcontractors and suppliers, dates of work undertaken and completed, times and dates of telephone calls made to the contractor and returned, oral agreements, and payments made. Homeowners should consider taking photographs of the work before, during, and after the contractor has left the site. There is no better way to resolve a dispute than to be able to point to specific evidence and details.

Hiring
a Contractor

Although some ambitious homeowners tackle home remodeling on their own, hiring a contractor is necessary for many projects. Working successfully with a contractor means trying to anticipate problem areas in order to avoid frustration, delay, and extra expense.

A good legal contract helps. The heart of a workable contract lies in communicating, negotiating, and agreeing on its terms. A necessary prerequisite is for the homeowner to have a base of knowledge and vocabulary to explain the job accurately and understand the contractor's jargon.

But a contract is only as good as the people who sign it. It is important to get recommendations of several contractors, interview them, and check their references. What the homeowner is seeking in a contractor is fairly simple: (1) completion of the job according to a reasonable timetable, (2) good workmanship, (3) attention to job specifications, (4) caution in preventing injuries or damage to other property, and (5) fair prices.

SEARCHING FOR A GOOD CONTRACTOR

Competent contractors know their business, are responsible, have integrity, are not overextended, do not overcharge for materials, respect the customer's property, can handle their own financial affairs, follow schedules, and return phone calls.

Some contractors may be good at certain jobs but not at others. The roofer who claims to know how to lay a driveway may be searching the bookstores for self-help books.

A key to selecting a good contractor is not to make price the deciding factor. Look for quality and competence combined with price.

A key to selecting a good contractor is not to make price the deciding factor. Look for quality and competence combined with price.

Make a list of contractors, getting names from friends, neighbors, real estate brokers, and local hardware stores or lumberyards. From a list of 5 to 10, call and ask for a bid in writing. The contractors should visit the site, and the homeowner should be sure to ask each contractor to bid on the same specifications. Even if elements of the plan ultimately change, having each contractor bid on the same plan is the only way to compare the bids. Of course, the contractor can be invited to make an alternate bid with the suggested changes.

Large general contractors have staffs who do the work. Many smaller general contractors are able to complete large projects by hiring subcontractors, or specialists who do one phase of the work. When a deck is being built, an excavating subcontractor may dig the foundation, and a brick and masonry subcontractor may lay the cement. It's important to know how the contractor will operate.

LICENSED CONTRACTORS

In some states and cities, contractors are licensed. In order to be licensed, the contractor pays a fee. Licensing does not guarantee that the contractor is good, because in many places there are no performance tests for licensing. But contractors with licenses may have had to contribute to a fund for homeowners who are victimized by dishonest or incompetent contractors.

The fact that a contractor has made an effort to be licensed is a good sign. Dishonest contractors regularly close and reopen, changing the name of the company. A lack of a license, a license in another name, or a recently issued license may give clues to which contractors to avoid.

A local consumer affairs office should have information about whether contractors are licensed in the community and whom to contact for further information.

SCREENING AND EVALUATING CONTRACTORS

Check with the local Better Business Bureau, city consumer agency, the local courthouse, and state attorney general's office to find out if there are complaints against the contractor and what the nature of the complaints is. Complaints indicate problems, but a lack of complaints is not a seal of approval—the company may be new or may be bidding in a new area.

The Home Owners Warranty Corporation (c/o H.O.W. Operations Center, P.O. Box 152087, Irving, TX 75015-2087), started by the National Association of Home Builders, has a list of 12,000 builder-members. H.O.W. builders have the benefit of an insurance program and mediation program to resolve homeowner disputes (see below).

In very large projects, homeowners should check or have their banks check on the financial resources of the contractor. There is a practical legal reason for doing this. A financially troubled contractor may not pay suppliers, workers, or subcontractors brought onto the job. Under mechanic's lien laws, homeowners can end up being responsible for those payments, even though the contractor has already been paid for them. It is wise to check cases filed at the local courthouse to see if there are significant claims pending against the contractor.

Get references of recent jobs completed by the contractor. In checking the reference, ask what problems arose, if the work was done on time, and if the work was good. If possible, visit the site.

For complicated projects, a homeowner's architect or engineer can evaluate the contractor's past work. For less complicated projects, the homeowner can consult with an inspector. The American Society of Home Inspectors, Inc. (1735 North Lynn Street, Suite 950, Arlington, VA 22209-2022; 703-524-2008) maintains listings of approved inspectors.

If subcontractors are to be used, get their names. Check their references and ask if the contractor is up-to-date on bills and payments. Subcontractors who don't get paid can legally pursue a homeowner for payment. Likewise, check with the contractor's suppliers to make certain that the contractor pays supply bills.

Keep notes of conversations and contacts with the contractor, beginning even with the precontract stage. If a contractor engages in misrepresentation or deceit, it very well may occur *before* the contract is signed as an inducement to get the job. Misrepresentation, especially if it is oral, is always difficult to prove, but by having contemporaneously written notes, the homeowner will at least be a step ahead.

PITFALLS

There is no government agency or other entity that can force a contractor to finish the job. When things go wrong, it is possible to sue for a return of money, but that can be a protracted procedure and a poor second to getting the work done, especially if the house is ripped open and the project is incomplete. Midconstruction arbitration may be a solution, but far from a perfect one. A clear and firm agreement with a good contractor can help provide alternatives through timetables, incentives, and a lockstep payment plan (one that is paid as phases of the project are completed).

Home renovation contractors come and go. Many fold up their scaffolding each year and leave the business (or lack of business) behind. If a contractor goes out of business or goes bankrupt, a homeowner has little recourse. There is no one available to remedy the situation or provide financial reimbursement. Performance bonds, insurance, and a lockstep payment plan can provide some protection.

Finally, in every state, the contractor carries a club known as the *mechanic's lien*. This allows an unpaid contractor, subcontractor, or supplier of the contractor to place a lien against a homeowner's property to force payment of money due. Homeowners may be able to protect themselves from the worst aspects of a mechanic's lien law by using contract waivers, lien releases, or direct payments to suppliers and by maintaining a complete record of the contractor's work.

CON ARTISTS

In addition to competent and incompetent contractors, there are con artists who masquerade as contractors. The con artists often go door-to-door and try to persuade people that their houses are in disrepair or that they can get an especially good deal by paying for immediate service. After collecting the money, these con artists don't do the job as promised or they vanish without a trace.

They appeal to greed, sometimes offering an incredibly good price for a job. Keep two principles firmly in mind: never sign a contract without careful deliberation and never pay cash on the spot.

Homeowners who encounter a questionable contractor should contact local consumer organizations and the Better Business Bureau to sound the alert. If ripped off, make a report to the police and to a state attorney general's office. In some cases, attorney general's offices have been able to track down the worst abusers and sue them on behalf of groups of homeowners.

NEGOTIATING THE CONTRACT

A good contract won't do anything to get a bad contractor to show up in the morning. Conversely, a good contractor will do the work well, even if the contract is minimal.

The point of a contract is to protect the homeowner *and* the contractor against disagreements. It is not necessary to accept the contract provided by a contractor. But if such a contract is used, it is possible to negotiate and change specific clauses. Any contract—even a form—can be altered by rewriting it or by simply changing portions of it by hand or typewriter, and initialing each change.

A written contract is important even for a small job. Contractors can honestly forget what they have agreed to. Some contractors have sales agents, who nod their heads but are not on-site when the nails are being hit. Other contractors deliberately mislead in order to land the job.

The homeowner may not be clear in presenting the job verbally. Writing down specifics makes a huge difference. No detail is too small, including special concerns such as cleanup every night, particular hours, or exact make or type of material. Make certain the plans are clearly and precisely worded and that the construction terms likely to be used by the contractor are understood.

On remodeling jobs costing $10,000 or more, have an attorney look at the contract. Even a few hundred dollars in attorney's fees will be a small amount compared to the total expense, particularly if things go wrong.

BASIC TERMS TO INCLUDE IN CONTRACT

Contracts commonly refer to and incorporate the plans for the project. They should also include permits, payment or performance bonds, warranties, and specifications for materials. Detail is best. It doesn't matter how many pages the contract is, just that it says what it needs to say. (Some sample contracts are available from the American Institute of Architects, 1735 New York Avenue, N.W., Washington, DC 20006; 202-626-7300.)

Some states have now passed consumer protection laws requiring that certain provisions be included in home remodeling contracts. The state consumer agency, contractor licensing board, or attorney general's office will have information.

At a minimum, a good contract should contain clauses that specify:

1. *The job.* General description of the work, including specific identification of materials to be used—brands, models, styles, finishing, minimum performance standards of the materials (that is, by an electrical code), specially tailored orders.
2. *ID.* Identification of the contractor, including name, address, telephone, and license number (if appropriate); and the names, addresses, and phone numbers of subcontractors who will be employed on the project.
3. *Pay.* Total cost and a complete payment schedule, including provisions for a beginning and final payment, any bonuses or incentives, and a lockstep payment plan.
4. *Dates.* Starting and ending dates for the job, with a possible clause for no work stoppages longer than a weekend.

5. *Permits.* All necessary permits and fees will be obtained by the contractor prior to beginning the work.

6. *Insurance.* Insurance coverage provided by the contractor, with copies attached; statement that the contractor will be liable for all injuries caused by the contractor, subcontractors, any employees, or agents.

7. *Guarantees.* Guarantees for the work provided by the contractor, and that all warranties and instructions for products used in the construction will be provided prior to final payment.

8. *Cleanup.* Agreements to supply Dumpsters or provide other cleanup, and how often cleanup will occur.

9. *Lien release.* The contractor will provide lien release forms from subcontractors and suppliers prior to final payment, and the possible inclusion of a no-lien clause by which the contractor (although in most states the contractor cannot speak for the subcontractor or supplier) agrees to waive the right to file a lien against the homeowner (lien waivers may not be valid in all states).

10. *No changes.* Changes in the contract are valid only if in writing and signed by both parties.

EXCAVATION CLAUSE

Digging up the ground in one yard can cause disruption to neighboring yards, and property owners can be held liable for any damage to neighboring property resulting from excavation.

Most cities require an excavator to get a special permit and to notify owners of adjoining properties. It may be necessary to shore up neighboring property and make test samples of the ground.

The contract should contain a clause that covers every aspect of the excavation process. Consider seeking excavation waivers from neighbors, where permitted (see chapter 8).

PAYMENT SCHEDULE

The payment schedule is key to the homeowner's ability to assure the completion of the project. The homeowner should make sure that the payment schedule in the contract never gets ahead of the work. Don't pay for work not done; it is the best protection against a contractor who loses interest in the job.

It is also unnecessary to pay hefty amounts up front. Contractors often seek half or a third of the cost of the entire contract in advance, but money may be the only incentive to get the job done. Even 10 or 15 percent can be too much to pay in advance, especially if the project is large and 10 percent amounts to a substantial sum. Evaluate how much is too much to pay in advance by imagining the worst-case scenario—if all the up-front money is lost to a contractor who never performs, will it still be possible to afford to complete the project?

Instead of a large advance payment, set up a lockstep payment schedule, by which periodic payments are made as each step of the job is completed.

The payments also should be connected to *work completed,* not just to dates. If the work is completed earlier, the contractor gets the reward of earlier payment. If the work is delayed, the homeowner does not end up paying for items that are not finished.

In order to set up a payment schedule, break down the entire project into logical subportions. The first payment should be paid on signing the contract, both to make the contract valid and as evidence of an intention to follow through on contract payments. If the contract is for the conversion of an unfinished attic into a usable room, other payments might be paid following the flooring and framing, after the installation of electrical service, upon completion of insulation, and so on. The contract should describe the exact work that must be completed before payment.

Contractors often demand the money in advance in order to buy materials. Instead, pay for the materials by writing a check to the supplier or jointly to the contractor and supplier.

If the contractor insists on payment in advance, offer to put the money in an escrow account. This assures the contractor that the money will be available when the work is done. A neutral third party can even be selected to monitor the account and cosign for release of funds.

FINAL PAYMENT

At a minimum, the contract should state that the final payment is not to be paid until the property is inspected and approved by the homeowner, any relevant building inspectors, and the architect, if any.

The contract should also specify that, prior to final payment, the contractor will provide the homeowner lien releases from all suppliers and subcontractors (see following). Also, the contractor should be required to give a comprehensive list of all product manufacturers and provide copies of written product warranties, instructions, guides, and warnings.

The final payment should be large enough so that the contractor is willing to return and finish the minor details on the job, rather than simply write it off. Fifteen percent is not an unreasonable amount.

A better contract clause provides for final payment after thirty to sixty days, during which time any hidden problems—such as insufficient wiring or a leak—might become apparent.

CONTRACT AND LATE PENALTY CLAUSE

A penalty for delay in completion is sometimes included in contracts; however, this presumes that the contractor has been paid in advance and will be fined for procrastination. Another approach is to include a clause withholding 3 to 5 percent from the final payment unless work is completed on time. There can be negatives to a late penalty charge—the contractor may decide it's cheaper simply to move on.

An alternative is to offer bonuses. The contract could provide that for each target date met (within 24 or 48 hours), there will be a bonus. The cost of the contract may be higher, but so is the likelihood of completion.

WORK STOPPAGE CLAUSE

What if the contractor stops appearing, won't answer phone calls, and has all but turned into a ghost? A work stoppage clause in the contract could permit a homeowner to take action.

This clause might provide that if the contractor failed to appear for a certain period of time, such as seven to ten days consecutively, the homeowner could consider it a work stoppage. The clause might state that after sending a written notice that the clause is being activated, a substitute contractor could be hired.

RESOLUTION OF DISPUTES, CONTRACT CLAUSE

Taking a case to court can be a grueling matter at any time. If an altercation arises while construction is under way, the problems can be even greater. Many homeowners are fearful that the contractor will leave the job with a couple of the walls still open to the wind.

A clause in the contract can bind parties to resolving problems through arbitration or mediation. Any individual—a lawyer, architect, engineer, or consultant—can be designated as a mediator. The American Arbitration Association provides minihearings for the resolution of problems. In addition, many communities have dispute resolution programs through the Better Business Bureau, a neighborhood counseling center, the local bar association or chapter of the American Bar Association.

The H.O.W. program also has a mediation service. If the contractor participates in the H.O.W. program, ask to see evidence of H.O.W. membership and specific registration for the home remodeling plan at hand if it is over $10,000. H.O.W. covers only registered projects (see following).

There are drawbacks to arbitration programs that should be considered before inserting an arbitration clause. Drawbacks include an inability to appeal and questions about the qualifications or preconceived biases of arbitrators (see chapter 21).

CONTRACT AND CANCELLATION

Under rules of the Federal Trade Commission, contracts for home-repair work that are signed in the home by the homeowner and in the presence of the contractor must provide three days in which to cancel (or rescind). The contract must contain a notice of this possibility.

The three-day time limit is strictly enforced and if a homeowner has second thoughts, the recision notice must be signed and delivered promptly. Use overnight mail, hand delivery with a receipt, or certified mail.

BONDS

Some cities and states require contractors to post bonds with a government agency. The pool of bond funds is then available to property owners when a contractor registered with the state fails to perform. This benefit is one of the central reasons to select a licensed contractor in those locations.

A bond is a contract issued by a third party—known as the *surety*—that guarantees some aspect of the work. A bond is similar to insurance in that it covers some financial loss. It differs from insurance, however, because three parties are involved—the contractor, the surety who is a guarantor for the contractor, and the homeowner whose property is the subject of the bond.

A *performance bond* pays for a loss if the contractor does not complete the job as promised. The language of many performance bonds is difficult to understand. In them, the term *penal sum* refers to the amount the bond will cover. What is covered is the cost of uncompleted work for which the contractor has already been paid. The performance bond does not guarantee that the job will be done; it merely pays back money that has been collected if the work is not finished.

A *payment bond* is a guarantee by a surety company to subcontractors that the contractor will pay for their labor.

A third type of bond, sometimes used in major developments such as high-rises, is a *bid bond* in which the bonding company guarantees that the contractor will complete the job in line with its bid.

Bonding companies decide whether or not to provide guarantees for a contractor based on a review of the contract and on the contractor's credit, ability to complete the job, sufficiency of the subcontractors, and reasonableness of the contract.

On the surface, bonds sound like excellent solutions to problems in dealing with a contractor. But the difficulties with bonds are twofold. One is that surety companies often resist paying. The second is that bonds are expensive, perhaps as a reflection of the high number of contractor defaults. Although the contractor actually purchases the bond, homeowners can be sure that the cost will be passed on and will significantly increase the cost of the project.

Other precautions against contractor failure to perform or pay subcontractors may be more useful than bonds, including a pay-as-the-work-proceeds schedule. This, along with clauses obtaining a lien waiver and lien releases prior to the final payment, may preempt the need for a performance bond. The best bond available is hiring a contractor with an excellent reputation at the outset.

WARRANTY PROGRAMS

Warranties offer an alternative to a performance bond. Some home builders offer warranties, as do some organizations and associations. There is a distinction. A warranty offered by the contractor may be worthless if the company is financially insecure or closes.

One warranty program that seems to be successful is the H.O.W. Warranty Corporation insurance plan. This plan was developed for the purchasers of new homes and new-home builders but has been extended to screened and registered remodelers. The program can be used by the 12,000 contractors who are registered with H.O.W. (see chapter 2).

Under the H.O.W. warranty program, the contractor's work is fully guaranteed to be free from defects in workmanship and materials for up to five years. Remodeling jobs that are over $10,000 must be registered in advance with H.O.W. in order to qualify for the warranty. If the contractor fails to correct a defect in compliance with H.O.W.'s Approved Standards, H.O.W. will step in and make the repairs at no charge.

Some states and cities apply license fees paid by contractors to a pool that can provide refunds to homeowners who have problems with licensed contractors. Other states protect homeowners by requiring home remodeling companies to put a percentage of each contract amount into an escrow account. State consumer affairs offices can provide details.

MECHANIC'S OR MATERIALMAN'S LIENS

Homeowners should not underestimate the power of mechanic's liens. A lien is a claim against the property for the purpose of securing the value of work performed or materials used in repairing a house or making other improvements to the property. A contractor, subcontractor, or supplier is entitled to put a lien on the homeowner's property for unpaid bills. The lien becomes an encumbrance to the property that must be paid off before the home can be sold or refinanced, and, in rare cases, can result in a foreclosure.

Mechanic's lien laws were developed in the eighteenth century to protect laborers and suppliers from unscrupulous contractors on the theory that if the contractor used services or supplies without paying, then the laborer or supplier should be able to recover from the party who benefited from the services or supplies—or the property owner. The mechanic's lien works well for major development projects, such as shopping centers, but it can be onerous for the individual homeowner.

Three types of people are entitled to a mechanic's lien for non-payment: the contractor, subcontractors or employees hired by the contractor, or a supplier of materials to the contractor (the claimant need not be a "mechanic" in the usual sense of the word).

CONTRACT CLAUSES AND MECHANIC'S LIENS

The right to a lien can be waived by the contract in most states, and a homeowner should ask for a lien waiver or a release from the contractor. But since only the contractor signs the agreement, in most states the contractor cannot affect the rights of subcontractors or suppliers.

A lien waiver clause by a contractor should state that the contractor waives any and all rights under mechanic's lien laws to file any claims or proceedings against the homeowner.

The contract can state further that the contractor will supply the homeowner with a waiver and release of lien rights from every subcontractor and supplier used on the job. These subcontractor lien waivers should be required prior to release of the final payment. The lien waivers should be signed (and notarized) statements by all subcontractors and suppliers that they have been paid in full and that they release the homeowner from any obligations under the mechanic's lien laws.

OTHER PROTECTION AGAINST MECHANIC'S LIENS

As protection against the supplier's lien, as discussed previously, the homeowner can pay the supplier directly for materials, either by a check to the supplier or a joint check to the supplier and contractor. This resolves the problem of the contractor who takes payment for supplies and spends it on other items, while buying the supplies on credit.

It may not be wise to pay a subcontractor directly. A homeowner doing so can then be subjected to other claims, such as worker's compensation, unemployment, or liability.

> *Check periodically with subcontractors and suppliers to make certain that they are being paid.*

Check periodically with subcontractors and suppliers to make certain that they are being paid. Some courts have even implied that a property owner has a duty to make certain that the contractor is paying the bills.

ENFORCEMENT OF MECHANIC'S LIEN LAWS

Every state has a mechanic's lien law, but the provisions vary. Some states make the law very difficult to enforce by insisting that technical provisions be followed to the letter by the contractor, subcontractor, or supplier; others have a simple procedure that favors the contractor (lienholder).

Some states require a contractor who is seeking a payment to provide a sworn statement to the property owner that includes the name of every subcontractor, laborer, and supplier and the amounts due to them. In some locations, subcontractors seeking payment must follow similar rules.

In order to enforce the mechanic's lien, the contractor or other person holding the lien must usually file a statement with a county clerk or designated public official. The statement is generally known as the *lien, lien paper,* or *claim.*

Mechanic's liens are enforced through a civil lawsuit. A summons and complaint are served on the homeowner. A summons and complaint must not go unattended. Failure to answer the complaint will result in a default, permitting the contractor or other lienholder to proceed with enforcement of the lien with little or no further notice to the homeowner.

In defending against the lien, the homeowner can show that payment has been made, the materials were not supplied, or the work was not done as promised. The homeowner may also have a defense on procedural grounds if the lienholder failed to file the lien in a timely fashion, failed to provide the homeowner with proper notice at the outset of the project, or signed a lien waiver.

If the contractor or other lienholder wins in court, the mechanic's lien then attaches to the property. The lien encumbers the property and can also be enforced by a sale of the property in some instances. A sale must follow the same procedures as the process of foreclosure (see chapter 12).

A mechanic's lien can be satisfied by payment. However, this payment often must be made before a judgment is entered. After the judgment, many states do not allow a homeowner to forestall foreclosure by payment.

Because a mechanic's lien can have such serious ramifications and because the laws in each state have their own technicalities, the homeowner should hire an attorney (see chapter 21).

INSURANCE

A remodeling contract should be covered by three types of insurance.

1.   The contractor should have insurance to cover damage to the property and that of the neighbors. If a piece of lumber is blown away and hits the neighbor's window, the contractor must be able to pay for the cost of replacing it.
2.   If the contractor has any employees, worker's compensation insurance is necessary to cover them in case of injury.
3.   Liability insurance is needed to cover injuries to third persons. If a bucket falls off the roof and lands on a passing child, the contractor must be covered for the injuries caused (see chapter 7).

When the contractor is supplying the insurance, copies of the policies and the name of the insurance broker should be attached to the contract between the homeowner and the contractor. The homeowner should also ask for the name of the agent and call to make sure that the insurance is in force.

The homeowner can supply or supplement this insurance. In some cases, a homeowner can even insure the project at a lower cost than the contractor's, in which case that insurance should be incorporated into the contract. In major building projects, a homeowner might supplement the contractor's insurance with an umbrella policy, which covers losses to higher limits (see chapters 1 and 7).

Independent contractors—solo odd-job persons—rarely have

insurance. The homeowner is responsible for any injury or damage caused by the contractor and should make certain that losses will be covered under the homeowner's policy.

FINANCING WITH CONTRACTORS

> *Some contractors offer to arrange financing, but this is invariably far more expensive than what a homeowner could arrange through a bank.*

Some contractors offer to arrange financing, but this is invariably far more expensive than what a homeowner could arrange through a bank or other financial institution.

If financing is arranged through a contractor, truth-in-lending information and other loan papers must be provided, giving clear and unambiguous details of the loan.

Home equity loans, refinancing, second mortgages, or home remodeling loans from banks will usually require that the property act as collateral for the loan. Under federal income tax rules, up to $100,000 in interest on home refinancing can generally be taken as a tax deduction. But since the house is used to secure the loan, failure to repay the loan can result in foreclosure on the property (see chapter 12).

HOMEOWNER CLAIMS AGAINST THE CONTRACTOR

Claims against contractors or about home remodeling fall in five broad categories:

1. Breach of contract, based on failure to complete the work specified in the contract. Usually, a homeowner has paid the contractor, but the job isn't finished.

2. Breach of implied warranties based on uninhabitability or poor workmanship. A homeowner claims that the contractor has done the job so poorly that warranties either stated in the contract or implied by the nature of the work have been breached. The warranty of implied habitability holds that the contractor should have done what was intended in creating a livable home—for example, the plumbing is correctly attached to the septic sys-

tem. The warranty of good workmanship holds that the crafts-
manship meets the standards of the profession in the
community—the gutters are properly fastened to the roof. When
implied warranties are broken, more work is usually required by
another contractor. What the homeowner seeks from the original
contractor is reimbursement for the costs of those repairs and
payment for any damages caused—interior water damage caused
by a poorly shingled roof that leaks.

3.   Injury to the property (secondary damage), to a person, or
to neighboring property. These claims are based on a breach of
contract or on negligence, and the homeowner is seeking to
recover the costs of damages to the property because of the contractor's negligence—repair of a downstairs co-op from a contractor who breaks a pipe in the wall, releasing a flood into
another apartment.

A contractor is considered negligent for failing to undertake
precautions that are reasonably necessary or for failing to foresee
problems that could be expected to occur. A swimming pool contractor who installs a latch on a gate that is easily reached by an
infant might be liable if the infant entered the area and fell into
the pool.

4.   Product defect or failure, causing loss of value or injury to
a person. When a product fails to perform, the homeowner may
have a claim against the manufacturer based on the breach of
warranty or a claim against the installer for negligence or breach
of contract. When someone is injured because of a product
defect, the homeowner might have a product liability claim
against the manufacturer, seller, or installer for the costs of medical bills and other damages.

5.   Negligence of someone other than the contractor. If a
homeowner discovers a basic design defect—doors that open
backward, heating vents that are installed under the floor—the
architect, designer, or engineer might be liable for drawing up
unworkable or negligent designs.

ARBITRATION

Difficulties with contractors can end up in court. These cases are
often unsuccessful and frequently fruitless on the collection end,
even if successful (see chapter 21).

Contracts can provide for binding arbitration through the

American Arbitration Association or other organizations. Although arbitration is less complicated than court and can be scheduled more quickly, the process is not necessarily informal, and its results are final. If the arbitration is binding, a homeowner cannot seek recourse in court.

Arbitration proceedings can be fairly useful for problems involving a breach of contract or failure to complete the work satisfactorily. But arbitration may not be the best forum if a personal injury or serious act of negligence by the contractor is involved.

If arbitration is instituted, approach it with all the seriousness of a trial before a judge. Be prepared with clear and specific evidence—photos, times, dates, bills, canceled checks, and a chronology. The proceeding may involve experts, and there may be rules of procedure to follow. An attorney may be advisable.

DEALING WITH CONTRACTORS

The legal aspects of a home remodeling project are inevitably intertwined with practical considerations. Before hiring a contractor, become thoroughly literate in building terms; have a clear and detailed plan; and check the references of bidding contractors for quality and reliability, as well as price.

Once a contractor is selected, the contract should set out in specific detail all of the work that is to be completed and how payment is to be made. As discussed previously, one way to reduce many of the common headaches with contractors is to design a home remodeling contract with a lockstep payment plan, by which the contractor is paid as each specific step of the project is completed.

In some locations, a homeowner may be able to get help when poor work is done by a licensed contractor by contacting state or city licensing bodies.

Injuries to Third Persons on the Property

The law places an obligation on homeowners to make certain that people who enter onto their property are not injured by unsafe conditions. Homeowners can be held responsible for injuries to business visitors, social guests, city officials, easement users, children—and, in some cases, even to trespassers.

To what degree they will be held accountable to someone who is hurt on the property depends largely on the seriousness of the injury, the dangerousness of the condition, and their opportunity to correct the condition.

Legal problems don't arise, of course, until someone tumbles down a broken step or is zapped by a dangling wire. The homeowner's property insurance covers most injuries to third persons, except those that are caused intentionally. Where injuries are extensive and the damages exceed the limits of the insurance, homeowners are responsible for the remainder.

As always, the wisest course is practical—fix dangerous conditions before someone is injured. At the very least, make sure that any newcomers to the property are warned about hazards. That means taking a meticulous inventory of the property to see what conditions might be unsafe.

DUTY OF THE HOMEOWNER

The responsibility for injuries occurring on property, or premises liability, falls in the general category of personal injury or tort law. The duty of the homeowner is to use "reasonable care under the circumstances" to prevent injuries to third persons entering the property. This standard is now accepted in almost every state.

Reasonable care is not easy to define. Legal jargon defines it as the actions of an ordinary, prudent person in the same situation. In simple terms, it means using plain common sense.

In defining reasonable care, several factors are weighed:

- Did the homeowner know (or *should* the homeowner have known) that a dangerous condition existed?
- Could the homeowner have foreseen the chance of someone being injured?
- Could precautions have been taken?
- How serious were the injuries?
- Was the injured individual warned about the danger in any way?

Many circumstances can be imagined. A party guest uses the bathroom faucet, which has been broken for weeks, and cuts a finger seriously. The court will note that the condition of the faucet existed previously, was known to the homeowner, and the owner failed to take the simple precaution of warning the guest. The homeowner would be liable.

Suppose, on the other hand, a friend picks flowers from the garden. While doing so, the friend is bitten by a snake and must be rushed to the hospital. The injury is not serious. A court might note that the snake in the grass was not a danger known to the homeowner, and, in this case, it wasn't foreseeable. The homeowner is probably not liable.

Take a more difficult situation. A homeowner puts an empty refrigerator behind the garage, planning to dispose of it. A neighbor's child sneaks onto the property, climbs into the refrigerator compartment, and suffocates. The danger of interior-latching refrigerators and unattended children is widely known, but the homeowner argues that there was no way to know a child would wander onto the property without permission. Yet, the precaution—removing the door or tying it up—was simple. A court could easily find that the homeowner was negligent and liable to the child's parents for the death, even though the child was on the property without permission.

In some cases, the duty of care required by the homeowner is linked to the status of the person injured—for example, business guest or social visitor. If the injured person was aware of the danger but proceeded anyhow, that individual is sometimes considered to have "assumed the risk" of the injury that occurs.

The crux of the modern approach to premises liability is whether or not there was negligence by the owner, summed up in four concepts of personal injury law: duty, breach, foreseeability, and proximate causation. Homeowners have a duty to prevent injuries to persons who come on the property. An injury that is caused by a breach of that duty will prompt an inquiry into whether, under the circumstances, the danger could have been foreseen and prevented.

DUTY TO WARN

In some cases, the dangerous condition cannot be corrected immediately. When part of a house is under construction, an open pit may exist in the backyard where an addition will soon appear.

> **When a homeowner knows about dangerous conditions, but they cannot be corrected immediately, the owner has a duty to alert anyone who enters onto the property.**

When a homeowner knows about dangerous conditions, but they cannot be corrected immediately, the owner has a duty to alert anyone who enters onto the property. The warning could be a posted sign, a fence surrounding the ditch, floodlights, an alarm—or all of these precautions.

Some circumstances are so dangerous that merely posting a warning is insufficient. If live electrical wires are lying on the construction site, a warning may not be enough. The danger must be alleviated prior to visitors entering or possibly entering onto the property.

STATUS OF INJURED PERSON

A small number of states consider the status of the injured person before considering whether the homeowner breached a duty of care. That is because different standards of care are applied to different categories of individuals—whether a business visitor, a social guest, or a trespasser. This was also the traditional way of evaluating a homeowner's responsibility.

In this scheme, a homeowner owes the greatest duty of care to prevent injury to a business visitor, known as an *invitee*—a repair person, interior decorator, or postal carrier, for instance. The highest duty of care requires a property owner to inspect the property and correct problems or provide warnings.

A less stringent duty of care was owed to a social guest—known as a *licensee*—and an even lower duty was attached to a trespasser.

Even states that use a standard of "reasonable under the circumstances" often hold the status of the injured person as one of the circumstances to be considered.

INTENTIONAL HARM

In all circumstances, a homeowner is liable for intentionally causing harm to a person entering on the property, even a trespasser.

> *In all circumstances, a homeowner is liable for intentionally causing harm to a person entering on the property, even a trespasser.*

A homeowner cannot install a fence that gives a high-voltage shock to someone who touches it, nor can one set up an automatic gun intended to fire at anyone who opens a door, nor put a cable across a dirt road used by motorcyclists. In these cases, the homeowner is liable, even if the injured people were intruders.

Homeowner's insurance generally excludes payments for intentionally caused injuries.

DUTY TO CHILDREN

When a child is injured, the courts have always been a bit tougher on the homeowner, since children don't have the same level of judgment as adults. Under a doctrine known as *attractive nuisance,* homeowners may be liable for injuries to children who come onto the property without permission.

If a homeowner knows that children are likely to trespass on the property and that a dangerous condition exists, the owner is required to exercise special care to eliminate the hazard.

The term attractive nuisance is reflective of the fact that children are drawn to certain environments. One big attraction is a swimming pool (see following). Take particular care to prevent injuries to children, even to uninvited ones.

DUTY TO TENANTS

In most states, landlords have a duty to protect tenants from injury. They are responsible for inspecting and repairing dangerous conditions in public areas, such as hallways, stairs, porches, bathrooms shared by tenants, elevators, and laundry rooms. Landlords also have the duty to disclose known dangerous conditions to tenants, particularly if the conditions are not readily observable or are latent defects.

If dangerous conditions are brought to the attention of the landlord, the majority of states hold that the landlord has a duty to repair those conditions. A failure to live up to these duties means that a landlord could be liable if a tenant or, in some cases, a guest of a tenant, was injured (see chapter 19).

WORKERS ON THE PROPERTY

Homeowners are liable for injuries that occur to certain types of workers on the property. If the worker is a household employee—someone paid by you to do a job, with the materials and goods paid for by you—then you are responsible for on-the-job injuries that might occur. Under this category might come domestic workers, gardeners, baby-sitters, home health care workers, and repair people such as a painter or carpenter who is supplied with tools and materials.

Homeowners should have worker's compensation insurance

for workers on the property. In a few states, such as New York, New Jersey, and New Hampshire, this insurance is required as part of a homeowner's comprehensive personal liability coverage.

If the workers are employees of a contractor or subcontractor, or if they are independent contractors who supply their own tools and materials, homeowners are not usually liable for injuries that occur on the property. The exception to this is if one fails to warn the workers of a known danger.

On the other hand, homeowners are responsible for injuries caused by an independent contractor to another person. The contractor who leaves debris on a sidewalk, tripping and injuring a passing pedestrian, subjects the property owner to liability.

If there are a large number of employees working on the property, a boost in the liability coverage limits on homeowner's insurance or the purchase of an umbrella policy might be in order, both as protection against injuries to the worker and by the worker.

RECREATIONAL USE LAWS

Nearly all states have tried to encourage the opening of private property to public recreational use by protecting homeowners from liability.

In Delaware, for example, property owners are not held liable for injuries caused to third persons engaged in outdoor recreational activities such as boating, hiking, hunting, fishing, winter sports, camping, or picnicking on the property, even if the property owner has been negligent. They are liable only for injuries caused by a known dangerous condition and willful or malicious failure to warn users about it—a difficult standard to meet.

Recreational-use statutes apply when there is no fee to use the property and when the activity is related to the outdoors and nature. Swimming pools are not included, nor are indoor recreational activities. Some recreational-use statutes exclude land near or in a city.

LIABILITY FROM ACTIVITIES

With increasing frequency, homeowners are defending themselves against people who are injured not because of a dangerous condition on the property, but because of some activity. So far, few people who have sued homeowners on this ground have been successful, but it is an important concern—especially when homeowners hosting a party serve drugs or liquor, or when a known violent or dangerous person is brought into a social situation.

The same standards of negligence—duty, breach, foreseeability, and proximate causation—apply. But courts have been more reluctant to attach duties to activities.

Suppose at a beach party on the property, one guest unexpectedly stabs another. The injured guest sues, claiming the homeowner had a duty to protect visitors from an out-of-control guest. So far, the courts have ruled against most injured persons in situations such as this. But if the homeowner knew that the guest had a tendency to become violent and carried a knife, the court might say that the property owner could have taken precautions to prevent a foreseeable incident.

Another area of concern is the so-called dramshop laws that make bar owners in some states responsible if they serve customers too much liquor and a car accident subsequently occurs. Some homeowners have been sued on similar grounds. When the guests are adults, suits against homeowners who served liquor to the driver have not usually been successful. The cases in which homeowners have been held liable for injuries that followed drinking generally involved circumstances in which the homeowner served liquor recklessly to someone who was visibly intoxicated and the homeowner knew that the person would be driving; or the homeowner served or permitted the serving of alcohol to minors. A logical extension will find homeowners liable for serving illicit drugs to guests. The number of cases raising this issue is increasing.

A ride home, calling a taxi, or urging someone to stay for the night may be important steps to preventing both an injury and a potential lawsuit.

PETS AND ANIMALS

Homeowners are held to high standards in exercising reasonable care when it comes to their pets and animals. The reasoning is that the pet's owner should be in control of the animal and has the best opportunity to restrain the pet and prevent an injury.

In nearly all states, a homeowner is held strictly liable for an injury caused by an animal if the owner knew that the animal could be dangerous. A dog need not have bitten anyone to be considered dangerous. Any dog that is bred to be dangerous—a guard dog, for example—will cause a homeowner to pay for damages if it bites someone. So will any animal that has demonstrated viciousness even without biting—for example, lunging at or attacking people. Some dogs, such as pit bulls, are considered to be known dangers.

If an animal has shown a dangerous streak, a property owner has a duty to muzzle, confine, or restrain it, and to warn both guests and intruders. The owner may have a duty to keep a visiting child away from a dog that is eating, or out of a corral with a horse that kicks.

A homeowner is also liable for any inury caused by a wild animal kept on the property as a pet. Examples include bears, tigers, snakes, monkeys, zebras, lions, and even bees that are kept close to a neighbor's property. A homeowner is not liable for wild animals that trespass on the property, such as the raccoon that wanders onto the property and injures a guest.

OBLIGATION TO AN INJURED PERSON

If injury occurs on a homeowner's property, the owner may have an obligation to see that the injured person is treated promptly.

> *If injury occurs on a homeowner's property, the owner may have an obligation to see that the injured person is treated promptly.*

In recent cases, homeowners have been charged with the duty to aid. If someone fell off the balcony of a house, the homeowner would have an obligation to make certain that the injuries were not worsened by failing to get immediate medical care. In one case, a homeowner was liable for not recognizing the seriousness of a guest's illness, when the guest was known to have a history of heart ailments, even though the homeowner did nothing to cause the illness.

PREVENTING INJURIES

Any obviously dangerous problem needs to be corrected, especially on the grounds or outside the home, where someone could
be unwittingly hurt. If the problem cannot be corrected immediately, put up a sign to warn persons who enter onto the property. Watch Out, Broken Step may prevent a fractured hip and a
lawsuit soon after. Verbal warnings should be provided to people
who visit the property.

In addition, pay particular attention to those problems in a
home that are most likely to cause injuries. According to experts,
several household areas can be safety traps:

- stairs or steps that are slippery, too steep, have an unexpected rise, fail to have handrails, or have rails through
  which children can poke their heads
- bathroom tubs and floors that are slippery
- garage doors, especially older electric versions that can
  drop on children crawling beneath them, or hand doors
  that don't have handles on each section
- sliding glass doors without safety glass or a railing or guard
  across the middle, or windows without guards
- electrical devices near tubs or sinks, bathroom plugs without ground fault circuit interrupters, or dangling bulbs
  over sinks
- heating devices that are incorrectly vented, fireplaces with
  poor chimneys or small hearths
- showers without temperature-regulating valves, sharp cabinet edges, hooks on the backs of doors at eye level

In addition, be aware of other responsibilities:

- Keep sidewalks and exterior steps free of ice, debris, toys,
  and dangerous cracks or breaks
- Be sure that pets and animals are not dangerous to people
  entering the property, are adequately chained or penned,
  and that clear warning signs are posted
- Take safety precautions when children are visiting, and provide adequate supervision
- Accompany elderly guests up steps and through difficult or

dimly lit passageways; make sure that stair edges are not masked by carpeting

- Store flammable liquids in proper containers and in well-ventilated spaces outside the home; use them with caution, especially lighter fluids for barbecues
- Keep products with built-in dangers—particularly those that can cut or injure, such as power mowers, electric saws, and guns—inaccessible and locked away

Owners of cooperatives or condominium buildings and landlords need to be aware of additional dangers that are not generally found on single-residence property (see chapters 17 and 19):

- elevator doors that don't work properly, open shafts
- inoperative incinerators or trash compactors
- hazards or faulty equipment in a laundry room
- hallway problems—accumulations of water, poor lighting, garbage, or debris

People living in a house often become accustomed to a hole in the driveway or a patched-together electrical connection. But visitors—who are the source of a liability claim—cannot be expected to know the territory.

Special Problems Related to Swimming Pools

Swimming pools cause special liability concerns, both because of the possibility of drowning and because they can be an attractive nuisance to children. A number of cities have adopted safety regulations for private swimming pools, whether in ground or above ground, so homeowners planning to install one should be careful to comply with all local regulations. Swimming pool owners should take all possible precautions to prevent injuries, including the following:

- Surround the pool by a fence that is at least five feet high and allows a clear view of the pool; make certain the fence cannot be scaled by young children and has no opening in it or beneath it that would allow a child to crawl through.

- The fence should have a self-closing gate with a latch that cannot be reached by small children.
- Use pool covers when the pool is not in use and remove them fully when the pool is in use.
- For an above-ground pool, remove steps to it when the pool is not in use.
- The pool should have clear markings at its edge denoting the depth of the pool and any ledges or barriers on the inside.
- Consider installing an alarm that warns when the water is significantly disturbed, as well as an emergency telephone near the pool.
- Remove accumulations of algae that make the inside of the pool slippery.

Children should not be allowed to use the pool unsupervised. Warn them (as well as baby-sitters) about pool safety rules and about not using the pool without permission. If children are using the pool without permission, reinforce gates and latches.

Supervise parties at the pool and restrict alcohol use. Prohibit rough play and limit the use of diving boards. Consider hiring a professional lifeguard.

Family members should also learn lifesaving techniques, CPR, and have emergency numbers on hand in case an accident occurs. An emergency kit, possibly including a mechanical inhalator, should be available.

In some cases, an injury occurs because the pool is badly designed. Consider exceeding safety standards, such as for the pool depth below a diving board. If an injury occurs because of a problem with the pool's design, the manufacturer or installer of the pool may be liable under a product liability claim.

Take similar safety precautions with any activity that is likely to draw people who are not members of the household—whether backyard archery, skateboarding, or a home chemistry lab.

HOMEOWNER'S INSURANCE

Liability insurance is one of the important features of homeowner's insurance, just as it is for car insurance (see chapter 1). But the number of premises liability cases are growing, and many homeowner's insurance policies provide insufficient coverage.

Homeowner's policies generally provide $100,000 in coverage; some offer only $25,000. The cost of personal injury cases can be high, and many experts recommend that a homeowner has $300,000 to $500,000 in coverage. (High-income earners should consider even higher limits.) The cost for increasing the coverage is less than $50 a year. Without the extra coverage, a property owner could be financially responsible for the remaining damages after the insurance policy has paid its maximum.

LEGAL ACTION ON AN INJURY

If someone is injured on the property, the homeowner may receive a notice of a claim. Immediately call the homeowner's insurance company or insurance broker. The company or the broker will handle the claim and provide legal representation. In most cases, it's best to let the company do the talking to the injured parties or their representatives.

If the claim is very small, for example, $300 to $500, the homeowner may want to settle it by simply paying that amount out-of-pocket. If so, the owner should obtain a *release of claim* from the injured party, stating the name of the injured person, the nature of the injury, the date on which it occurred, where it occurred by address and property location, the exact amount the owner is paying to the injured person in satisfaction of the claim, and that this payment covers the entirety of the injured person's claim for damages of any and all types and for all time.

The release form should be signed and notarized by the injured party (or parent, if a child is injured). Legal stationery stores carry forms for release of claim, but to be certain that the matter won't come back to haunt in a year or two, a brief consultation with an attorney is a good idea.

If the claim is beyond the limits of an insurance policy, the homeowner may eventually have to hire an attorney to handle the case. A lawyer will also be needed if the insurance company refuses to represent the homeowner's claim—stating, for example, that the injury was intentionally inflicted. In either case, the financial risks of a serious injury could be unacceptably burdensome, and the fee for a competent personal injury defense lawyer is a smart investment.

PROTECTION FROM LIABILITY CLAIMS

Under modern premises liability law, homeowners have an obligation to use reasonable care under the circumstances to prevent injuries to nonfamily members entering onto the property. Reasonable care means acting as an ordinary, prudent person would in the same situation and can include correcting dangerous conditions, warning visitors about dangers, stopping dangerous activities such as drinking by minors, and coming to the aid of an injured person.

The best way to protect against a liability suit is to take preventive action against common dangers—uneven stairs, slippery floors or walks, glass doors that are difficult to see, or dangerous electrical outlets. In addition, owners with swimming pools must take exceptional cautionary measures. The liability portion of homeowner's insurance covers injuries to third persons on the property, but it is often written with limits that are too low; homeowners should consider increasing the limits.

Water,
Air,
and Earth Support

A homeowner buys more than a house and the lot on which it stands. Owners also gain rights in the airspace above the land, including light, air, and view; in the earth support, oil, and minerals below the surface; and in any water that flows on, under, or next to the property.

These ownership rights are *rights incident to the possession of land* and can be used and enjoyed by the homeowner or can be sold, leased, or licensed. But these same resources are shared by neighboring landowners. The enjoyment of the resources must be placed in context with the rights of neighbors. A property owner's right to use a stream could be defeated by another property owner's damming of a river.

Environmental considerations increase the concerns about incidental rights. Pollution released into a stream can destroy the usability of the water for everyone along the stream. Corroded underground tanks that leak gas can spread damage without regard to property boundaries.

Disputes about incidental rights are inextricably linked to the other users of those same resources. When claims and lawsuits develop, they are usually between neighboring landowners, up- and downstream users of a river, or homeowners challenging a nearby airport's appropriation of airspace. The law about incidental rights actually involves competing claims of right in the same limited resource.

WATER RIGHTS IN GENERAL

Concerns about water rights focus on three areas: adequate supply, flooding, and pollution. Land that borders on a natural watercourse is known as *riparian land,* giving rise to *riparian rights.* The rights of riparian owners to use or divert water vary depending on the exact type of body of water involved—underground aquifer, stream, or lake.

Basic to the understanding of water rights, especially when flowing streams or lakes are involved, is that no property holder owns the water in the same way that the land is owned. At best, a property owner is permitted the right to use water that flows across, under, or adjacent to the land (owners can do what they want with ponds that are entirely contained on the property, subject to environmental regulations). No upstream owner will be permitted to defeat the water rights of a downstream owner by using all of the water or polluting it beyond an acceptable level.

NAVIGABLE WATER

When a stream or river is navigable, the federal government has the constitutional power to regulate and control both water traffic and the building of structures in or along the water. This power limits the rights of any private owner of land along the same watercourse. Private riparian owners are said to be subject to a *servitude,* or greater interest of the government. State governments also have some power over navigable streams, subject to the primary interest of the federal government.

Navigable water is defined as water that is used as a highway of commerce or is capable of being so used. It includes the oceans, rivers, and some lakes, such as the Great Lakes.

In general, the federal government can use or control the water as it sees fit. The public can be given a right to use the water for swimming and boating without consideration for the rights of private landowners along the shore. The government can also permit the building of power dams along navigable water, even though the dams significantly alter the water level and water flow to downstream users.

Claims raised by private landowners challenging the government's use of a waterway usually allege that the government has so reduced the value of the private owner's land that the property has been taken by the government. The argument is that the owner's are entitled to compensation under theories of eminent domain (see chapter 16).

EASTERN STATES—
REASONABLE USE OF STREAMS

In the majority of nonwestern states, every property owner is entitled to make reasonable use of any water that is on or adjacent to the property. Disputes arise when one owner's use affects or damages the reasonable use expected by another owner along the watercourse.

The reasonable-use doctrine reflects a belief that water has a utilitarian use—it can feed cattle, serve domestic water needs, or run a power supply. In most locations, this means that a property owner who has a use for the water will prevail over another property owner who does not need the water.

For example, if an upstream owner diverts water to provide a continuous flow to an artificial spawning pond, and a downstream user has a reduction in the flow of the water but does not use the water in any way, the upstream owner will be permitted to continue. If, on the other hand, a downstream owner uses the water to power an alternative energy source, the fish spawner may be required to adjust the use of the water. The key is whether there is actual damage to the downstream owner's reasonable use of the water.

The concept of reasonable use supersedes an older notion (still incorporated in some locations) that each property owner has a right to the natural flow of the water uninterrupted by anyone else's use.

In practice, in populated areas, water is managed by a municipal agency. Water is withdrawn by the agency for public use, and overflow systems discharge storm waters. The interests of riparian owners are often pitted against the use and redirection of water by these agencies.

Another area of concern has to do with pollution, resulting either from discharge by a company or from a sewage plant created by a city agency. Homeowners with water rights frequently must join their complaints into a class action, or lobby extensively for state or local regulations to protect their water interests (see following).

WESTERN STATES—PERMITS TO USE STREAMS

Seventeen states* west of the Mississippi, where water is a scarce resource, follow a different system of legal rights, known as the *appropriation system.* The appropriation system holds that water rights fall to the owners who make prior, beneficial uses of the water. This means essentially, first come, first served.

Central to the appropriation system is the assertion of public control over water by a state agency that oversees water use. The agency collects information on stream records, makes surveys, has a process for issuing water permits, and enforces a water code through local water masters. The exact rules on water use vary among the states.

In appropriation states, a property owner must prepare a written application for a permit to take unappropriated water. The application is submitted to an administrative body such as the water control board. It must state the time and purpose of use, the quantity of water, and the legal description of the point from which the water is to be taken, and must include supporting maps, plats, diagrams, or photos.

Applications for permits are published, and affected parties

*The states are Arizona, California, Colorado, Idaho, Kansas, Montana, Nebraska, Nevada, New Mexico, North Dakota, Oklahoma, Oregon, South Dakota, Texas, Utah, Washington, and Wyoming.

are contacted so that any objections can be filed within a set time period. In some states, water permits can be granted to people who own no property at all along the watercourse (nonriparian owners), but who have a use for the water. If objections are filed, the administrative agency holds a public hearing.

After hearing from an applicant and a state engineer, the water agency makes a finding about whether or not to issue a water permit. The primary consideration is whether the proposed use is beneficial. The agency also considers the availability of water and the harm to other water users with permits and to the public interest. The decision can be appealed, but the court considers only whether the decision of the water agency was made in an appropriate manner.

When all the conditions for a permit have been met, the state issues a license or certificate of appropriation, which is recorded like a property deed. The date of issuance of the water permit determines priority of use if the water level runs so low that all permit holders cannot enjoy the use of the water.

The state agency also adjudicates grievances among competing water users.

FLOODING STREAMS

Most streams overflow as the result of natural causes. Since there is no one to sue for damages when this occurs, there are few legal remedies for a naturally flooding stream. Owners of property along a body of water or in a flood district can protect themselves only by purchasing special flood insurance (see chapter 1).

A property owner was allowed to proceed with a claim against an upstream property owner who had failed to clear debris after a freak snowstorm. The debris washed downstream in a later rainstorm and caused flooding and erosion to other properties. The court found that an upstream property owner could be liable for failing to protect other property owners on the watercourse.

Sometimes, however, the actions of an upstream owner cause flood damage downstream. The installation of a dike or storm system may result in damage if the stream overflows, in which case the downstream owner may have legal recourse (see following).

SEWAGE, MUNICIPAL WASTE, AND STORM DRAINAGE

The release of sewage, municipal waste, and runoff into a waterway can have an effect on waterfront property through overflow, backup, and flooding.

What makes municipal-waste cases unique is the type of legal action that is usually taken. Because a government agency is involved, the property owner's claim would assert that the government should provide some compensation for taking away the beneficial enjoyment of the land, known as *inverse condemnation* (see chapter 16).

Property owners have also sued municipalities when private drainage systems cause flooding, claiming the municipality should not have approved the plan, but they have not had much success. (The homeowner could also make a claim against the people who installed the drainage system.)

There are other restrictions on cases against municipalities. Under a doctrine of sovereign immunity, some state laws make municipalities immune from lawsuits unless they acted in an outrageous manner. When claims are allowed, the homeowner might be required to file a notice of claim with the municipality quickly. If a storm system problem arises, promptly notify the appropriate city agency in writing about the problem and seek corrective action.

SURFACE WATER

All property owners are affected by surface water. Surface water is drainage—water that moves along the ground from rain, snow, swelling springs, or flooding. Succumbing to laws of gravity, surface water moves from higher ground to lower ground. Changes in the flow of surface water also occur from nearby construction.

Legal disputes about surface water arise because it is generally unwanted. This contrasts to the rules about streams, in which the property owners usually want to increase or preserve their access to the water.

Homeowners frequently try to protect their property from the flow of surface water by cutting a new channel, draining the water onto other property, or barricading the flow of water from higher ground. States have taken three very distinct attitudes about how a property owner may treat surface water.

1.   *As is.* Half the states hold that a property owner must suffer with the natural condition of the property toward receiving surface water and cannot redirect it to other land. This is known as the civil law or natural servitude rule.

2.   *Enemy.* One-third of the states take an opposite approach, holding that surface water is a common enemy to property owners, and they can do anything to get rid of it, no matter how it affects neighbors.

3.   *Reasonable.* The most recent approach, adopted in about 10 states, holds that a property owner may drain or channel water from the land if it is reasonable under the circumstances. This means that the owner takes reasonable care to avoid injury to others and adopts the best drainage method with the least effect on other landowners, and that the benefit from draining outweighs the harm to neighbors. Landowners who fail to meet the reasonable use test can be liable to neighbors for damage caused by draining surface water.

Before engaging in expensive drainage systems or efforts to redirect surface water, homeowners should find out which standard is followed in their state.

Underground Water

Underground water is important in digging wells or tapping aquifers or basins that hold water.

The law about underground water is still catching up to the fairly recent understanding of engineers about the nature of underground water and how it extends beyond a single piece of property. Underground water is valuable because it is not quickly replaced. In addition, powerful new pumps can draw water in quantities and from depths that previously could not be reached.

Disputes are created when one landowner believes that another is unfairly using up the underground water.

Several states now require a water-well permit. Nearly all of the western states have developed systems for registration, permits, and administration of underground water (as they have for streams).

Underground water is divided into two types: underground streams and percolating water. An underground stream has defined banks and a bed and is determined by test borings. Most states apply the same rules to underground streams as they apply to aboveground stream water.

Most underground water, however, is presumed to be percolating, or trickling, through many layers of rock and earth. For percolating water, states have adopted three different views.

1. *Reasonable.* The majority of states hold that every property owner has the right to make reasonable use—on the land—of the water underneath. The key is how it is used. If the water is pumped but used on other land, the use is probably not reasonable. Conversely, when the water is used by the owner of the land from which it is pumped, and the use is reasonable, the property owner can even deplete the supply of water to the detriment of a neighbor.

2. *Absolute.* A smaller number of states believe that a property owner has absolute ownership of underground water on the land and may use as much as desired in whatever way. A neighbor's need or use can be disregarded. This is more or less an all-persons-for-themselves approach.

3. *Relative.* The third view, developed in California, is that owners have *correlative rights* to underlying water basins. Each property owner with an aquifer under the land is considered to have equal rights to use the water in beneficial use on the property. But these rights do not mean that a landowner can deplete a neighbor's supply. If water is in short supply, each property owner must reduce use so that some water is available to all.

GROUNDWATER CONTAMINATION

Tanks buried underground can leak into the groundwater and cause contamination. This is an area of growing and significant legal concern. Estimates indicate that there are over 1 million underground storage tanks for fuel and chemicals in the United States, largely made of corrosive steel. Many of these tanks are on the sites of former gas stations.

The contents of leaking underground tanks can find their way into drinking water through groundwater and well water. Federal legislation under the Resource Conservation and Recovery Act (RCRA) and the Superfund Act are beginning to address compensation for damages caused by underground tanks. Nearly half the states have rules governing underground tanks. In addition, individual property owners have brought many cases for tank leakage on theories of trespass and nuisance (see following).

LAKESIDE PROPERTY

The owners of lakeside property are entitled to reasonable use of the lake and are obligated not to harm it in any way. Reasonable use includes boating, fishing, and swimming.

A lakeside property owner cannot discharge waste into the lake or contaminate or pollute it. Lakeside owners also cannot drain the lake by pumping water beyond that necessary for their own reasonable use.

In one case, a lakeside owner was prohibited from placing a barrier around a portion of the lake, since all owners were entitled to the full enjoyment of the entire lake and could not be excluded from a portion. Other states hold that lakefront property owners may use barriers to keep a portion of the lake within their exclusive use.

If a lake is navigable, the bed of the lake usually belongs to the state or federal government. The public is free to use a navigable lake. Owners of property on a navigable lake may not have exclusive use of the water, even though they may own the shore points.

PRIVATE LAKES

Property owners control lakes or ponds that are fully contained on their properties. They may fence the lakes, drain them, close them off, or fill them with pebbles.

Some private developments are built along lakes and offer the purchasers certain rights to use the lake. But the ownership of the

> *Property owners control lakes or ponds that are fully contained on their properties. They may fence the lakes, drain them, close them off, or fill them with pebbles.*

lake may not be exclusive. A private development may claim the rights to a lake only if the bed of the lake is entirely owned by the private development and no part of the lake is open for public use.

Planned communities developed along a lake may be subject to covenants in the deed (see chapters 3 and 17). The covenants may specify the type of boats that can be used, the hours of lake usage, the type of docks that can be built, and any other restrictions that the developer wishes.

Oceans and Wetlands

Ocean water belongs to the federal government. Coastal land is also subject to regulation by each state. Competing with the rights of oceanfront property owners are the rights of the public to have access to the ocean. In some states, the law explicitly states that the public has a right to access even to privately held beach property.

Questions about oceanfront rights arise from the proximity of the land to what is essentially a public thoroughfare. Oceanfront property owners can suffer injuries because of activity in the ocean, such as an oil tanker spill, which could give rise to legal claims.

Dumping waste in the ocean is regulated by the federal government under the Ocean Dumping Act and other laws and by state legislative enactments. Ocean dumping is not prohibited (excepting high-level radioactive waste), but it is not to be done at distances so close to the shore that it affects beach property. Nonetheless, trash lands on beaches and, theoretically at least, dumping could give rise to claims by homeowners. But problems in developing evidence make it difficult—the source of the waste and the company or person who dumped the waste must be identified and it must be demonstrated that the waste was dumped illegally within a distance prohibited by the law.

Beachfront property can also be affected by direct discharges of industrial or municipal waste and both urban and agricultural runoff in coastal zones. Streams and rivers polluted with discharge carry their contaminants to the ocean. Public sewage plants release a large percentage of both treated and untreated sewage into ocean waters. Sand can be diverted by the building of dams and jetties that alter the natural sand flow. Generally, legal remedies are so complex that homeowners wishing to pursue them must join forces with citizen's groups (see following).

In some areas, the government has prohibited building near the ocean, such as beach setback requirements. Regulations of wetlands—the swampy lands between the ocean and land in some areas—also prohibit building on the property. Property owners have claimed that their property has been taken from them and that they deserve compensation from the government (see chapter 16).

GROUND SUPPORT

Property owners are absolutely entitled to have their land supported laterally by the land of a neighbor.

If a piece of property were sliced from the earth like a piece of pie, the sides of the property would be subject to slippage and erosion, and the center could crumble and holes and depressions could be formed. Lateral support is that provided by the land standing next to the property.

EXCAVATION

If excavation by a neighbor disrupts a homeowner's land, the homeowner has a total right to recover damages.

If excavation by a neighbor disrupts a homeowner's land, the homeowner has a total right to recover damages. It does not matter whether the excavation was done with extreme care or carelessly—the right to recover for damages to the land itself is absolute.

There is one hitch—this right applies to the land, but not necessarily to buildings on the land. The reasoning is that a neighbor should not have to refrain from building simply because adjoining land was built up first.

Under this rule, if a house is damaged by a neighbor's excavation, the homeowner would have to show one of two things:

1. The excavation was done haphazardly or negligently: negligence has been found when an excavator failed to notify the neighbor with adjoining land, in order to allow the landowner to shore up the property, or in some cases for failing to conduct soil studies in advance.
2. The excavation actually damaged the land and the harm to the house is a consequence of the land being disrupted.

The harshness of the common-law rule on neighboring landowners, particularly in urban areas, has been corrected by local ordinances in many cities. These ordinances may require the issuance of a special permit before excavation begins and notification to neighbors of pending excavation (see chapters 5 and 6). If the excavation is to go below a certain depth, the excavator may be required to shore up the building of an adjoining landowner.

If cracks appear in a house's foundation after a neighbor's excavation, a homeowner can also proceed legally on other theories. Some homeowners have successfully argued that excavation was a nuisance (see chapter 10). Another argument is that the excavator could have avoided the harm, and that the law generally favors the avoidance of harm wherever possible. In one case, a property owner argued that an excavation was an ultrahazardous activity and made the excavator liable without any negligence.

The damages for a wrongful or negligent excavation can be either the cost of repairs or the depreciation in the market value of the property.

In some states, even noncontiguous property owners have been allowed to recover for damages from a negligent excavation.

When the adjacent property is a public highway, a property owner who is excavating is required to prevent disruption to both the land and to the highway. The excavator is unquestionably liable for any damages.

Homeowners are, at times, asked to sign waivers permitting excavation on neighboring property. A waiver could prohibit the owner from rightfully obtaining compensation for damages. Before accepting any payment or signing any document agreeing to excavation on neighboring property—whether waiver, license, or easement—consult an attorney.

Before homeowners permit contractors to undertake excavation on their land, they must make certain that all notification and permit procedures are followed (see chapter 6).

RETAINING WALL

The right to lateral support also applies to the right to build a retaining wall and to prevent an adjoining landowner from interfering with it. A retaining wall bolsters the land's strength and prevents erosion and deterioration.

A retaining wall built by one landowner cannot cross the boundary line of the property. The builder cannot compel the adjoining owner to contribute to its costs. On the other hand, the neighbor cannot do anything to harm, damage, or remove support from the retaining wall.

If both property owners agree jointly to build a retaining wall, they should get a written agreement about costs and maintenance.

GRADING OR FILL

Questions of lateral support arise when one property owner raises the level of the land by grading or fill. The rule is that a homeowner cannot fill the land in such a way as to cause damage to a neighbor's property by letting mud and dirt be carried onto it.

This is an affirmative duty. A property owner who lets changes in the surface of the land affect a neighbor's land will be liable for damages.

PARTY WALL

The right to lateral support also extends to a common wall between two attached houses, or a party wall. Party walls are typical in cooperatives, condominiums, and town houses. A party wall is essentially an easement that each homeowner has in the other person's property.

The legal rules concerning party walls can be further specified in the rules and covenants of a planned development, cooperative, or condominium association.

In general, both parties are responsible for the costs of repairs to a party wall. If a repair is necessary but affects only one property, the owner of that property bears the cost of repairs.

Neither party may damage a party wall to the detriment of the other. If damage occurs, the party who caused it must pay for the damages. This does not prevent a homeowner from making alterations to the property or even to the party wall, so long as the lateral support and strength of the wall are not reduced in any way.

The one time that one person may destroy a party wall is when the wall is dangerous. In that case, the neighbor needs to be notified in advance about the condition of the wall and intended action.

SUBJACENT SUPPORT

Under traditional law, the ownership of land extends to the center of the earth. Landowners have the right to mine or pump oil from their land and the right to lease the underground property for various purposes. A neighbor who digs a mine shaft at an angle that, beneath the ground, crosses the property boundary is committing trespass.

Subjacent support is that ground support underlying the property. The subjacent support can be undercut by a tunnel, water mains, or a mine shaft. If the cutting of such a structure impairs a homeowner's property, even if the owner gave permission, for example, to mine, the person causing harm is absolutely liable.

In one case, the holder of an easement to build a railroad tunnel under certain property was held absolutely liable for injuries caused by the removal of subjacent support from the surface land. In cases of subjacent support, courts extend the right to recover damages to the land and buildings on the property, particularly when the buildings were standing without problems before the subjacent support was disrupted.

Courts have declined to find liability when the damage was caused by neighbors drawing groundwater from their own land. Subjacent support applies only when the land has been cut directly underneath.

AIRSPACE

A homeowner was once presumed to own the property from the ground up to the heavens. Airplanes changed that. Congress declared the upper airspace to be a public highway and it is now equivalent to navigable waters—controlled and regulated by the federal government for the use and benefit of the public.

Lower airspace still belongs to the property owner. You own as much airspace as is reasonably needed. The exact airspace accorded varies from state to state, but is generally the area from 20 to 50 feet above the land or above the highest point on the building. The property owner can sell an easement or license in the lower airspace, such as to cable companies or for power lines.

The lower airspace itself can be sold, as sometimes happens in New York City, in which a developer buys the air rights over a smaller structure and designs a building around the structure. Condominium and cooperative buildings often sell air rights to increase their common funds. Air rights can also be accumulated by major developers in order to increase the space with which to juggle zoning requirements on bulk and size of buildings.

Air rights are subject to zoning limitations and local ordinances that restrict the height of buildings.

Because the airspace above the property belongs to the homeowner, anyone who crosses the airspace is committing a trespass. A low-flying plane could be trespassing, as could shots fired across the land (see chapter 9).

Airspace is also susceptible to encroachments from overhanging eaves or tree branches. An airspace encroachment could ripen into a property right by another through adverse possession, if the homeowner did nothing to object and the encroaching use existed openly for many years.

Even though the upper airspace is in the control of the government, homeowners often raise claims about the nuisance, sound, and lights of airplanes taking off from a nearby airport. The common claim is that the flights so interfere with the enjoyment of the property that it amounts to a taking of property by the government (see chapter 16). In some cases, courts have agreed with homeowners.

Light, Air, and View

Despite owning the airspace above one's property, under traditional law a homeowner has no incidental right to have light, air, or view protected from being blocked by adjoining property owners. Some cities have changed the classic rules through zoning or other ordinances.

Traditionally, owners could not complain if a neighbor built a structure so close to the boundary that light, air, or view was cut off or even obliterated. The law provided an exception to this rule if the adjoining landowner maliciously or intentionally sought to block light or view, such as by building a tall spite fence.

Homeowners can protect light, air, or view by obtaining an easement from a neighbor. A homeowner and a neighbor could sell each other mutual easements that would, for example, prevent building additional stories.

In one case in Minnesota, a court ruled that property owners had an implied easement of air, light, and view, and that the property owner could be compensated when the government built a skywalk that blocked air, light, and view.

In many cities, zoning regulations provide setback requirements and bulk limits on structures. Planned communities and subdivisions often have extensive regulations in their covenants and restrictions that protect homeowners from light, air, or view obstructions by neighbors (see chapter 17). A few cities have also passed view ordinances, in which a homeowner can take steps to get a neighbor to cut back a tree that has destroyed the original view existing at the time of purchase.

Property owners have been permitted to sue a seller who misrepresented the continuing nature of a special view, knowing very well that planned new construction would block it. The purchasers did not discover the problem until after the sale was complete.

In a few locations, homeowners who install solar panels, which require constant light, have been protected by ordinances that prohibit neighbors' trees from interfering with sun access. One state ruled that a neighbor's construction, which interfered with the solar panels of a homeowner, could be considered unreason-able, possibly entitling the solar homeowner to damages. For the homeowner considering solar panels, it is a good idea to ensure a degree of protection by buying an easement over a neighbor's property.

Although there is no incidental right to receive free-flowing air, if an owner's enjoyment of the property is damaged by air pollution, it may be possible to have a claim in trespass or nui-sance (see chapters 9 and 10). In one case, a property owner was awarded damages as a result of the release of dust from a cotton mill. Property owners have been held strictly liable for damages caused by an herbicide that blew onto neighbors' property in aer-ial crop-dusting.

Pollution from Neighboring Property

Concern about pollution and its affect on neighboring land has brought new attention to incidental rights. Legislation is setting higher standards for air, water, ground, and noise pollution. Among these are the 1972 federal Clean Water Act; the Resource Conservation and Recovery Act of 1984 (RCRA); the Comprehensive Environmental Response, Compensation & Lia-bility Act (CERCLA); the 1986 Superfund Amendments and Reauthorization Law (SARA); the Clean Air Act Amendments of 1990; the Endangered Species Act; the National Environmental Policy Act (NEPA); and the Coastal Zone Management Act of 1972 (CZMA).

The laws reflect concerns about hazardous waste dumping or underground burial of it; about discharge into streams, lakes, and oceans; and about noxious materials emitted into the air. In many cases, the federal government is responsible for overseeing the enforcement of these laws, sometimes in conjunction with state agencies. In addition, many states have passed environmen-tal protections of their own.

The enforcement procedures under these laws are difficult and success is far from complete. These difficulties are underscored by the highly technical nature of proof, such as demonstrating what is being emitted or discharged, its harmful nature, from where it is being emitted, and the damage that it has caused or might cause.

Many environmental laws give citizens the right to sue for damages, known as a *private right of action* (compared to the government's public right of action). The owner of property along a stream being polluted by discharge from a paper mill could possibly bring a lawsuit under the Clean Water Act, seeking compensation for damages and for the devaluation of the property.

Similarly, under RCRA, a homeowner who owns land next to a dumping ground used by a chemical company, from which hazardous waste is seeping into groundwater and flowing onto the property owner's land, could bring a lawsuit.

These lawsuits are extremely complicated. They must be brought in federal court, and there are many restrictions and technical concerns that require the assistance of a specialized attorney. This makes proceeding under a federal environmental law prohibitive for the average individual. However, citizens' groups have brought several hundred actions.

If concerned about damage to property from pollution, homeowners should contact local and national environmental interest groups to see if a citizens' action is under way or is being considered.

As noted previously, recent attention among citizens' organizations is being directed to the ways in which minority and low-income communities may suffer disproportionately from a lack of environmental law enforcement or from dumping and hazardous waste siting.

In severe cases, the state attorney general's office undertakes to represent citizens. In the infamous Love Canal case, the state attorney general's office took action on behalf of the homeowners who were forced to flee their properties. Hundreds of homes were built on land that was formerly a company's chemical waste dump. Homeowners experienced chemicals seeping into their homes, explosions emanating from buried chemical drums, fires, and other difficulties. The property was declared a national disaster area.

Individual property owners can file a formal inquiry for documents collected by federal or state agencies under the Freedom of Information Act. By writing to the agency's freedom of information officer, paying a fee (or requesting a waiver of fee), and stating the information sought, owners can get copies of government records on the pollution.

Individual property owners who suffer the damages of pollution from some identifiable source can also sue on their own, just

as they might sue any adjoining landowner who interfered with
their property.

Lawsuits against a polluter proceed on a basis of trespass or
nuisance.

In some instances, property owners might be able to claim that
the adjoining property owner engaged in an ultrahazardous
activity and that the polluter should be held strictly accountable
for any damage, such as from aerial crop spraying.

When the pollution has occurred for many years, the polluter
often asserts that the time limit, or statute of limitations, for
bringing a claim has passed. Polluters also claim that they have
acquired a prescriptive right to pollute—stating that since they
have been doing it for so long, they have acquired what is essentially a property right to continue to do so. Under theories of
adverse possession these polluters claim that they have gained an
easement or other right to discharge the offensive materials (see
chapter 3). Homeowners should act as soon as possible, if damage from pollution is discovered.

In the case of long-term environmental hazards, homeowners
can also consider bringing an action against the seller if the problem was not disclosed prior to the purchase (see chapter 2).

As with environmental contaminants found inside a home,
brokers, lenders, developers, or a title search company could
bear responsibility if they knew or should have known that the
property was environmentally damaged or hazardous (see chapter 15). In one case, a court ruled that banks, builders, and real
estate agents could be liable for harm resulting from a housing
development built on land once used for a wood-creosoting
operation.

There is one other problem with environmental hazards.
Under CERCLA, property owners may have to pay for cleaning
up toxins, even though they had no part in their discharge or
dumping. Further, if they sell the property, they could be liable
if they do not disclose environmental conditions to the new buyer
(see chapter 20).

LEGAL STRATEGIES

Homeowners seek two types of solutions when incidental rights
are invaded: compensation for damages and a cessation of the

activities. Following is a discussion of the legal strategies most often used.

Negotiation Negotiation should always be the first approach. Incidental rights invariably involve neighbors. Some problems can be solved by a simple letter or phone call. Homeowners can help keep the peace by trying a friendly, nonthreatening approach first.

Trespass Trespass is a common legal claim used to rectify an incidental rights issue. Trespass usually applies to intentional acts and involves an actual physical invasion on the property. The dumping of oil into a stream, which then washes up onto the homeowner's property, could be a trespass. In order to pursue a trespass action, the homeowner needs to have suffered only nominal harm or damages. In the case of a continuing trespass, the homeowner would seek an injunction to stop the activity.

Nuisance The most widely used theory in cases of incidental rights is a private nuisance action (see chapter 10). An adjoining landowner could be liable for a nuisance if the activity in question creates a substantial and unreasonable interference with the owner's use and enjoyment of the land. The homeowner must have suffered actual property or personal damage.

In a nuisance action, the court balances the importance of the activity to the public with the harm caused to the individual. In a pollution case, for example, the benefit to the public from the operation of a mill could be matched against the harm caused to the individual by lowered air quality.

Negligence In a negligence case, a homeowner would claim that a neighbor had a duty of care, the duty was breached, this caused injury, and the homeowner suffered damages. The failure of an upstream owner to clear dead tree limbs from a river, causing damage to a downstream owner, might be attributable to negligence.

Strict Liability If the adjoining property owner engages in ultrahazardous activities, a homeowner could proceed on a theory of strict liability—that the neighbor should be liable for damages even if not negligent. Aerial herbicide spraying, a chemical spill, and possibly the siting of an underground gas tank might be considered ultrahazardous activities.

Absolute Liability   Other activities that subvert incidental rights are subject to absolute liability, regardless of negligence by the person causing the harm. A disruption in subjacent support when a miner's shaft below the surface collapses and causes the land to cave in is subject to absolute liability. The landowner is entitled to be compensated for damages.

Covenants and Restrictions   When a property is part of a sub-division, planned-unit development, condominium, cooperative, or vacation community development, rights and responsibilities for incidental rights may be stated in the covenants in the deed or in the rules and regulations of homeowner's associations (see chapter 17). The use of a lake or the responsibility for a party wall, and the means of enforcement for breaches, may be specified in the homeowner documents.

Local Ordinances and Zoning   Local agencies can be called upon to enforce certain regulations related to incidental rights. Excavation requires permits in many urban areas, and without a permit can be halted by the city. Permits are required in many states to discharge water or to draw water from a well. In some cities, zoning regulations protect air and light access by prohibiting the construction of tall buildings in residential neighborhoods. If local regulations apply, the proper enforcement agency may be able to stop the offensive activity.

Eminent Domain   Many cases involving incidental rights also involve government action—damming a river, installing a drainage system, building an airport. In these cases, the homeowner generally brings a lawsuit against the government on theories of eminent domain, asserting that the value of the property has been lost because of the government's action (see chapter 16).

Administrative Law   In cases involving government decision making, such as the issuance of water permits, homeowners are required to follow the rules of a regulatory agency. If this is unsatisfactory, the case can go to court, but the homeowner must then show that the administrative agency acted in an arbitrary and capricious fashion.

Quiet Title   If the violation to incidental rights—for example, airspace—involves an overhanging eave or other encroachment, the homeowner could bring an action to quiet title. The homeowner seeks to have a declaration that the encroachment is a violation of the owner's property right, so that the neighbor does not gain a prescriptive right to continue it (see chapter 3).

Federal or State Pollution Laws and Citizens' Action   When the matter involves pollution, various federal laws provide protection. Homeowners can sue under many of these laws, but suits are complicated. Consider joining with citizens' action groups to pressure for changes or to bring a lawsuit. Particularly in cases with aggravated circumstances, a state attorney general's office might pursue a polluter on behalf of homeowners.

Easements   Some peace and solace can be provided by buying an easement from an adjoining landowner. For example, light, air, or view easements from a neighbor could protect a homeowner from property development on that parcel of land. An easement to divert water could permit a property owner to drain land even though some water will flow onto a neighbor's property.

Protection of Full Rights

Home ownership entails rights beyond the mere ownership of the house and land, and extends to rights in water, ground support, and airspace. But these rights are subject to the competing rights of adjoining property owners.

Therefore, homeowners have both rights and responsibilities—the right to expect that their property will receive lateral

In most states, a homeowner may not unreasonably interfere with a neighbor's use of water in a running stream by damming, withdrawing, polluting, or flooding.

support from neighboring property, but also the duty to provide lateral support to their neighbors.

Homeowners also have an obligation with regard to shared natural resources. In most states property owners may not unreasonably interfere with a neighbor's use of water in a running stream by damming, withdrawing, polluting, or flooding.

The interdependent nature of air, water, and the earth necessarily becomes part of the landowner's world in protecting and enforcing incidental rights.

Trespassers,
Unwanted Visitors,
Intruders,
and Security

Trespassing is a concept understood by most people—in everyday language, it is simply entering onto another person's property without permission. But trespassing also has a specific legal application that is part of civil, not criminal, law. A civil action for trespass is possible when a homeowner suffers any physical interference with the possession of the property.

This type of trespass encompasses a wide range of activities. A trespasser is the person who walks across the lawn without permission. But a trespass can also occur when the branches of a neighbor's tree overhang into a homeowner's yard, when a neighbor dumps asphalt on the edge of a lot and it flows onto another person's property, when a neighbor's horse breaks through a fence, when eggs are thrown at the garage, and when someone gathers wood on the homeowner's property without

A civil action for trespass is possible when a homeowner suffers any physical interference with the possession of the property.

permission. The invasion of the homeowner's space by any tangible item can constitute a trespass.

When a trespass occurs, homeowners may take legal action, including bringing a lawsuit for the costs of injuries or damages or suing to stop the activity if it is continuous (see chapter 21).

Ordinarily, property owners have a case or cause of action against only a trespasser who knows or is warned that the activity is a trespass. For this reason, the first step to take when faced with a situation of trespass is to warn the individuals that they are trespassing and to ask that they stop. Often, a posted No Trespassing sign warns people who might enter onto the property or cause some other trespass that they are interfering with private property rights.

THE NATURE OF TRESPASS

A trespass claim is a civil action against an offending party for any unwanted physical intrusion onto another's property. An unwanted intrusion is without permission and without privilege. Trespass is one of the oldest types of civil law claims.

A trespass claim can be brought even if the property owner has suffered no observable damage. The owner's right to exclusive possession of the land is considered of prime importance. Just intruding physically upon another's land without permission is a sufficient claim for a lawsuit. In this regard, trespass is an unusual kind of civil claim, since nearly all other cases rest upon injuries of some sort.

Nevertheless, trespass lawsuits usually involve damage to the property. In a trespass claim, landowners are entitled to seek compensation from the trespasser for all damages caused by the trespass or as a result of the trespass. A property owner can also seek an injunction to put an end to the intrusive activity.

PLACE OF TRESPASS

A trespass usually occurs on the surface of the land. But since a property owner's rights extend up into the air and down into the ground, a trespass could also be airborne or subterranean. The shot from a gun fired across the land is a trespass, as is a low-flying airplane. An angled underground shaft that crosses the boundary below the surface is a trespass (see chapter 8).

INTENTION

A trespass claim will be successful where the action of the trespasser is intentional, negligent, or the result of ultrahazardous activity.

Most trespass claims focus on intentional trespasses. Intention in this case means only that the people intend to be where they are or doing what they are doing, not that they intended to trespass. An example of lack of intent is a person who is kidnapped and taken onto someone else's property.

PERMISSION TO BE ON A PROPERTY

A person who has permission to be on another's property is not trespassing. Invited social or business guests are not trespassing. Workers hired to make repairs on the property are not trespassing.

A neighbor who has an easement to use another's driveway is not trespassing either. In addition, under the conditions of the easement, the easement owner may have a right to be on the property to maintain the easement. Utility company easements generally give the company the right to enter onto the property to maintain the wires and to cut trees that are threatening to fall on them.

A trespass can occur when someone exceeds the scope of permitted or privileged entry. Permission to use or be on the property can be exceeded by time, space, or scope of activities. A person who is invited to a party, but refuses to leave when the party is over, crosses over from a guest to a trespasser. A construction worker who is to fix the roof but is found rummaging through clothes in a closet becomes a trespasser. The neighbor who has an easement to dig beneath another's ground to install a sprinkler system but instead builds a bomb shelter is committing a trespass.

PRIVILEGED ENTRIES ONTO PRIVATE PROPERTY

In some circumstances, an entry onto the land is permissible, even though the property owner has not invited the person or consented to the entry. If the entry is permissible, the homeowner may not sue for damages or take other action, such as ejectment.

One such entry is for reasons of necessity. People are permitted to trespass if they find themselves in a dire situation and necessity requires that they enter the land. A boat that encounters a sudden storm has a privilege to dock without permission. Indeed, a landowner could be liable for injuries that occurred after turning away the distressed boat. On the other hand, after the storm is over, the boat owner cannot decide to stay for another week and enjoy the scenery.

Similarly, if an airplane loses an engine, the pilot has the privilege of landing on private property. (The airline company or its insurance carrier still might have to pay for damages that occurred to the property.)

Emergency is a similar privilege. A neighbor would be privileged to enter another's property if the house were on fire or to save a child from drowning in a swimming pool. Fire fighters may string a fire hose across any property if doing so is the shortest route to a hydrant when attempting to put out a fire.

Hot pursuit is a privileged entry onto property, as well. If the police are chasing a robber who jumps a fence and runs through someone's backyard, the police may also run through the yard.

A person may also have a limited privilege to trespass to abate a nuisance. A property owner has a right to undertake self-help to abate certain nuisances, even if it means entry onto another's property (see chapter 10). If water were flooding a homeowner's property from a running outdoor faucet on a neighbor's property, the homeowner might be privileged to enter onto the property for the sole purpose of turning off the faucet.

A privilege also exists for people to enter onto another's property to retrieve their property or pets. They may do so only by acting in a reasonable manner. For example, breaking down a door is not reasonable.

A landlord has a limited privilege to enter the rental property to inspect the premises, correct problems, let workers in, or show the premises to new renters. By most state laws, these visits need to be announced reasonably in advance. A landlord cannot repeatedly enter rented premises without permission (see chapter 19).

If an entry is privileged, the trespasser may not extend the entry beyond the specific privilege. It is limited in time, activity, and location.

GOVERNMENT OFFICERS

In some cases, a government officer may have a privilege to enter upon private property. This privilege, however, is weighed against serious constitutional provisions that protect homeowners from unwarranted intrusion by the government.

The Fourth Amendment holds that a police officer may not make an unreasonable search of private property. *Unreasonable* means without a search warrant, with certain exceptions. A *warrant* is an order by a judge who has reviewed the reasons the police offer for conducting a search on private property. The police must show that there is probable cause to believe illegal activity is occurring, or that they expect to find evidence of illegal activity.

If a police officer comes to a homeowner's house and requests to search the premises, the owner has a right to see a search warrant. If a warrant is presented, the property owner is unjustified in refusing the search. If no warrant is presented, the homeowner can refuse the search—without giving a reason.

On the other hand, if a police officer does not have a warrant but is acting on a reasonable belief of illegal activity, the officer may be able to conduct a search if the property owner consents. Granting consent to a search can amount to waiving Fourth Amendment rights against unreasonable search and seizure. In theory, if a person grants consent to a search, the individual can revoke it at any time. Homeowners can consent only to a search of property in their control, not to a search of a tenant's property, or even, in some states, of a child's room.

Police officers carrying a warrant are supposed to "knock and announce" their purpose. This obligation is excused if the officers believe that evidence will be destroyed, such as illegal drugs dumped down the drain. If the police knock and no one answers, they may enter and conduct the search. A search is supposed to be limited to the description in the warrant. If the police are in hot pursuit of a suspect and believe that he or she has entered the house, an exception to the warrant rule is made. Police may also enter without a warrant if they believe there is someone inside who is in need of aid or that a crime is in progress.

The law of search and seizure is fairly complex and usually arises when someone is charged with a crime, in which case an attorney can raise the question of whether the search was justified.

A privilege to enter private property is also extended to persons carrying out a court order, such as serving a summons or to repossess property under a valid court order.

Questions arise when other government employees request entry. These may be health department officials, building department officials, assessors, child-welfare workers, and so on.

A government official may have a limited right to enter onto the property for official purposes. A person's consent extends only to permitting the inspection requested and not a broader search of the premises. If the homeowner refuses to allow a search of the property, the official may seek a search warrant.

LIABILITY AND THE TRESPASSING INDIVIDUAL

A trespasser is liable for any injuries or damage that occur on the property as a result of the trespass, even if they were unforeseen. A trespasser whose cigarette burns down a shed is liable for the damage caused.

On the other hand, property owners have a limited duty to trespassing individuals not to cause them harm by reckless, willful, or malicious conduct (see chapter 7). This is especially true if

A trespasser is liable for any injuries or damage that occur on the property as a result of the trespass, even if they were unforeseen.

the homeowner knows that there are trespassers who use the property and also knows of dangerous uncorrected conditions. A wire stretched across a private road subjected a property owner to liability when a motorcycle rider, known to use the road, struck the wire and was thrown from the bike.

Homeowners can be liable especially for injuries suffered by child trespassers, whose judgment is considered poor and who can be attracted to dangerous conditions on the property, known as the theory of attractive nuisance (see chapter 7).

THE TRESPASSING ANIMAL

Animals come in four basic varieties—claimed and unclaimed, wild and domestic. How the landowner can respond to the trespassing animal depends on its category.

The responsibility for an animal's activities lies with its owner. If the trespassing animal is wild and roaming in nature, it has no owner and there is no one to take to court for trespass. Protective measures against the animal can be taken, or the property owner can contact state or local animal wardens. Shooting or trapping the animal is permissible only if it is allowed under state hunting and wildlife laws, which apply to activities on private as well as public property.

If someone owns a wild animal—whether horse, tiger, or monkey—the owner is responsible for the animal's wanderings. If a homeowner's property is damaged by the wild animal owned by another, money for any damages caused can be sought. Attempts to remove the animal can be made, but only by using reasonable means. Killing the animal is reasonable only if there is a present danger to a person or property.

When the West was being settled, many cases were concerned with roaming cattle. For example, a cow leaps over the fence, kicks over a lantern, and a fire burns down the barn. For this eventuality, states adopted "fence out" and "fence in" laws. The "fence out" laws decreed that a property owner could recover for damages caused by another's livestock only if the property owner had taken precautionary steps in building a strong fence to keep the creatures out. Other states held that the livestock owners were responsible unless they had strong fences to keep the animals in. These laws are still in force in some localities.

Domesticated pets fall in a separate category. In most places, courts give a bit of leniency to the owner of a dog or cat that ambles away from home. The dog or cat owner is not likely to be held liable for a mere trespass. Even if the pet does minor property damage, the owner is often not held accountable without a local ordinance that makes pet owners responsible for a clear act of negligence. If the pet owner knows that the animal is trespassing and causing damage, he or she becomes liable for not taking steps to prevent the harm. The owner is always responsible for personal injuries caused by a pet (see chapter 7).

Many communities are now taking stronger measures against pets. Pets are expected to be leashed or fenced at all times. If the pet gets out and causes property damage, the pet owner is required to pay the bill. Some subdivisions governed by homeowner's associations have passed strict rules on animal ownership and leashing (see chapter 17).

Faced with an animal that trespasses, the first recourse is to talk to the owner. Even if this doesn't solve the problem, it does establish that the pet owner knew about the animal's intrusions, so that if the problem continues, the homeowner may have a case against the owner for negligence. After talking to the pet owner, write a short note explaining the problem or the damage and ask that the owner restrain the animal.

If a leash law exists in the community, contact the local animal warden. It is possible that others have made similar complaints, and the city might take steps against the pet owner.

If the animal continues to intrude, the animal can be removed, but the property owner may not harm it. Only reasonable force can be used; otherwise, the property owner could be held liable for damages. It is a rare case when killing or trapping a trespassing pet is justified. In addition, local animal protection laws may restrict the force that can be used against a trespassing pet.

Finally, if the animal continues to be a problem or causes severe damage, a homeowner can sue the pet owner for the animal's trespass and harmful deeds.

The pet owner probably has a privilege to enter onto another's property to retrieve the pet. In so doing, the owner could remain on the property without permission only for as long as necessary to recover the pet, and could take only reasonable steps to recover the animal.

Trespass by Object or Substances

Objects or substances can also be the source of a trespass, and the person who set the objects in motion or who is responsible for them can be liable for the trespass.

Digging a quarry that throws rocks onto another's property is a trespass. Dumping into a river, causing trash to land on the shore of another's property, is a trespass. Stringing a clothesline that loops over another's property is a trespass. Leakage from an underground gasoline tank that causes an explosion or defiles a well is a trespass. Airplane overflights into lower airspace are trespasses (see chapter 8).

The cases that turn into civil lawsuits are most often this kind of trespass. At times, a distinction is made between a trespass and a nuisance—for example, from air pollution. It is considered a trespass when the matter coming onto the land has a fixed, tangible nature. Dust that is observable to the eye and lands on the property could be a trespass. If there is something less tangible, such as particulates floating in the air, it is likely to be considered a nuisance (see chapter 10).

Making a civil claim based on trespass is preferred over one based on nuisance because there are fewer defenses to a trespass. It happened or it didn't; if there was no consent and no privilege, the reasons why it happened are inconsequential. In a nuisance claim, a property owner can allege that there was an unreasonable interference with the use or enjoyment of the property, but the offending party is allowed to show that his or her activity benefits society in general even though it annoys an individual property owner.

Both trespass and nuisance are used to enforce a property owner's rights against adjoining landowners. Often, homeowners combine claims of trespass and nuisance when they feel their rights are suffering from interference.

Trespass, Adverse Possession, and Encroachment

A trespass claim is also used to stop encroachments to property and to prevent others from gaining rights to the property. An ongoing encroachment, if not stopped, can become a legal right of the other party through adverse possession (see chapter 3).

If someone is using another's property without permission, a trespass action is a way to stop it formally. A neighbor building a shed that crosses a boundary line is making an encroachment on the owner's property, and the homeowner can bring a trespass action to stop it. Conversely, by doing nothing, the neighbor could ultimately gain a legal right to that portion of the land through adverse possession.

Someone who regularly takes a shortcut through property to get to a lake could ultimately gain a prescriptive easement, or a legal right to use the path if the landowner does nothing to object.

An action in trespass prevents other persons from gaining the legal right to use the homeowner's property.

USE OF REASONABLE FORCE TO REMOVE
A TRESPASSER OR TRESPASSERS

Property owners have the right to eject and remove trespassers from their property, but only reasonable force can be used to accomplish this. Reasonable force can be described as no more force than is necessary to accomplish the removal.

In nearly all circumstances—except those posing danger— property owners are expected to ask the trespasser to leave prior to taking any forcible action. The trespasser must be allowed an opportunity to leave. People essentially become trespassers when they are advised that their presence is an intrusion or unwelcome and they intentionally stay on the property.

No Trespassing signs are one way of notifying intruders that they are not welcome. The intruder who ignores the notice is a trespasser.

A second step to reasonable force might mean calling police or security to handle the situation. If there is no imminent threat, the property owner should contact officers of the law before there is any physical confrontation.

> *Property owners have the right to eject and remove trespassers from their property, but only reasonable force can be used to accomplish this.*

Homeowners have the right to remove someone bodily from the property. But physical force is not permitted when words would do. In addition, physical force is unacceptable if there is no imminent danger, or the danger is past; for example, the person is turning to leave.

Physical force cannot be greater than is necessary under the circumstances. No force can be used that would cause death or serious injury to the trespasser, unless there is also a real threat to one's personal safety or that of a family member. In one case, it was held that a property owner was not justified in overturning the ladder upon which a trespasser was standing, since such an act could clearly cause serious physical harm.

It would be equally unreasonable, of course, to require the homeowner to ask a burglar to leave the property.

Property owners may be able to use great and even deadly force if there is imminent personal danger, but they may not kill in defense of their property. Most states have turned away from such an interpretation of the law and now hold that people can use deadly force or a gun against an intruder only in self-defense, if they have a reasonable fear of personal bodily danger.

Even when deadly force may be used against a trespasser, the number of tragic accidents caused in such situations, including injuries to children, friends, and relatives who are mistaken for intruders, advises against such use of extreme force.

People may not, under any circumstances, set a trap to catch or injure intruders. A trap gun set to shoot someone who opens a window is illegal and would subject the person who set the trap to significant personal liability for any injuries caused (see chapter 7).

Of course, ejection is not a possible action against many trespasses. There is no way to eject a low-flying airplane that buzzes the property. It would be meaningless to eject a trespasser who has already cut down half a dozen trees for timber—the damage is done. In cases like these a civil lawsuit, seeking damages or an order to cease the activity, is the appropriate remedy.

SECURITY

The standards that apply to trespassers can be applied to home security systems in general. Simply, a home security system cannot use unreasonable force, set a trap, or be designed to injure or harm a person who enters onto the property, even if the person does not have permission to be there. If someone—even a trespasser or burglar—is injured by such a device, the person who set the trap will be held liable.

A security system cannot be designed to shock an intruder physically or to have a gun go off if someone opens the door. A property owner was liable for setting dynamite to explode when a wire was tripped by an intruder. Similarly, keeping vicious dogs without a posted warning could result in liability.

On the other hand, when someone enters onto the property without authorization, it is permissible to have a security system that sets off a siren, lights, or a tape recording. In addition, a barbed wire or spiked fence would not create liability since its danger is obvious and the damage that it causes less severe.

CRIMINAL LAW ENFORCEMENT

When someone is notified that he or she is trespassing and refuses to leave the property, the trespasser violates the criminal law. Trespassers could be arrested, sent to criminal court, fined, and possibly jailed.

Sometimes trespassers cannot be arrested. Trespass—without other damage—is generally classified as a misdemeanor. In order to make an arrest in most misdemeanors, the police officer must have witnessed the incident.

For this reason, when heinous trespassing occurs—a nightly voyeur, for example—an injunction or restraining order from a court ordering the offender to stay off the property can be obtained. A restraining order is commonly used in domestic-violence situations to prohibit an abusive spouse from going onto the property for several days or weeks until a fuller hearing can be held. When a restraining order is in effect, the police can arrest the trespassing person because the court order has been violated.

A trespasser may have violated other criminal laws in some communities, including ordinances that prohibit door-to-door salespeople from indiscriminately knocking on doors without obtaining a permit. These ordinances are known as "Green River" ordinances.

Leash laws or other laws prohibiting animals from roaming

free may be misdemeanors and subject the pet owner to a fine or penalty.

CIVIL LAW ENFORCEMENT

The trespass that ends up as the subject of a civil lawsuit is usually a continuing one, such as the continual trespass of pollution, an encroachment, or other actions of a neighbor or nearby company. In those cases, notify the offender about the trespass and ask that it be stopped. Also, keep a day-by-day record of the trespass (see chapter 21).

In some situations, property owners can be in danger of losing property rights by failing to stop the trespass. An encroachment can ripen into a prescriptive right to the property. A neighbor's nonconsensual use of a driveway is a common example. In cases like these, a civil trespass suit can be used to protect full rights to the property.

In a civil lawsuit, a property owner could recover a nominal sum for the act of trespassing. If the property is damaged, an owner can also get compensation for the cost of repairs and loss of value. A trespasser or person who causes a trespass is liable for all injuries suffered because of the trespass, even if unintended.

In a civil case, a property owner can also seek an injunction or order from the court to stop the activity. If a company continuously lets factory discharges flow across the neighboring property, the property owner could ask for an injunction to stop it. An injunction is granted only after a hearing in which the property owner shows that money damages are not sufficient compensation. In pollution cases or airplane overflights, neighbors ban together to sue.

HOW TO EXERCISE CONTROL OVER THE PROPERTY

A landowner has the right to full control over the property, and can put an end to unauthorized physical intrusions or trespasses. Trespasses can occur above the ground, on the ground, or under the ground, and they can be of a person, animal, or inanimate object.

In order to prevent trespassing, the first step to take is notifying trespassers that their entry or use of the property does not have the consent or permission of the property owner. Posted No Trespassing, No Dumping, No Hunting, No Solicitations, or No Parking signs can act as a warning. Individuals can also be verbally notified that they are trespassing and asked to leave.

The more serious trespasses are continuing encroachments, pollution, and other physical intrusions. The trespasser should be notified in writing that the intrusion is a trespass, and if it is not stopped or abated, the property owner has the option of going to court either to stop the trespass or to seek compensation because of it.

10

Private
and Public Nuisance

The word *nuisance* means annoyance, and a nuisance action is a lawsuit to stop an extreme annoyance or to seek compensation because of the harm it is causing. Nuisance actions are of two types, private and public. They have similar features, but they are not the same.

A *private nuisance* is an intrusion on the property owner's freedom to enjoy use of the property because of another's obnoxious behavior. The all-night whining of a neighbor's dog could be a private nuisance, causing sleep deprivation and an erosion of emotional well-being. A private nuisance is handled in civil cases brought by a complaining homeowner against the offending individual. It is the primary tool of a homeowner in securing peace and quiet.

A *public nuisance* is an offense against the community that results from conduct so uncivil as to interfere with health and welfare of people in general. The massive dumping of toxic solid waste on a public highway could be a public nuisance. A public nuisance is handled in criminal cases brought by the city or local government against the offending party.

A *private right of action for a public nuisance* permits some individuals who have suffered disproportionately from a public nuisance to sue in a civil lawsuit. The homeowner whose driveway is blocked every time waste is dumped on the highway may have a private right of action to sue the offender.

PRIVATE NUISANCE

The right to the use and enjoyment of the property is one of the hallmarks of home ownership. When that ideal is disrupted because of the unreasonable and substantial interference of neighbors, the claim of private nuisance can bring relief. Unlike a trespass, which is a physical intrusion onto the property, a nuisance involves nonphysical invasions, often against the senses— sounds or smells.

In a nuisance claim, a homeowner seeks damages in civil court for injuries suffered because of the actions of another. The injuries can be physical, such as burning eyes caused by the emissions from a smokestack; they can be physical damage to property, such as the cracks on a wall from the vibrations of a battering ram; they can be severe emotional damage, such as the inability to sleep because of the sound from a high-pitched security device.

In addition, you can seek to have the offensive activity stopped by order of the court through an injunction.

Nuisance claims are almost always against neighbors or nearby property owners or residents. By proximity, the activities of one person can be disruptive to another. Of course, not every annoyance amounts to a nuisance claim. In a society of conflicting interests, it is assumed that people must live with a certain amount of ordinary intrusions—street noise in a city, the smell of pigs on a farm, a foghorn near the ocean.

When actions become intolerable or unreasonable—a decorative foghorn on top of a restaurant in a suburb blasting away hourly or the smell from a slaughterhouse located next to a subdivision—nuisance claims arise. A private nuisance is really the wrong thing in the wrong place. A nuisance claim is also one of the standard legal tools to use when the incidental rights of water, land support, or airspace are disrupted (see chapter 8).

Unlike a trespass claim, in a nuisance claim, the offensive activity does not have to cross the property's boundaries physically. The offending activity need only affect enjoyment of the property.

The annoyance that brings about the private nuisance action may consist of noise, smells, pollution, vibration, toxic emissions, hazardous waste, bugs, rodents, dangerous animals, dust, stored chemicals, fire hazards, excessive light, overgrown weeds, a blockage of air, criminal activities, and a seemingly endless list of harms that one neighbor can visit upon another.

DETERMINING WHETHER AN ACTIVITY CONSTITUTES A PRIVATE NUISANCE

The resolution of nuisance claims often rests on finding a balance between competing rights. A property owner and a neighbor have equal rights to the use and enjoyment of their properties. Resolving a claim often means balancing the value of one person's use and enjoyment with the annoyance suffered by another person.

In weighing this balance, no single factor is conclusive, but all of the facts work together. A court considers several factors.

Interference with Property Right   The offending activity must have, in fact, interfered with the use or enjoyment of the property.

Substantial Interference   The interference must be of consequence. Normally expected activities do not rise to the level of substantial and unreasonable. Traffic noise in an urban area is expected. A single puff of smoke is not meaningful. Most visual or esthetic annoyances are not considered substantial. The extent of damages suffered is an indication of how substantial the interference is.

Unreasonable Interference   The interference must be such that an average person would find it offensive. The complaining party must not be extrasensitive. The ringing of church bells is ordinarily not unreasonable, even though they may be intolerable to a person who is ill and easily distressed.

Harm   The interference must cause some harm, which could be (1) harm to the land, such as erosion caused by excessive overflow into a creek; (2) harm to other property, such as a ceiling cave-in because of vibration from constant drilling; (3) a depreciation in the value of the property, such as lowered market value because of the smell from an oil refinery; or (4) real physical discomfort or unusual mental anguish, such as runny eyes from the dust discharge of a cotton gin or sleep deprivation because of the unending noise of a windmill motor.

Intentional Nature of the Interference   Only an intentional interference is a nuisance, but intention comes from setting in motion or undertaking any activity that the offending party knew would result in harm. A company that discharges pollutants into the water acts intentionally. A factory that explodes and spews noxious fumes probably did not intend to do so.

Negligent or reckless behavior also constitutes intention. A neighbor who constantly leaves unsealed rotting garbage out may be negligent. A drunken truck driver whose vehicle overturns and smashes open, causing leakage of poisonous fumes, is reckless. Malicious behavior, such as building a 10-foot wall to block a neighbor's view, is intentional, as is engaging in ultrahazardous or dangerous activities, such as storing gunpowder.

DEFENSES TO A PRIVATE NUISANCE CLAIM

Even when the existence of a substantial and unreasonable interference with another's property can be proven, offending parties raise several common defenses that can defeat the nuisance claim.

Priority   The offending activity existed first, and the complaining party was "coming to the nuisance." A paper factory in a once-remote area finds a city continually growing until a new residential subdivision is built near the factory. A homeowner in the subdivision, waking up daily to the unpleasant smell of pulp processing, sues the factory in a private nuisance action. The factory responds that it should not be liable because it was there first and the homeowner moved to the nuisance.

Courts usually hold that the fact that a nuisance was there first does not alone excuse the activity. Changing circumstances may take precedence, and if an activity is so offensive as to interfere with another's property right, the activity can be stopped or the person suffering from the annoyance can be compensated.

In some states, special farm statutes have been passed to protect farmers from having to respond to nuisance claims by new residential neighbors.

Prescription   The offending party claims that it has conducted the activity for so long without complaint that it has now gained a property right to continue it under a theory of adverse possession or prescription (see chapter 3). A polluter might claim that it had been spewing red dust into the air for many years and that the dust had continually encroached on the homeowner's airspace. Over time, the polluter states, it has gained adverse possession in the homeowner's airspace.

Compliance with Laws   The offending party asserts it was in compliance with laws and regulations permitting it to operate, such as zoning regulations or environmental laws. Most courts have found that compliance with these laws is not a sufficient defense to a nuisance claim.

Social Utility   The social utility of the activity outweighs any harm done. The activity may have a value to society as a whole, and avoiding harm to one property owner may be impractical or costly. The operator of a power plant might state that the importance of having electricity outweighs the damage to an individual homeowner from electrical discharges by high-voltage power lines near the plant. A cement plant claims that its employment of local workers outweighs the problems with dust being released into the air.

Not Responsible   The party charged with committing the nuisance states that it was not, in fact, responsible or was only partially responsible for the activity; or that the complaining party knew of the activity and assumed the risk.

DAMAGES

> *If homeowners suffer unreasonable interference with property because of another's activities, they can seek monetary compensation or damages.*

If homeowners suffer unreasonable interference with property because of another's activities, they can seek monetary compensation or damages, including

- payment for injuries suffered to the land
- damages for the loss of use and enjoyment of the land, even if a nominal sum
- damages for injuries suffered, including physical ailments, medical care, and severe emotional damage, such as sleep deprivation
- special damages for loss of crops or injuries to animals or other occupants on the property
- compensation for a loss or depreciation in the market value or rental value of the property
- restitution for repair or corrective action, such as replacing a floor after a neighbor's repeated sewer backups ruined it
- punitive damages for malicious or recurring behavior

INJUNCTION

A homeowner saddled with a private nuisance can also seek an order from the court, or an injunction, to stop the activity. In some cases, a partial injunction is issued, such as limiting the activity to certain hours or methods.

One way of deciding whether an injunction is appropriate is for the court to determine whether the order would do more good than harm. Courts have ordered offending parties to pay damages for the nuisance, even for damages likely to be inflicted in the future, but have declined to order offenders to stop. What homeowners want the most, however, is that the annoyance be ended, and, given the choice, an injunction is generally preferred over damages.

PRIVATE NUISANCE TEST

The ultimate test applied in a private nuisance action is whether the interference is unreasonable (and therefore compensable), given

- the character of the neighborhood
- the extent of the harm
- the social utility of the activity
- the ability of the complaining homeowner to avoid the activity

Natural conditions on the land—even if annoying—do not constitute a nuisance.

TYPES OF CLAIMS

Nuisance claims come in so many shapes and varieties and are so dependent on the individuals and circumstances involved that courts often seem to make a broad decision about what is fair and supply the exact reasoning later.

Examples of activities that have resulted in nuisance claims are the following:

- dirt, smoke, and vibration from a cement plant
- noise of low-flying airplanes landing or taking off from a nearby airport
- persistent barking of a dog in the night
- emotional fear aroused by a wild or vicious animal
- smell from a neighbor's defective septic tank
- a holiday display that attracted volumes of traffic to a residential neighborhood
- leaked radiation from a company's computer that interfered with the reception of television sets in a nearby repair shop
- landfill leaching into a stream
- acid fumes that destroyed irreplaceable trees
- aerial spraying of an herbicide, damaging crops
- loud noise from a band
- the establishment of an offensive pig farm in retaliation against a neighbor who opposed building plans

- smoke from burning rags
- smells and flies from a slaughterhouse
- sand from construction that regularly blew onto and destroyed a house's paint

TAKING ACTION

To press a private nuisance claim, file a civil lawsuit at the courthouse (see chapter 21).

Prior to filing a claim, a homeowner should take informal steps. Tell the offending party about the problem. Write a short letter explaining why the activity is a substantial and unreasonable interference with use and enjoyment of the property, and ask the offending party to end the activity or, if appropriate, to pay for damages that have been incurred.

Keep a log of the offensive activity and any injuries, such as sleep deprivation or visits to a doctor. If experts or specialists are contacted for opinions on the problem—a consumer agency on unlicensed activity, an exterminator on rodent activity—keep names, bills, and fees.

Some communities also have mediation panels or neighborhood resolution programs that are adept at handling nuisance claims. In other cases, homeowner's associations or zoning boards can take up the fight. For certain problems, the intervention of a local legislator, consumer hot line, or even the police can serve to get the offending party to stop the nuisance.

In some circumstances, homeowners may use self-help to end a nuisance, but only if the actions involve the use of reasonable force in a reasonable manner. They bear the risk of stepping over the line and will be liable for any damages that are caused.

If the situation presented is an emergency, homeowners may be permitted to act to abate the nuisance. If a falling tree threatens to knock over an electrical power line, they might be empowered to cut the branches. In nonemergency situations, it is not reasonable to undertake self-help without first contacting the offending party and requesting that the problem be corrected.

If the damage is small and homeowners seek only to be reimbursed for it, they could file a nuisance claim in small claims court. If the problem is serious and they want the offending activity to stop, they have to go to a county district court or another court of general jurisdiction over civil claims (see chapter 21).

In filing a lawsuit based on a nuisance claim, address each of the items listed on page 159 to show that the activity interferes with a property right, is of a substantial nature, is unreasonable, causes harm, and is the result of intentional or purposeful activities.

COVENANTS, CONDITIONS, AND RESTRICTIONS

Subdivisions, planned units, condominiums, and cooperatives have covenants, conditions, and restrictions (CC&Rs) that are closely allied with the subject of nuisance (see chapter 17). The whole point of covenants and restrictions is to ensure that every homeowner gets maximum enjoyment and use of the property without unreasonable interference from a neighbor—the same goal as in private nuisance theory.

CC&Rs are often specific about typical annoyances and how they are to be resolved. Hours and levels of noisy activities are limited; certain disruptive activities or those out of character with the neighborhood are prohibited.

For a resident in a planned community, turning to the organizational association should be the next step after talking personally to the other property owner. The managing agent or board of directors can investigate the annoyance, contact the offending party, and enforce the CC&Rs to abate the nuisance.

In some cases, a nuisance is common to an entire neighborhood or cooperative building. The all-night blasting of the air drill in a car-repair shop next door might keep everyone awake. In those cases, the managing agent or board of directors can act on behalf of all of the members.

PUBLIC NUISANCE

A public nuisance is an activity that interferes with public health, safety, or morals of the community, under the standards of the local government. It is a different concept from a private nuisance, although there is some overlap in cases in which similar activities are involved.

Examples of public nuisances are maintaining a gambling establishment, conducting illegal dogfights, engaging in public profanity, obstructing a highway, keeping diseased animals, pol-

luting a stream, emitting toxic fumes, failing to dispose of garbage, and permitting ice to accumulate on a sidewalk.

Public nuisances are something of a catchall criminal offense.
In addition, every state has a huge variety of laws that make specific activities a public nuisance, such as dangerous multiple
dwellings, dogs running at large, or buildings where drugs are
sold.

When faced with a public nuisance, a police officer or other
government official, such as a housing inspector, can write a
ticket and charge an offender with a violation of the law. The
party will have to appear in court and can be fined or ordered to
end the nuisance.

Failure to fulfill certain community obligations—whether
improperly disposing of trash or burning leaves in contravention
to a fire ban—can result in a charge of public nuisance.

Aside from the criminal law, restraining nuisancelike activities
is at the heart of many zoning regulations, which are designed to
minimize annoyances to neighbors by eliminating uses that are
not in character with a neighborhood (see chapter 4).

PRIVATE ACTION ON A PUBLIC NUISANCE

Unlike most criminal laws, the public nuisance laws can be used
by a private individual to sue an offender in civil court. This is
known as a *private right of action* based on public nuisance, and it
has become especially useful when taking action on environmental laws (see chapter 8).

People can sue to end a public nuisance if they have suffered
harm that is even greater than the harm felt by the public at large.
The homeowner who lives along a stream may be more damaged
by stream pollution than other people who live elsewhere and use
the stream merely for recreation.

The private right of action is preferred as a legal strategy in
some cases because (1) citizens' groups can band together as
property owners and non–property owners, whereas a private
nuisance claim applies only to property owners; (2) for political
reasons local government is unwilling to enforce laws on certain
offensive activities; and (3) some defenses used in private nuisance claims are summarily tossed out in a public nuisance case,
such as the claim to a prescriptive right to continue the offensive
activity because it has gone on for a long period of time.

How to Use Nuisance Law

Private and public nuisance laws, although different, both provide civil recourse for serious annoyances that disturb the homeowner's use of the property.

A private nuisance often involves a claim against a neighbor or nearby company that is causing a substantial and unreasonable interference with the use and enjoyment of property, whether from noise, smells, vibrations, hazards, or pollution. A homeowner who suffers damage can sue for monetary compensation or for an injunction to stop the offensive activity. If the nuisance presents an immediate danger, homeowners can take steps to stop or abate the nuisance directly.

In determining whether the activity amounts to a nuisance, a court will apply a balancing test that weighs the offensiveness of the activity, its extent, the character of the neighborhood, and the social utility of the activity.

Prior to bringing a lawsuit, property owners should write the person responsible and ask that the activity be stopped at once. It is also important to keep a record of the harms and injuries caused by the offensive activity.

A public nuisance, on the other hand, is the interference with public health, morals, or safety, and is prohibited by criminal statutes enforced by the government. A so-called private right of action also allows private individuals to enforce public nuisance laws in civil court, a tactic that has been used successfully in some environmental litigation.

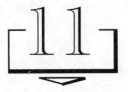

Taxes
and Abatements

Tax implications—both benefits and drawbacks—usually weigh in a person's decision to purchase a home. Throughout the period of home ownership, and even after selling it, taxes have a significant impact. The main taxes that affect homeowners are of two types:

1. Real estate taxes and assessments charged by a local municipality, in exchange for providing city services
2. Federal income taxes, for which the government provides significant tax breaks in the form of deductions, and the possibility of shielding from taxes money made from sale of a home by reinvestment in another one.

Records are vital. Keep track of all expenditures made on the property throughout the entire period of ownership.

PROPERTY TAXES

Property or real estate taxes are strictly state and local affairs. These amounts are collected by the local government and, in some cases, by state governments. Property taxes are determined according to the value of the property, or *ad valorem*. Value is determined by assessment.

The money collected in property taxes pays for the costs of local government services, everything from traffic lights to tap water, police, fire, garbage pickup, sewers, schools, public hospitals, and the salary of the mayor. Sometimes these taxes are packaged into one property tax; in other cases, taxes are assessed separately by various districts—the fire district, the school district, the sanitation district.

In addition to property taxes, special assessments may be levied on a local district for services provided directly to that neighborhood. For example, making curbs on roadways may be financed by a special assessment. A special assessment can also be directed to an individual homeowner. Repairs of sidewalks in front of a home may be assessed to the owner.

The system for collecting property taxes varies according to the municipality and the state, but there are many similarities in these systems. One similarity nearly everywhere is that decisions about property taxes—tax rates, assessments, public expenditures—are tied to the local political system. Homeowners are likely to be voters, and they can have considerable influence.

AMOUNT OF TAX A HOMEOWNER PAYS

Property tax can be defined as tax rate multiplied by the property value, which results in the *ad valorem* amount.

The actual amount of tax a homeowner is asked to pay is determined by several variables:

1. Limits on taxation set by the state.
2. The tax rate established to meet budgetary needs. Tax rates are different for various categories of property— commercial, residential, and so on.
3. The value of the property as determined by government assessment. Value is assessed in various ways, and the

exact valuation will depend on the frequency and accuracy of the assessor's determination, as well as fluctuation in market values of property and the extent to which they are considered by the assessor.

4. The proportion of the property value that is applied to the tax rate.

5. Addition of any special assessments for local improvements.

6. Adjustment in the tax can occur because of an exemption for which the homeowner qualifies or by a limitation in state law, such as a prohibition on an excessive rise in the taxes. Adjustments can also result from an appeal by the individual homeowner or a determination by a board of equalization that the taxes are out of line with the taxing district or community.

Because of these variables, merely knowing the tax rate does not enable a homeowner to compare taxes from one city to another.

AUTHORIZATION FOR PROPERTY TAXES

Some property tax is calculated and collected by the state. By and large, however, cities, towns, or counties are responsible for collecting property tax and also receive the benefit from the tax.

The state has a role in any case since it authorizes the collection. State legislatures can put conditions on the collection of real estate taxes. They may, for example, demand that all property in a district be reassessed at the same time.

States may provide particular exemptions—veterans or senior citizens below a certain income may be exempted from property tax.

TAX RATE

The tax rate can vary from year to year. Sometimes it is established by vote of the local governing body, such as a city council. In some communities, an increase in property taxes must be put to a public vote.

The tax rate can be different for various categories of property—commonly, commercial property is taxed at a higher rate than residential property. There may also be differences in the tax rate for single-family residences, duplexes, cooperatives, condominiums, apartment buildings, residential property with some business use, and so on. Another common distinction is based on whether the structure on the property is newly constructed, recently rehabilitated, or long-standing. In essence, this scheme establishes tax brackets based on the type of property that is being valued.

A second crucial component of the tax rate is the budget for government appropriations. The city or other taxing unit plans and estimates the money that will be required to pay for needed services, and calculates income from other potential sources of revenue, such as local sales tax, rents, or bonds. The shortfall is designated for property-tax collection.

The Assessment

Every piece of property in a taxing district must be assessed. Since each house and building is unique, the assessment must be conducted individually—there is no blue book for houses as there is for cars.

The goal of the assessment is to set a value on the property. Value can be determined in many ways. For instance, a house could be assessed at its value at the time it was purchased, even if that was many years ago, or at the amount it would demand on the market today. If the market declines, the community must decide whether the assessed value will decline also; such a reassessment will result in a consequent loss in taxes to the community. In some communities reassessments are made every year; in others, every five or ten years.

To determine the current market value of a house, assessors must know the market value and current sales prices of houses in the area. An assessment is also based on the condition of the house. Assessors make an outside inspection of the property. Improvements add to the market value and are reflected in higher taxes. In some communities, assessors also try to look at the inside of the house, and aggressive communities make a policy of visiting all homes for which building permits were issued. Architectural style, construction quality, and the number of bathrooms or fireplaces can change the figure on an assessor's clipboard. Assessing is not an exact science but involves a good deal of subjectivity. It is not uncommon for an assessment to be wrong.

In some communities, the projected assessments are reviewed and equalized, with the hope that no community or neighborhood is assessed unfairly. Many communities apply only a proportion of the assessed market value to the tax. If the property is assessed at $100,000, this amount is reduced to 80 percent of the property value, or $80,000, and is then multiplied by the tax rate to calculate the actual taxes owed.

All of the assessments are compiled in an assessment roll, which is maintained in an appropriate city office. It may also be published. A homeowner whose assessed value has been increased gets notification in the mail.

EXEMPTIONS

Certain categories of property can be given exemptions to reduce their property tax in whole or in part.

Many states give exemptions to veterans or disabled veterans. Several states provide partial exemptions to senior citizens, particularly those whose income falls below a certain established minimum. Some states provide tax exemptions to homesteads, widows, or farmers. Property may be exempted from taxation because it serves a religious, charitable, or educational function.

APPEALING THE ASSESSMENT

Homeowners frequently disagree with the assessment of their property, and many are, in fact, erroneous.

The errors can be mechanical, typographical, or judgmental. The most common complaints are that the property has been overvalued or that it is not valued comparably to similar property. The assessment can be appealed through an administrative procedure. Appeals must be made promptly, as set out in the following discussion.

Research   Investigate the matter. In many locations, the notice received has little concrete information about tax rate, market value, or how the assessment was calculated. Look at the assessment roll and the listing of properties in the neighborhood to get an idea of how comparable houses are valued.

Speak to Assessor Try to talk informally to an assessor. In small communities, this can be accomplished easily. In cases of obvious error, the assessor may be willing to make an ad hoc correction.

File Notice of Protest An appeal must be filed as soon as possible after the assessment is received. In some municipalities, appeals are heard on certain days or certain months—usually several months prior to the date upon which the assessment is to take effect (an assessment to take effect in July might be sent in January and appeals heard in February or March).

In metropolitan areas, lawyers, accountants, private assessors, and specialized companies handle appeals, some on a contingency basis. If they lose the appeal, the homeowner pays nothing; if they win, the owner pays a percentage of the amount saved.

The owner or agent files an appeal of the assessment, sometimes in a document known as a *notice of protest*. The appeal must be in writing, stating why the assessment is incorrect or in error.

Review The review of the assessment is handled by a board of equalization, tax appeal board, or other local body. In some states, the decision of the board can be appealed to another board; in others, to a court. However, this is an administrative proceeding, and it is important that it be handled properly at the first level. Upon further appeal, the court will review only to see whether the grievance was treated with procedural fairness in the administrative hearing.

At the appeal before the board of equalization, present careful documentation about why the assessment was incorrect. Evidence should be organized, typewritten, and presented in signed and notarized affidavits. When permitted, an appraiser or other essential person can testify before the appeals board.

If, for example, the assessment was based on an exterior observation, but the interior of the house is in shambles, show photographs. If the appeal is based on the assertion that the property was overvalued, present the sworn statement of a qualified appraiser, stating that the true value of the property is actually lower than suggested by the assessor. If the appeal is based on a lack of comparability, and other properties of similar style are valued lower, provide evidence concerning the valuation and similarity of other properties.

The board of assessment can make a determination to accept the assessment, lower it, or, in rare cases, raise it.

In some cases, the assessment of an entire neighborhood, condominium, or cooperative can be challenged by the homeowner's association.

Court Appeal The decision of the board of equalization can also be appealed in court. Strict time limits for filing apply. Appeals to court are likely to be expensive and subject to technicalities that require the services of an attorney.

A few states, including Michigan, New Jersey, New York, Ohio, and Oregon, have developed a small claims court procedure to permit homeowners to appeal the decision of the tax appeals board more easily. The owner can file an appeal for a small fee and present the tax case to a judge.

SPECIAL ASSESSMENTS

Special assessments may account for a large increase in a real estate tax bill. A special assessment pays for a specific improvement to the locality—sewers, lighting, street paving.

Some assessments are for local and general benefit. Building a bridge or constructing a city library might be considered a general benefit for which an assessment is tacked onto the real estate tax bill.

For local improvements, the costs are divided up according to the property to be benefited. Unlike real estate taxes, special assessments are not necessarily deductible from federal income taxes. They are considered an improvement that will increase property value. Special assessments for repair and maintenance are deductible.

BANK ESCROW

When a homeowner has a mortgage loan, the bank collects the property taxes as part of the monthly mortgage payment. The tax portion is put into an escrow account and is paid to the taxing authorities on the due date. (In some places, there can be multiple due dates for the various taxing authorities, such as September 1 for the fire district, November 1 for the school district, and so on.)

There are good and bad effects from the escrow process. Certainly, the collection process is more convenient for homeowners. The homeowner is automatically setting aside funds for the payment of property tax and can avoid the prospect of being unable to pay a large tax bill when it is due.

Banks also receive a substantial benefit—they can hold and use the escrow money until its due date. The homeowner, in the meantime, doesn't have use of the money and rarely earns interest on it.

Federal law allows a lender to collect excess escrow amounts in case charges on the home go up during the year, but the excess is not supposed to amount to more than one-sixth of the anticipated need. In some cases, lenders have withheld excess escrow fees. In one case, twelve state offices of the attorney general sued a lender and obtained refunds for thousands of homeowners.

Most banks do not permit a homeowner to pay property taxes directly, except if the bank holds only a small portion of the equity in the property.

Another drawback of the escrow system is that it serves as a buffer between the homeowner and the assessment process. The bank does not object to increased assessments since it merely collects and holds the money.

COOPERATIVES

Cooperative association boards are responsible for collecting and paying real estate taxes for its members. In the eyes of property tax authorities, the property being taxed is the building, which is held in common by the cooperative association, with the individual unit owners holding shares in the association. Cooperative buildings are often taxed at the higher commercial building rate. The percentage of taxes charged to each unit is based on the number of shares the person owns and becomes part of the maintenance fee.

This scheme puts the burden on the board of the cooperative to scrutinize and challenge questionable tax bills. As with bank escrow accounts, this often distances the individual unit owner from careful attention to assessment increases.

DELINQUENCY OR FAILURE TO PAY

Taxing authorities apply a series of penalties to homeowners who fail to pay their property taxes.

If the tax date and a grace period are missed, the homeowner is charged a penalty and interest. If the homeowner continues to be delinquent, the taxing authority can place a lien on the property for the amount of the taxes, penalty, interest, and costs.

The taxing authority can enforce the lien by foreclosing on the property and holding a tax sale. In most states, property owners have an opportunity to redeem or regain their property by paying the back taxes and costs before a tax sale purchaser takes title.

Members of the military are protected from a tax sale under the federal Soldiers and Sailors Civil Relief Act, which bars a tax lien forfeiture of the property if the owner's failure to pay has been affected by military service.

Tax authorities can also collect property taxes by a personal judgment against the homeowner.

CONSTITUTIONAL CHALLENGES

Taxing schemes are sometimes challenged in state or federal court, often by groups of citizens, businesspersons, or public interest groups.

In reviewing the taxing plan, the court ordinarily looks to see if the system is a rational exercise of governmental power; if the system has been adopted and is operated with adequate notice, opportunity to appeal, and other standards of due process; and if all taxpayers of similar categories are treated equally and fairly.

Some tax challenges have been successful and have forced communities to modify their taxation systems.

DEDUCTIBILITY

Local real estate taxes for a primary residence and a second residence are deductible on federal as well as state and city income taxes in most places. Special assessments are not deductible.

FEDERAL INCOME TAXES

Federal income tax rules are, of course, subject to change. In general, however, taxpayers can take advantage of federal income tax rules in several ways:

- Deductibility of property taxes and interest
- Protection from taxation of income from a sale if the sale proceeds are reinvested in another home or if the homeowner is over 55 years of age and meets other conditions
- Deduction for expenses associated with a qualifying home office or rental property in the home
- Adjustment in gain because of improvements on the property

DEDUCTIBILITY OF TAXES AND INTEREST

The lawmakers in the nation's capital smile favorably on homeowners by providing them with generous tax breaks in the form of deductions from taxable income for those who itemize.

The deductions apply to a primary residence and to a second home that is used as a residence—for example, a vacation home. Income tax deductions are available for cooperative and condominium owners also. In order to claim these deductions, the homeowner must itemize all deductions on Schedule A and fill out the Form 1040 or long form. (IRS booklet 530, *Tax Information for Homeowners,* can be ordered for free by calling 800-829-3676.)

Property Tax   Regular payments of property tax are deductible. Taxes to local fire, school, sanitation, and other districts are included in the definition of property tax. Special assessments for neighborhood improvements are not deductible, since they are expenditures to improve the property. Special assessments for repairs and maintenance can be deducted.

Interest on Mortgage   Interest charged on the mortgage loan is deductible from income taxes. Each monthly mortgage loan payment includes a payment on the principal and a portion designated for payment on the interest, but only the amount of the interest is deductible. The interest portion is usually the highest at the beginning of the mortgage, then declines with each successive payment through the years of the mortgage loan.

Interest payments can be deducted for two residential properties, so long as the total indebtedness on both houses does not total more than $1 million. Interest paid on home equity loans is deductible, as are interest payments on second mortgages and home improvement loans. The IRS has set a limit of $100,000 on deductibility of loans secured by the home but used for a purpose not related to the property, such as paying off credit cards or taking a vacation.

On a first mortgage, mortgage *points*—which are really prepaid interest to protect the lender against an increase in interest rates—are also deductible. If the mortgage is for a principal residence, the points can usually be deducted entirely in the year in which they are paid; for vacation or second homes, the deduction for points must be spread out over the period of the loan.

Points associated with refinancing are deductible, but are allocated to each year of the loan. If the refinancing is for home improvement, then the points deduction may be taken in the year that the loan is made.

After calculating their full tax return, families with an adjusted gross income in excess of $150,000 may face a limitation on deductions, which can reduce the value of the mortgage interest deduction.

The bank normally sends a statement of total interest paid during a year; if not, it can be requested. Penalties for late payment are not deductible.

As a way of reducing the principal amount outstanding on the mortgage loan, some homeowners make prepayments on their mortgage loans (see chapter 13). As is true with regular payments, principal prepayments are not tax deductible.

HOME OFFICE

The prorated costs of operating a home office can be deducted from income taxes under certain circumstances (see chapter 18).

To qualify, the office must be a separate space that is used exclusively and regularly for business purposes. The major activity of the business must be conducted in the home office. The deductions for the home office (but not other business expenses) cannot be greater than the income received from the activity.

Self-employed persons are most likely to qualify for a home office deduction. A person employed by someone else qualifies for a home office only if it is for the employer's benefit and not merely for the convenience of the homeowner/employee. The IRS has extensive rules covering the deductions for home office expenses.

RENTAL

Homeowners who rent out a portion of a home, or a second home, can, for income tax purposes, deduct from the rent collected a great many of the costs associated with operating the rental space (see chapter 19). Within strict limits set by the IRS, certain losses from the rental of property may reduce the homeowner's overall income and tax payment.

Business costs associated with renting the property, including the costs of repairs, may be deducted. Costs might include the fees of a lawyer, accountant, or contractor, or expenditures for new appliances or advertisements. Record keeping is important.

Rental property can also be depreciated. Depreciation assumes that some portion of the total value of an item is lost every year because of its aging. Nonrental property does not qualify for depreciation deductions.

HOMEOWNER REINVESTMENT ON SALE

When a homeowner sells a home, there is another enormous benefit. The profits from the sale of a primary residence (sale price minus the selling expenses and the purchase and renovation costs, or adjusted basis of the home) ordinarily have to be reported as income. However, if this money is reinvested in another residence, the homeowner does not have to pay income taxes on the profit from the sale, provided that the purchase price of a new home is as much as the adjusted sales price of the old one. Homeowners have 24 months before or after the date of sale to reinvest the profit into a new home. If so invested, income taxes are deferred (see following and chapter 20).

This provision applies to condominiums and cooperatives used as primary residences but not to a second home or vacation home.

OVER-55 SELLER

> *A homeowner over the age of 55 can use a once-in-a-lifetime exclusion to avoid paying taxes on up to $125,000 profit from the sale of a residence.*

A homeowner over the age of 55 can use a once-in-a-lifetime exclusion to avoid paying taxes on up to $125,000 profit from the sale of a residence (see chapter 20). In order to qualify, the homeowner must have owned and resided in the residence for three of the five years prior to the sale. The property must have been the principal residence, not a vacation or second home.

CAPITAL GAINS AND IMPROVEMENTS UPON SALE

Ordinarily, homeowners must report the profit on the sale of a home as a capital gain and pay income taxes on it (see chapter 20). Capital improvements to the property can reduce income taxes due on sale. IRS rules allow the homeowner to add the costs of home improvements to the adjusted basis of the home, which is used to calculate capital gain.

Suppose a person bought a home for $100,000 and sold it for $180,000. The profit of $80,000 is a capital gain. Unless this money is reinvested in a new home, the capital gain is taxed as ordinary income, and there would be federal income tax on the amount.

But suppose the homeowner had invested another $50,000 in the home, adding a deck in the backyard. The $50,000 is added to the original cost of the home (the *basis*), for a total of $150,000 adjusted sales price. (Costs of repair or maintenance, such as patching a roof or replacing a broken window, do not qualify as capital expenditures.) If the home sold for $180,000, the home-owner would profit by $30,000; therefore, taxes would be due only on the $30,000.

Qualifying improvements are expenditures that increase the value of the property. Adding a room, converting a den, or installing a major structural system such as plumbing or new electrical wiring qualifies.

Special assessments paid to local authorities for neighborhood improvements can also be added into the pool of improvements. On the other hand, special assessments related to general maintenance and repairs do not qualify as improvements.

In order to benefit from this provision, keep complete records of the costs of improvements, no matter when they were done during the course of home ownership.

If the property is sold by an installment sales agreement or contract for deed, the seller has to report as income only the gain that is realized in each year of the sales agreement.

SPECIAL DEDUCTIONS OR TAX PROVISIONS

Under shifting IRS and state income tax rules, homeowners are permitted special deductions from time to time.

- Deductions for energy-saving modifications to the home may be allowed, and some historic property can qualify for tax credits for rehabilitation.
- Homeowners who suffer unusual losses—whether by a natural catastrophe or by theft—may be able to deduct some of their unreimbursed losses. Deductions available for casualty and theft are granted if the loss exceeds 10 percent of the homeowner's adjusted gross income and after a loss of $100 is absorbed. Be sure to document the losses.
- Costs of selling a home, such as commissions, advertising, legal fees, fix-up costs to improve marketability, and loan charges can be deducted from the amount realized on the sale.
- Costs of buying a home (aside from points and interest) are not deductible, but they may change a homeowner's income tax liability upon sale of the home. These costs, like improvements, can be added to the purchase price of the home, or the adjusted basis, for the purpose of calculating capital gain. Costs that can be added to the purchase price include attorney's fees, abstract fees, transfer taxes, costs of surveys, costs of title insurance, charges for the installa-

tion of utility service, recording or mortgage fees, selling commissions charged to the buyer, and back taxes or interest of the seller that the buyer paid. Keep records about costs paid at the time of purchase.

FAILURE TO PAY FEDERAL INCOME TAXES

The federal government can penalize an individual who fails to pay income tax or evades income tax in several ways: penalties, fines, seizing assets such as a bank account, criminal action in severe cases, or placing a lien on the property. Only in rare cases is a lien on a home subject to foreclosure by the federal government.

STATE AND CITY INCOME TAX PROVISIONS

States are autonomous and individualistic when it comes to determining state and local income tax rules. Some follow the lead of the federal law and offer the same deductions for interest and property tax; others offer special benefits for certain classes of persons, such as homesteaders below a certain income. Homeowners should consult their state and local tax rules.

MISCELLANEOUS:
TAXES FOR HOUSEHOLD WORKERS

If the homeowner employs any personnel to work regularly in the home on a full-time or part-time basis, Social Security and Medicare taxes on wages should be paid to the federal government.

Social Security taxes are partially deducted from an employee's pay, and partially contributed by the employer. These taxes should be paid for child-care workers, domestic employees, or other household personnel who earn more than $50 a year.

Social Security and Medicare taxes are paid quarterly on Form 942, Employer's Quarterly Tax Return for Household Employees. Failure to do so can result in the assessment of back payments for the amounts that should have been paid by the employee and the homeowner/employer, as well as interest and penalties.

The homeowner/employer is responsible for deducting income tax payments from the employee, if the employee requests it. Income taxes withheld are reported quarterly on Form 942. IRS Publication 15, Circular E, *Employer's Tax Guide,* explains how to calculate the amount to withhold. (For more information, see IRS booklet 926, *Employment Taxes for Household Employers.*) If a household employee earns more than $1,000 a year, the homeowner is also liable for Federal Unemployment Tax (or FUTA). FUTA is paid annually (by January 31), on Form 940 or 940-EZ, Employer's Annual Federal Unemployment Tax Return.

In addition, a homeowner/employer may be required to pay state unemployment tax, and some states require homeowners to pay into a worker's compensation fund on behalf of household employees.

Challenging Federal Tax Decisions

A taxpayer who disagrees with a decision of the Internal Revenue Service has a right to appeal the decision to an appeals office. The request to appeal must be in writing, and must come promptly—within thirty days, in most cases—after the decision that the taxpayer is contesting.

The appeals office is an administrative agency that is intended to resolve taxpayer claims without having to go to court. Decisions of the appeals office can, in turn, be appealed by pursuing the matter in the U.S. Tax Court, the U.S. Claims Court, or the U.S. District Court.

If the IRS determines that a taxpayer owes money and sends out a *notice of deficiency,* the taxpayer has 90 days to appeal. A case of under $10,000 can be heard in a simplified small tax case, after which the decision is final (see IRS Publication 556, *Examination of Returns, Appeal Rights, and Claims for Refund*). The filing of a federal tax lien can be appealed, as well.

The IRS is generally willing to work out a payment plan for tax-payers who owe money. A problem resolution office is located at each IRS service center, and is supposed to assist taxpayers unable to clear up difficulties through normal IRS channels (the numbers of problem resolution offices are available by calling 800-829-1040). Remember that IRS rules and regulations are subject to frequent and constant change.

Preserving Rights Under Tax Laws

Local property taxes are assessed according to the value of the property. Property tax appeals can be made to a board of assessment or tax appeals, where the homeowner is allowed to show that the assessment was incorrect or inconsistent for other similarly situated properties.

> *All tax decisions—whether local property, state, or federal income tax—can be appealed.*

All tax decisions—whether local property, state, or federal income tax—can be appealed. Appeals are usually made first to an administrative board and can be appealed further in court. Tax appeals must be made immediately—sometimes within 30 days of the notice received from the tax office.

In order to take advantage of tax benefits and to be prepared to challenge tax inequities, keep excellent financial and property management information throughout the period of home ownership.

12

Financial Difficulties and the Home

When a homeowner faces difficult financial times, payments on the mortgage loan can slip behind. The safety of a homeowner's ownership claim in the home also can be threatened by nonpayment of other debts: second mortgage loans, home equity loans, maintenance fees, or certain liens.

External circumstances can cause economic strain, such as the bankruptcy of a developer, the failure of a bank, the default of a cooperative sponsor.

All of these factors can put a home in jeopardy. The worst consequence of financial difficulties could result in loss of the home, sale of the property, and even in some cases a remaining personal debt.

To provide some protection to homeowners, foreclosure proceedings must follow strict rules. Since foreclosure is undertaken by the bank or other lender, the procedure varies depending on the type of loan arrangement, whether the loan is a mortgage loan or a share loan, a contract for deed, a deed of trust, or other arrangement. State laws also have a significant impact on foreclosure proceedings.

For some financially pressed homeowners, there may be less drastic solutions than foreclosure, such as an agreement to restructure the debt or filing a bankruptcy petition.

MORTGAGES

The most common method of financing the purchase of a home is through a *mortgage* loan with a bank. In return for a loan, the bank obtains the promise of the homeowner to pay back the loan plus interest. In addition, the homeowner signs a document that allows the bank to claim the home if the homeowner fails to repay the loan.

The latter document is the mortgage. (And in a somewhat confusing twist of terms, the bank or lender is the *mortgagee* or recipient of the mortgage, and the homeowner is the *mortgagor* or giver of the mortgage.) The mortgaging process is a secured transaction, and the mortgage makes the home the security or collateral for the loan.

If a default occurs on the loan, the lender can claim the house and resell it in foreclosure proceedings. Many mortgage loan documents also make the homeowner personally liable for the loan. This means that if the lender takes back the property and resells it, but the sale price is not sufficient to pay back the original mortgage loan, then the lender is entitled to seek the remaining balance, or *deficiency,* from any of the other assets of the original borrower.

Although rare, the lending institution also can act on the default without foreclosing by seeking recovery on the loan alone. The bank could sue a homeowner personally for the full amount due on the loan instead of exercising its option to foreclose on the property. If a person had substantial nonhomestead assets such as savings, and the property was not especially valuable, this procedure might be attractive to a lender. Some states do not permit a bank to seek a personal judgment against a homeowner without undertaking foreclosure proceedings first.

If a loan application or mortgage loan was taken out with a cosigner, the cosigner is also liable on the loan.

Second Mortgage Loans or Home Equity Loans

> *If a homeowner misses payments on a second mortgage loan (even though continuing to pay the first mortgage loan), the bank or lender has the same rights to foreclose on the property.*

Second mortgage loans are secured by the property in the same manner as the first mortgage loan. If a homeowner misses payments on a second mortgage loan (even though continuing to pay the first mortgage loan), the bank or lender has the same rights to foreclose on the property.

A home equity loan is simply another name for a second mortgage loan. A home equity loan is secured by the home and gives the bank the right to claim the home if a default occurs.

Installment Sales Contracts

An installment sales contract, or a contract for deed, is sometimes entered into by a seller and a purchaser. The purchaser makes a down payment to the seller. The seller accepts the balance of the purchase price in monthly installments from the buyer. The deed to the property doesn't pass to the buyer until the final payment is made.

One frequent feature is a balloon payment. The buyer pays the seller a monthly payment for a period of time, for example, three years. On an agreed-upon date, the balance of the original price and interest can be due all at once, which is the balloon payment. Such a large amount can become a looming threat. Failure to pay the balloon payment on time can put the home buyer in default.

If payments are missed under a contract for deed, the consequences can be severe. The seller can take back the property, and in some states can do so without following the rigors of a judicial proceeding or foreclosure sale (see below). Some states have enacted legislation to reduce the harshness of default under an installment sales agreement.

Other problems with the installment sales agreement can arise if the seller who signs the agreement also is still making payments on a mortgage loan from the bank. Most mortgage loans have a "due-on-sale" clause, which would require the seller to pay off the full amount of the loan at the time of signing the installment sales contract. Often, neither the seller nor the buyer has the funds to pay the balance, leaving the sale and the property in jeopardy.

DEEDS OF TRUST

A less frequently used type of financing permitted in some states is the deed of trust. This involves three parties—the buyer of the property, the lender, and a trustee. The trustee holds the deed as security until the buyer has paid off the loan from the lender.

The practical difference between a deed of trust and a mortgage for a homeowner with financial difficulties is that the foreclosure proceedings under a deed of trust usually are not regulated as strenuously. While most foreclosures under a mortgage require a judicially approved foreclosure sale, with a deed of trust, the lender can proceed sometimes by an out-of-court foreclosure sale, known as the *power of sale*.

SHARE LOANS

People who take out a loan to buy a unit in a cooperative building do not really have a mortgage, although it is commonly referred to as such. The cooperative homeowner receives a share loan or an end loan (see chapter 17).

In essence, the purchaser buys shares in the cooperative corporation that, in turn, owns the building. In exchange for the shares, the purchaser gets an exclusive lease on the apartment.

In terms of legal transactions, the unit purchaser is not buying real estate, but rather shares, and it is the purchase of the shares that is financed by the lender. No deed passes hands, since the deed to the building belongs to the cooperative corporation, which pays for the mortgage loan by passing on a portion of the maintenance fees collected from shareowners. A cooperative owner can go into default by failing to pay either the share loan or the maintenance fee.

The difference in cooperative financing is critical if financial difficulties arise. Since the bank does not hold a mortgage, laws about mortgage foreclosure do not apply. The foreclosure happens in an out-of-court proceeding that is not subject to the same strict rules or court review. Foreclosures on co-op shares are conducted under rules of the Uniform Commercial Code, not unlike the foreclosure on a car, a boat, or other sizable personal property, in which the notice of sale is published in the paper for approximately three weeks prior to the sale.

There is another difference with the cooperative. Lenders may be quicker to foreclose on cooperative units because the lender is responsible for maintenance payments if the purchaser is not paying them. After paying maintenance charges for a defaulting purchaser for a couple of months, bank officers will quickly take steps to sell the cooperative unit.

TYPES OF FORECLOSURE

In broad practical terms, foreclosure involves the lender taking back and selling the property. There are three types of foreclosure:

1. Foreclosure by judicial sale, which is permitted in every state, regulated by certain state rules, and used most often in mortgage foreclosures
2. Out-of-court foreclosure or *power of sale,* which is permitted in approximately half the states, regulated by fewer state rules, and used in deed of trust situations and a small number of mortgage foreclosures
3. A Uniform Commercial Code foreclosure proceeding, which is less rigorous than a judicial sale and used for foreclosure on shares in cooperative units

The exact procedure for foreclosure varies from state to state, but is, at best, loaded with technical requirements and complications.

STEPS IN JUDICIAL FORECLOSURE

The most common foreclosure on a home involves the judicially permitted foreclosure. There are several steps involved in a judicial foreclosure. Along the way, homeowners may be able to take action to prevent the loss of their home.

The process of a judicially permitted foreclosure includes the following:

1. *Default*—missed payments or other default.
   a. Notice of Default—letter that if payments are not made (or other nonmonetary default corrected), lender can require full amount to be paid within 30 days after receipt of notice.
   b. Curing the default—homeowner pays up delinquent amounts before further action occurs; if the default is cured, foreclosure proceedings usually cease.
2. *Acceleration*—option by the lender to demand the entire loan and interest be paid at once.
   a. Activated after notice of default by filing a foreclosure complaint in court and, in some states, a notice of acceleration in advance.
   b. Option by lender to take over property and receive rent that is due from tenants during intermediate period.
3. *Negotiated solutions*—homeowner tries to work out new arrangements with the bank, including a refinancing or payment extension.
   a. Deed in Lieu of Foreclosure—homeowner voluntarily signs over deed to lender, sometimes in exchange for money, or an agreement from the lender to stop collection efforts; the mortgage loan is considered paid off.
4. *Notice and court hearing*—homeowner has an opportunity to present defenses, such as a mistake, fraud, or unfairness, to a reviewing court.
5. *Equity of redemption* or Right of Late Payment—homeowner can avoid a property sale by paying off the entire debt. If homeowner doesn't redeem, another party with a lien on the property can redeem and take over property.
6. *Foreclosure* by judicial sale—property sale by sheriff or other official.

7. *Confirmation of sale*—the court approves the sale.
8. *Statutory redemption*—right granted in approximately half of the states that permits a homeowner to pay the amount of foreclosure sale price and all costs for six months to several years after the foreclosure; after payment, the homeowner can retain ownership.
9. *Disbursement of sale proceeds*—the money from the foreclosure is dispensed to the lender or others who have liens or are owed moneys, and to the homeowner if any amount remains.
10. *Deficiency judgment*—if foreclosure price does not pay off the debt on the loan, in many states, the lender has a right to collect remaining amount from the homeowner personally.

OUT-OF-COURT FORECLOSURE

An out-of-court foreclosure or power of sale skips some of the steps in a judicial foreclosure. Excluded steps might include notice, court review, and possibly rights of redemption or buying back the property after the sale. Out-of-court foreclosures, permitted in approximately half of the states, generally apply to deed of trust loans and not to mortgages.

DEFAULT

The homeowner can default on the mortgage loan whenever a payment is missed or late. Other acts can also amount to a default, including failure to pay taxes or insurance, failure to pay condominium association dues, or causing severe damage to the property. Also, mortgage loans usually have a "due-on-sale" clause, which requires immediate full payment if the homeowner sells the property, for example by an installment sales agreement; and failure to pay constitutes a default. Technically, the breach of any clause in a mortgage amounts to a default.

Although it is not obligated to do so, the lending institution generally ignores one or two late payments or even missed payments. The homeowner may get a phone call or a reminder in the mail. Late payments do subject the borrower to a penalty charge.

When the homeowner voluntarily pays up the amount owed before any further action is taken by the lender, the default is taken care of or *cured,* and the lender is precluded from taking further action.

ACCELERATION

When a homeowner is in default, the lender has the option of speeding up the payment plan and declaring that the entire amount of the loan must be paid at once, known as *acceleration.*

A homeowner in default normally receives a notice in the mail from the lender that foreclosure will occur if payment is not received. The homeowner usually has 30 days to pay.

Acceleration takes place when the lender initiates foreclosure. The homeowner may hear nothing else about acceleration, but simply receive the notice of foreclosure.

Some states and some lenders still permit a homeowner to cure the default even after the acceleration by paying up the amount originally due. This right is available if a clause in the mortgage allows the homeowner to reinstate the loan as it was originally written. Without this opportunity, the homeowner is faced with paying the entire remaining loan, which is frequently a huge amount of money.

Upon default, the lender has a further right in nearly all states to take over possession of the property. If the homeowner is permitted to stay on the property, a fair market rent may be charged. In addition, the lender has the right to receive the rent from any tenants on the property.

WORKOUT

When a default occurs, many banks prefer to avoid the foreclosure process because it is difficult and requires a good deal of time and effort.

One solution is to negotiate. The bank may be willing to rewrite the loan with lower payments but over a longer period, or take other conciliatory steps. Homeowners facing foreclosure or default situations should contact a bank officer or an attorney at once.

DEED IN LIEU OF FORECLOSURE

A second type of negotiated solution in a default is for the home-owner to sign over the property to the lender. When a person cannot afford the payments, signing a deed in lieu of, or instead of, foreclosure may be sensible.

In the procedure, the lender is saved from the difficult fore-closure process. The homeowner can possibly salvage some credit and can be spared from personal liability if the property is sold at a price below the debt, leaving a deficiency.

The drawback is obvious. The homeowner loses the home to the lender.

DUE PROCESS AND PRESALE NOTICE

In a judicial foreclosure, the homeowner is entitled to due pro-cess, a concept in the law that means fair notice of the action and the opportunity to be heard about it.

Fair notice in foreclosures used to mean tacking the foreclo-sure to the post outside the county courthouse. Today, the con-cept of notice has evolved to providing a homeowner with actual physical notice. The homeowner normally receives a letter of judicial foreclosure proceedings. The lender also may be required to publish a legal notice in a newspaper, although usu-ally these notices are in fine print and placed in a section most people do not read.

In some cases, the notice might not come from the bank or original lender, but from another firm or entity. This notice still may be a valid foreclosure, because lenders often sell or transfer their loans. Loans are sold to private mortgage loan companies or to quasi public-private agencies, such as the Federal National Mortgage Association (Fannie Mae).

Once notified, the homeowner has an opportunity to present defenses. Any other people who have a claim on or financial interest in the property, such as a second mortgage lender or the holder of a mechanic's lien, also are provided with notice and can present their claims.

In most states that permit an out-of-court foreclosure, notice need be provided only by an advertisement in the newspaper. The lack of protection from the due process rigors provided by a judicial foreclosure is a drawback to financing by a deed of trust or cooperative share loan.

If a federal government agency such as the Veterans Administration or the Federal Housing Administration has made the loan, notice by mail and the opportunity for a hearing must be provided.

DEFENSES TO FORECLOSURE

In a judicial foreclosure, a judge holds a hearing on the proposed foreclosure and reviews defenses offered by the homeowner or homeowner's attorney. Many states have stringent foreclosure proceedings, and the judge can stop the foreclosure if the lender has not followed the technical requirements of the law.

Other defenses can be raised, although they are limited and, in some cases, complex. They include assertions that the lender was negligent in the first place by delivering an unmarketable title; that a mistake was made by the lender in applying payments or in the calculation of the interest; or that the homeowner was induced to enter into a fraudulent loan agreement. Some cases have raised a question about lender liability when it agrees to lend money for property that it knows has been sold at an inflated price.

Technical claims about the sufficiency of the lender's notice can be raised, as can claims that the lender failed to comply with federal loan laws, such as the Truth-in-Lending Act.

A bankruptcy petition puts a hold on all foreclosure proceedings. Bankruptcy may not stop the foreclosure, but it can delay it for weeks or months (see following).

The owner might be able to raise a defense "in equity," which is the equivalent of a plea for mercy to the judge because the sale would be unfair. If an elderly homeowner had paid off 80 percent of a loan, but because of the death of a spouse forgot to make several payments, the court might find that foreclosure was unduly harsh.

A homeowner on active duty in the U.S. military has special protection from foreclosure under the Soldiers' and Sailors' Relief Act. The military homeowner may request that the default be set aside if it was incurred before or during the military service. The foreclosure proceeding cannot continue if the soldier is not before the court. If the foreclosure takes place anyway, the individual in the military can apply to have the sale put aside, or rescinded.

If no defense is accepted, the court will order a judicial sale of the property by the lender.

In an out-of-court foreclosure, or power of sale, the opportunity for a hearing before a judge is not available—the lender has the right to sell the property without a court review.

Period of Formal Presale Buy-Back

Before the actual foreclosure sale takes place, a homeowner can get the property back by paying the mortgage debt and costs, known as the *equity of redemption*. This right, existing in all states, was designed to offset the harshness of foreclosure and to be fair to those property owners who had invested significant sums in the property.

With a judicial foreclosure, the right to redeem lasts until the court finally confirms the sale.

Persons other than the homeowner can use the equity of redemption, as well. Those with an interest in the property—because they have a lien, were a cosigner, were in the process of buying the property, or will otherwise find their rights closed off by the sale—also can pay the mortgage loan debt and obtain title to the property.

At this point in the foreclosure proceedings, a homeowner cannot get the property back by simply making the overdue payments. Unless an agreement is negotiated with the lender, the entire loan balance plus costs must be paid. In one recent case, a property owner whose land value had dropped dramatically attempted to pay the lower market value of the property as the equity of redemption, but that was rejected.

Foreclosure Sale and Review of Sale

At the foreclosure sale, anyone can bid on the property. The property is often sold at less than the full amount of the mortgage loan. If the property is sold for more than the mortgage loan debt, the homeowner is entitled to receive the surplus.

Questions often are raised about the foreclosure sales price—

not only by the homeowner, but by others who have liens on the property and may not get paid if the sale price is too low. If the sale price is at least 70 percent of the full debt, it is generally considered sufficient. The lender must act in good faith to get a fair price at the foreclosure sale by exercising due diligence.

If a homeowner raises a question about the price obtained at the sale, the lender has to show that the sale price was a fair bid.

The lender can also be the buyer of the property at the foreclosure sale. This occurs frequently since the lender does not have to come up with cash but often can buy the property for the amount of the remaining debt.

After the sale, the court confirms the foreclosure. Most judges, at this point, sign off only that the sale was properly conducted. Without an objection from the homeowner, judges are not likely to reject the sale on their own because the price was too low.

In an out-of-court foreclosure, the lender does not need to have the sale confirmed by a judge.

POSSIBLE POSTSALE BUY-BACK

After the sale, approximately half the states give the homeowner yet another chance to get the property back under a rule of *statutory redemption*. Statutory redemption laws are different from the equitable redemption, which is allowed in every state but before the foreclosure.

Statutory redemption laws give the homeowner the right to pay the same amount that the property fetched at the foreclosure sale, along with costs and fees. The homeowner must do this within a certain time frame, ranging from six months to three years, depending on the state. During this time, the homeowner may even be permitted to live on the property.

If the property is not redeemed within the time period, the purchaser at the foreclosure sale takes over the property.

REMOVAL OF FORECLOSED HOMEOWNER

After all proceedings have been completed, including the passage of the statutory redemption period where it applies, the foreclosed homeowner no longer has any right to the property and can be evicted.

In order to evict, the new purchaser may have to go through eviction proceedings, not unlike a landlord who wants to evict a tenant (see chapter 19). After legal eviction proceedings are complete, the homeowner can be removed from the property forcibly by a sheriff or officer of the law.

In the case of foreclosures on cooperatives, the unit owner is occasionally protected from eviction under state rental laws. A cooperative unit owner who has undergone foreclosure and wishes to remain on the property as a paying tenant should consult an attorney.

Stopping FHA Foreclosure

A person who bought a home with a Federal Housing Administration (FHA) loan may qualify for a program that can save homeowners from foreclosure if they go into default.

Under Department of Housing and Urban Development (HUD) regulations, a homeowner can apply for a mortgage assignment. If a mortgage assignment is granted, the bank that holds the loan "assigns" or transfers the mortgage loan commitment to HUD for up to three years, and HUD will cover the loan for that time period. The homeowner and the lender are released from the mortgage obligation.

To qualify for the HUD Mortgage Assignment Program, homeowners must show that the default is for reasons beyond their control and that they can make up the payments later when their financial situation has improved. People who are laid off or face unemployment and are looking for a new job may qualify.

After the HUD assignment period is over, HUD will extend the loan for up to three years or arrange for a slight increase in mortgage loan payments to make up for the lapse. As with all government programs, the mortgage assignment program is subject to change and revision.

Applications for the FHA Mortgage Assignment Program need to be filed promptly upon receipt of notice of foreclosure. Banks should have information about the program. Legal services offices also may have information (see chapter 21). For further information and assistance, contact HUD, Washington, DC 20410.

DEFICIENCY

If the lender undertakes a foreclosure proceeding and sells the property for less than the debt on the loan, the difference between the sale price and the full debt is called a *deficiency*.

In some states, the lender is entitled to seek the rest of the amount owed under the loan by suing the foreclosed homeowner for a deficiency judgment. If granted, the homeowner could be personally liable to pay off the remaining debt on the loan.

The debt, at this point, is the amount remaining on the mortgage loan, plus costs and fees incurred by the lender in foreclosure proceedings. When faced with a deficiency proceeding, it is not uncommon for the former homeowner to challenge the sufficiency of the sale price obtained by the lender. The lender will have to show that the price obtained was a fair bid.

Under a theory of enough is enough, some states passed anti-deficiency laws limiting the amount of money that a lender can claim against a former homeowner in a deficiency judgment if the property is sold for less than its fair market value. The lender might be able to seek the difference between the original debt and the fair market value of the property—but not the difference between the original debt and the lower sale price obtained on foreclosure.

If a homeowner does not object to a deficiency judgment, the lender may get the right to attach wages, bank accounts, or any other property the individual owns.

LIENS

Mechanic's liens, tax liens, bail bond liens, environmental law liens, and judicial liens—which arise after a civil court judgment on a lawsuit won against a homeowner—are paid off in a priority order after a judicial foreclosure sale.

These liens usually exist as an encumbrance against the property, so that they must be paid off before the property is sold and title can be perfected for a subsequent buyer.

In most states, homestead laws protect a homeowner from having a home sold to pay off liens (see following). There are some cases, however, in which liens can be enforced and the property can be sold by foreclosure. The difficulty of these proceedings and other limitations on the ability to foreclose a lien prevent many lienholders from forcing the issue.

INSTALLMENT CONTRACT DEFAULT

An installment sales contract, or a contract for deed, used to have an extraordinarily harsh impact on someone who fell into arrears on payments. Most states have now taken steps to ease the pain.

Under prior practice, the party who held an installment sales contract—such as the seller of the property—could take back the property and keep all the money that had been paid. Foreclosure proceedings weren't necessary, since the seller already held the deed to the property until all of the payments were made. Even the purchaser who made 99 out of 100 payments, but missed the last, could lose all rights to the property. Further improvements or investment in the property were lost.

Now, installment sales contract purchasers have some protection, but the extent of it varies greatly from state to state. The thrust of the laws is to protect the buyer from patently unfair forfeitures.

Some state courts, when presented with a forfeiture on an installment sales contract, examine the amount paid by the buyer, the extent of the default, and the reasons for the default and will balance the home buyer's rights against the seller's. A judge could then come up with a reasonable solution, such as permitting the buyer to cure the default.

Some states formally give the buyer a grace period after the default to make back payments. The seller usually has to notify the buyer that the contract is in default and that forfeiture is likely.

Other states permit the buyer to pay the full amount of the debt under the same theory as an equity of redemption.

Yet another approach is for the court to order the seller to conduct a foreclosure sale, as if the installment sales contract were a mortgage. In this way, a purchaser who has nearly completed the payments under the contract could get a share of the investment back from the surplus after the sale.

For example, where a buyer paid $21,000 of the $36,000 purchase price on an installment sales contract and would have lost all of it by a complete forfeiture, the judge ruled that the damage suffered by the seller, because of a default, was not equal to the amount being retained, and ordered a foreclosure sale, with the excess proceeds to go to the defaulting buyer.

In order to enforce their rights, the installment sales buyer usually must take the seller to court to stop the forfeiture (the opposite scenario from a mortgage foreclosure, in which a bank takes the homeowner to court). When faced with the prospect of going to court, many sellers are willing to negotiate a solution.

COOPERATIVE DEFAULT

Cooperatives face delicate problems when the holder of an individual unit, the cooperative corporation, the sponsor, or an investor faces financial difficulties.

Each shareholder is a member of the whole cooperative association as well as an individual unit holder. Generally, if a shareholder has financial difficulties, the lender of the share loan must pay the monthly maintenance fee to the cooperative corporation and is responsible for initiating foreclosure proceedings.

The cooperative foreclosure does not have to follow the judicial foreclosure of a mortgage loan because there is no mortgage, only a loan to purchase shares. The sale can happen much more quickly and there is less protection for the unit owner.

The cooperative corporation itself can be affected if unit foreclosures occur. If several unit holders stop paying dues, the association can find itself with payment lags and a strain on its mortgage loan or reserve fund. An increased assessment to other unit holders may become necessary.

A very sticky situation can arise when a cooperative sponsor faces financial difficulties. A sponsor is the developer who converts rental apartments into cooperative units and then sells the units. If the units are not sold, or are rented at below-market rates to existing tenants, the sponsor normally has to make up the difference between the maintenance fee collected from the vacant or rented unit and the amount paid by shareowners. If the sponsor runs out of money, the payments on these units can go into default, requiring the lender to take legal foreclosure action.

Some sponsors use unsold apartments as collateral on further loans, leaving a tangle of confusion in the wake of financial difficulties. In addition, a sponsor default means that the cooperative has empty units on which maintenance fees may not be forthcoming, a situation in which new purchasers will not want to invest.

If an entire cooperative corporation defaults on the mortgage and ends up in foreclosure, all of the unit holders may face dispossession. The law has not yet dealt with many such situations, since the cooperative corporation often arranges a payment plan with a lending institution to prevent foreclosure. In one case where refinancing was not possible and a foreclosure occurred, a judge held that the former unit owners (shareholders) had a right to stay in their apartments as tenants, and a new owner of the building could not evict them.

CONDOMINIUM OR SUBDIVISION DEFAULT

The owners of condominiums have title to their individual units, and if a default occurs it is between the homeowner and the lending institution. The condominium owner's association, which maintains only common areas through dues, is not likely to be as seriously affected by unit defaults as the cooperative association (see chapter 17).

Where condominiums or subdivisions can get into trouble, however, is when the developer defaults. Developers take out huge loans for construction with liens against the property and pay back loans from the proceeds of unit sales. If the units are not selling, the entire project can be subjected to liens from the developer's activities.

The condominium owners may then face legal implications from the developer's financial shortfalls. These cases are complicated and require an attorney.

BUYING FORECLOSED PROPERTY

There are many difficulties in buying foreclosed property, which underscore the process of foreclosure.

For example, in states with statutory redemption, the buyer may not be able to take title to the property until a year (or the statutory time period) passes, during which period the former homeowner can pay up the sale price and get ownership status reinstated.

The buyer of foreclosed property must make certain that the title is clear and marketable, and that the title accurately reflects the chain of ownership. The buyer also is liable for any existing liens or claims against the property.

When a cooperative is involved, the buyer may still need to be approved by the cooperative board and, in addition, may be liable for outstanding maintenance fees. Unlike liens, there may be no formal or clear notice of the amounts that are outstanding.

The buyer of foreclosed property has no guarantee that the former owner or a tenant has vacated the property. Eviction proceedings may be necessary.

Also, the buyer of foreclosed property should truly beware. The property is sold as is and defects to the property will be the full responsibility of the purchaser.

BANKRUPTCY

Bankruptcy is written in the U.S. Constitution as a means of permitting people with excessive debts to begin anew. Bankruptcy petitions are handled by special federal courts, and they apply a mixture of federal bankruptcy rules and state laws from the jurisdiction in which the court is located (see chapter 21).

For homeowners facing financial difficulties bankruptcy may be helpful because, to a certain extent, a homestead is protected under bankruptcy laws as exempt property. The extent of that protection varies from state to state.

Exempt means that the property is not counted or is only partially counted in the available assets of the person filing for bankruptcy, or the petitioner. Property is exempt when the federal government or the state has determined that it is part of a person's basic living needs and should not be taken away, even to pay debts.

In its simplest terms, bankruptcy involves a petitioner filling out a list of all existing debts and a list of all assets. Then the exempt property is crossed off the assets list. Any remaining assets are divided among the qualifying creditors.

Two types of bankruptcy procedures can be used by the average homeowner—Chapter 7 liquidation and Chapter 13 adjustment plan. Other forms of bankruptcy apply to corporations or to farmers.

Chapter 7 or straight bankruptcy is a settlement of all assets and debts. After the nonexempt assets are distributed to creditors, most remaining debts are discharged and wiped off the books.

Chapter 13 bankruptcy is an adjustment of debts for employed persons. Creditors must stop collection procedures and are put on a payment schedule that can last for several months up to three years. Often, creditors are paid only a portion of the amount they are owed, as determined by the bankruptcy court. After the payment schedule has ended, remaining debts are discharged. Chapter 13 is preferred by people who have many assets that are not protected by homestead or other exemptions.

Some debts cannot be discharged in any case—tax liens that are fewer than three years old, child-support payments, some student loans, criminal penalties. Some debts that cannot be discharged under a Chapter 7 liquidation can be resolved under a Chapter 13 adjustment plan.

THE HOMESTEAD EXEMPTION

Critical to the homeowner with financial difficulties is how the home will be treated in a bankruptcy proceeding. Each situation requires an independent analysis based on the state's laws and the amount of principal paid off on a loan to purchase the home.

When applicable, a homestead exemption makes the home exempt from being sold to pay off creditors. A homestead exemption can be complete—for the full value of the home, no matter how great the value is—or it can be partial—protecting homes with limited equity or paid-up investment.

Homestead exemptions of varying amounts are permitted in every state. In about 15 states, bankruptcy petitioners have a choice of following state exemptions or exemptions listed in the federal bankruptcy law. The federal law has a homestead exemption of $7,500. State homestead exemptions range from $2,500 to $100,000 or beyond.

Homestead exemptions are determined by the value of the equity in the home. Equity value in this case is the price the home would get if it were sold on the open market, less the outstanding mortgage loan amount and any other liens. A few states describe the homestead exemption by acreage.

The homestead exemption in bankruptcy applies to a single individual and can be doubled if a couple files a bankruptcy petition together. A separate exemption applies to household goods—$4,000 per individual under federal law.

EFFECT OF HOMESTEAD EXEMPTION IN BANKRUPTCY

Not every house is protected by a homestead exemption in a bankruptcy proceeding. Exemptions depend on the relative value of the home, whether or not the mortgage loan payments are in default, and whether or not there are other assets that can pay off that portion of the mortgage loan payments that are in default.

If a homeowner is filing a Chapter 7 (liquidation) proceeding and the equity value in the home is fully exempt, the home will be protected during the bankruptcy proceedings from seizure or sale.

If the equity in the home exceeds the exemption limits, the house could be added to the assets of the bankruptcy estate and sold, in which case the exempt amount would be paid to the homeowner from the sale.

BANKRUPTCY AND FORECLOSURE

If a homeowner has defaulted on the mortgage and declares bankruptcy, the bankruptcy petition first of all will put an automatic stay or hold on the foreclosure proceedings. That does not mean that the foreclosure won't go forward, but the bankruptcy trustee has an opportunity to present defenses to the foreclosure.

A homeowner also may be able to stay in the home longer or arrange a workout or restructuring of the loan, making a new payment schedule with the lender while the automatic stay is in place. If a workout is arranged, the foreclosure proceeding can be brought to a halt.

Under bankruptcy rules, the trustee and the court also want to make certain that a foreclosure proceeding by a lender is fair to other creditors. If the lender is using the foreclosure proceeding to swallow up a homeowner's available assets to the detriment of other creditors who might have priority, the bankruptcy court may step in.

If a former homeowner does not declare bankruptcy until after the foreclosure sale, some courts hold that the bankruptcy trustee can still challenge the validity of the sale and whether a fair price was obtained.

In some cases, when bankruptcy is filed during or after the foreclosure proceedings, courts consider the bankruptcy filing to be in bad faith and permit the foreclosure. In one case, a bankruptcy filing 50 minutes before the foreclosure sale was held to be in bad faith.

Discuss the details of bankruptcy filings with an attorney knowledgeable in the field.

MEDICAID AND THE HOME

Senior citizens with substantial medical bills may need to turn to Medicaid. Medicaid places strict limits on the assets an applicant may have. Seniors are often required to *spend down* any savings or assets to an acceptable level of impoverishment before they are able to obtain assistance from Medicaid.

For many seniors, their sole asset of value is a home in which they invested many years earlier. How a house is treated in Medicaid eligibility varies from state to state.

States may adopt federal guidelines, but they are not required to do so. The federal guidelines permit an individual to retain a house, regardless of value, without being disqualified for Medicaid. Some states have their own rules that put a limit on a house's value for Medicaid eligibility.

In addition, federal rules require that a Medicaid application must be denied if assets, including a house, are transferred at less than the fair market value within 30 months prior to the application. But a transfer can be made for less than fair market value to a spouse, a dependent or disabled child, a son or daughter who has lived in the house for two years and has cared for the senior parent, and a sibling who has lived in the house for a year and has a claim to it.

Seniors should consult a legal services office or other attorney about protecting the homestead.

COPING WITH FINANCIAL STRAINS

When a homeowner becomes financially strained, the home can be placed at risk. A mortgage gives a lender the right to reclaim the property if there is a default on the loan. However, prior to a foreclosure, there may be opportunities to make up missing payments, work out new payment arrangements, or agree to give up the property in lieu of foreclosure to salvage a credit rating or further debt. If foreclosure proceedings are begun, a homeowner generally has formal rights prior to the sale of the property, including a chance to present defenses in court and the opportunity to pay the full debt before the property is sold.

After a judicial foreclosure, some states permit a former homeowner to buy back the property for the same price for which the house was sold at the foreclosure sale, plus costs. In some cases, a former homeowner has a legitimate claim that a house was sold at a price that is too low, cutting off the right to any moneys beyond those owed under the loan, or opening the possibility of a deficiency claim for amounts that are still unpaid on the loan even after the sale.

Defaults on cooperative purchases do not follow the same rules as mortgage loan foreclosures. Cooperative buyers take out share loans, not mortgage loans, and the property can be sold quickly under a nonjudicial foreclosure.

In bankruptcy proceedings, homestead exemptions can protect homes from being sold to meet the claims of creditors, depending on the laws of the state and the value of the home. A bankruptcy filing can delay foreclosure proceedings, although it does not necessarily prevent foreclosure entirely.

The intricacies of foreclosure and bankruptcy laws vary from state to state. Homeowners should consult an attorney who specializes in these areas.

13

Refinancing, Home Equity Loans, Prepayment, and Reversible Mortgage

After purchasing a home, a homeowner may at some point want to renegotiate or rearrange payments on the mortgage loan.

Refinancing can benefit the homeowner by lowering monthly payments, making a pool of cash available for remodeling or other needs, or by resolving a default situation through a loan workout. However, the homeowner will end up paying out-of-pocket costs for the refinancing, which may wipe out the gain. Anyone contemplating refinancing should carefully evaluate and compare the terms of the agreements offered by lending institutions.

If problems do arise in refinancing or prepayment, a homeowner should remember that financial institutions are regulated by government agencies, which can sometimes take action on the owner's behalf.

REFINANCING: COSTS AND BENEFITS

Refinancing a mortgage loan becomes attractive when interest rates drop. A change of even 1 percent can make a difference of tens of thousands of dollars over the period of the loan.

Refinancing is not easy, nor is it inexpensive. The homeowner is essentially obtaining a new mortgage loan and virtually all of the costs paid to a bank at closing for the original mortgage loan are paid again. In addition, the paperwork must be completed once again.

Expenses can include a new appraisal, title insurance, credit report, new termite and other inspections, a loan origination fee, points, and processing. This typically amounts to $3,000 to $4,000 for the refinancing of a $100,000 mortgage loan. The amounts vary because points are determined as a percentage of the amount being financed. Some banks permit these costs to be amortized over the period of the loan.

In addition, in times of high demand for refinancing, lenders have added on new charges for application fees, either as a flat amount or as a percentage of the amount being financed. These fees can be as high as $1,500 to $3,000.

Refinancing used to be considered financially viable with a 2 percent drop in the interest rate, as long as a homeowner planned to stay in the home for at least two more years. This formula does not always predict the value of refinancing, though. Drops of 1.5 points may work to the homeowner's advantage, or 3 points may be necessary to make a difference. Much depends on the type of mortgage that was originally signed, the remaining equity, and the amount borrowed, as well as the rate.

Refinancing can benefit a homeowner in other ways. When rates are reasonable, the homeowner with an adjustable-rate mortgage loan might want to lock in the mortgage loan at one interest rate and avoid the uncertainty and constantly shifting costs that are connected with an adjustable-rate mortgage loan.

Refinancing is a consideration for people who want to trade the built-up equity in their homes for cash. When the homeowner has paid off a substantial proportion of the home equity, the home can be remortgaged at its full value, the equity is reduced, and the homeowner takes the cash difference. A similar objective is accomplished by a home equity loan, which creates a second mortgage loan on the property instead of rearranging the first mortgage loan.

Homeowners who fall into default may also want to consider a workout—which is essentially renegotiating the terms of the loan with the bank. If the homeowner has equity built up in the property, in refinancing, the equity is reduced and used to retire the homeowner's default.

Points associated with refinancing are deductible on federal income taxes, but the deductions must be prorated over the entire period of the loan. If the refinancing is for home improvements, the homeowner can take the total deduction for points in the year of the loan (see chapter 11).

REFINANCING PROBLEMS

Some people may not qualify for refinancing, even though they qualified for the original financing. Approximately 20 percent of the equity or the fair market value must be paid off before most financial institutions will consider refinancing. A homeowner who made a low down payment may not have accrued that amount of equity.

If the home has increased in value but income has remained the same, the homeowner may no longer qualify under bank guidelines. On the other hand, income may have declined, or the property value may have declined, such that the bank no longer considers a new (or refinanced) mortgage to be a good deal.

In addition, standards for loan approvals change constantly, and in many cases may be tougher than when the original loan was obtained. Although a homeowner qualified on purchase, this owner may not fit within new guidelines, even though nothing in the person's financial profile has changed.

Co-op owners often have difficulty finding a bank willing to refinance because the nature of their original loan is not a mortgage on the property, but a loan to buy shares in the cooperative association. If units are still unsold in the building, the financial institution may consider refinancing too risky.

In addition to comparing the long-range financial picture, homeowners should compare the mortgage instruments to see if they will be different on refinancing. The original mortgage might allow assignment of the loan, but the refinancing instrument does not. Assignment allows the borrower to assign or put the loan in the name of a purchaser, a tactic that can aid in selling property by making financing available to purchasers who might not qualify for a bank loan.

MORTGAGE BROKERS

Mortgage brokers do not actually provide refinancing, they search for the best deal. A mortgage broker can be useful for the marginally qualified homeowner because the broker can sometimes persuade the financial institution that the homeowner is a better prospect than appears on paper.

The cost to the homeowner is not supposed to be higher than bank closing costs—the mortgage broker splits the fees that the lender collects. Some brokers charge application fees, and the homeowner should ask detailed questions about all costs and fees and make certain that they are set out in writing in advance.

A majority of states have laws regulating mortgage brokers, in which mortgage brokers must be licensed and a regulatory agency monitors their activities and investigates complaints. For more information or a local referral, homeowners can contact the National Association of Mortgage Brokers, 706 East Bell Road, Suite 101, Phoenix, AZ 85022; 602-992-6181.

HOME EQUITY LOANS

A home equity loan is the same as an additional mortgage loan. A homeowner gets cash from the lending institution, using the equity in the home as collateral.

The opportunity to take a loan on the equity may be possible either because of the amount of equity that has been built up through down payment and mortgage loan payments or because the market value of the home has increased.

Home equity loans have all the benefits and drawbacks of a mortgage loan. They differ from refinancing, because they are a new and additional obligation on the property. The mortgage loan and the home equity loan use the same property as collateral, with the home equity loan providing a new source of funds to the homeowner.

Because the home is collateral, a default in payments can result in action to foreclose on the home (see chapter 12).

In some cases, homeowners use the concept of a home equity loan to establish a revolving line of credit, a constantly available loan fund. The home is used as collateral against this account.

Home equity loans have significant benefits that other types of loans no longer have. Under current IRS rules, taxpayers can deduct the interest on a home equity loan up to a total of $100,000 financing or the equity of the home.

Banks charge application fees on home equity loans. A large fee may counteract the tax benefits. *Tips on Home Equity Loans* is available for $1 from the Council of Better Business Bureaus, Inc., 1515 Wilson Boulevard, Arlington, VA 22209.

PREPAYMENT OF MORTGAGE PRINCIPAL

A homeowner can gain significant benefits from prepayment of the principal. Prepayment of the principal takes place when the homeowner pays the lender more than the monthly payment. The extra amount should be applied to the principal.

Lenders generally don't favor prepayment, and some banks don't allow it. The refusal to permit prepayment has been challenged by homeowners. In the early 1990s, states moved to enact rules requiring banks to allow homeowners to prepay the principal. In other states, court battles are under way.

The reason prepayment makes a difference comes down to mathematics. The interest on a home mortgage is enormous: Typically, over the total term of a standard mortgage, the borrower pays more than $200 in interest for every $100 that is applied to the principal (for a 30-year mortgage at a 10 percent interest rate). But only amounts that reduce the principal pay off the purchase price and build up the investment or equity in the property.

In the standard monthly payment arrangement, the portion of the payment that is applied to interest in the early years is extremely high and the portion applied to principal extremely low. The initial payments on a 30-year loan apply over $200 to the interest on the loan for every $10 that is applied to the principal.

The balance between amount applied to interest and principal changes each month, but very slowly. Only after two-thirds of the loan term has expired does the amount applied to the principal begin to exceed the amount applied to the interest. As much as one-half of the principal is paid in the final five years of a 30-year mortgage loan.

Prepayments of the principal also lower the total interest that will be paid. The interest on the principal is calculated in advance to set regular payments, but if the principal is paid off early, then the same interest is not necessary, and the total interest is reduced.

Banks don't favor prepayments because they lose interest income that they anticipated earning. But prepayments can save borrowers a lot of money.

Banks don't favor prepayments because they lose interest income that they anticipated earning. But prepayments can save borrowers a lot of money.

Some banks charge a penalty on prepayment. The term penalty often frightens homeowners from making a prepayment, but it shouldn't. The penalty is usually limited to prepayments that come to more than 20 percent of a mortgage loan in a year, or $20,000 on a $100,000 home. Most homeowners who use pre-payments pay an extra $50 or $100 a month or $600 to $1,200 a year, so the prepayment penalty would not apply. Even when a prepayment penalty does apply, ultimately prepayments may benefit the homeowner anyhow, since the penalty is substantially less than the amount saved from prepayment.

The bank practice of charging penalties has been outlawed in many states, and several of them have passed laws requiring banks to allow prepayment. If a homeowner purchased a home prior to changes in the law that required banks to permit prepayment, the loan documents might say that prepayment is not permitted, or is penalized, but the law might now say otherwise. Check with the bank or state banking authority.

In addition, homeowners have argued in recent court cases that prepayment should be permitted as a matter of public policy. Some courts have agreed with this position, but others have not.

The clear trend, however, is to require banks to permit prepayment. In states in which these laws have not been adopted, homeowners should consider contacting their state legislators about the idea.

If a homeowner is making prepayments, good record keeping is essential to make certain that the payments are properly credited. Homeowners should write prepayments on separate checks from the normal mortgage payments, and mark them prepayment of principal. They should also keep an account of every prepayment made and the canceled checks throughout the entire period of ownership.

Bank errors in applying the prepayment are not uncommon. Homeowners should periodically check their personal records against bank records. Most financial institutions will provide a statement of all transactions on the account, if requested.

Private companies also offer mortgage auditing services. If a homeowner suspects a bank error, an auditing agency can be engaged to calculate the payments clearly. These companies perform services for a set fee or for a percentage of any recovery from error in the bank statement.

REVERSE MORTGAGE

Elderly homeowners who have paid off the principal on their homes sometimes consider a reverse mortgage, technically known as the reverse-annuity mortgage or RAM.

In a reverse mortgage, cash is paid to the homeowner in monthly payments. This is considered a loan, secured by the mortgage on the property. The homeowner is assured of receiving a payment each month, approximately equal to what a mortgage payment would be. The loan is paid off from the proceeds of a property sale or the proceeds of the estate after the homeowner's death.

The monthly payments can last until the fair market value of the property is paid out, in which case the situation reverses again—the homeowner must start making payments back to the bank. One disadvantage of a reverse mortgage is that at this point the owner must often sell the home.

Not all lending institutions permit reverse mortgages, and reverse mortgage agreements can vary. For more information and a list of institutions that have them, homeowners should contact the National Center for Home Equity Conversion, 1210 East College Drive, Suite 300, Marshall, MN 56258; 507-532-3230.

CHALLENGING BANKS AND FINANCIAL INSTITUTIONS

The rules of banks and other financial institutions can seem arbitrary, unfair, and obnoxious at times. Homeowners do not have to accept that all rules are legal or that the institution is always right. Challenging the requirements of a bank is never easy, but borrowers do have recourse.

The types of complaints against bank policy or lending requirements are many. A homeowner might suspect that a bank is discriminating in refinancing, preventing lower-income neighborhoods from taking advantage of good interest rates. Or the multiplication of fees that make refinancing prohibitive might come under question, as might a bank's reasons for denying refinancing or rejecting prepayment.

Financial institutions are subject to various government regulations. Homeowners can contact the agency that monitors the bank (see below). In addition, legal challenges can be made, and particularly onerous practices of banks can be changed by new legislation.

Aside from questionable policy decisions, banks also make accounting errors in calculating the complex home mortgage loan schemes. Homeowners can undertake an audit of their accounts and challenge these errors.

LEGAL RESPONSES TO FINANCIAL INSTITUTIONS

Legal responses to questionable banking practices fall into three areas: regulatory complaints, lawsuits, and legislation to change bank rules.

A lawsuit against a bank is often impossible for an individual. Banks are very wealthy; the amount of money involved may be rapidly exceeded by legal fees.

Of course, there are David vs. Goliath attempts that sometimes work. If a homeowner has been charged a refinancing fee that seems inappropriate, an action in small claims court is possible. Small claims courts have limits on the dollar amounts that can be recovered, ranging from several hundred dollars to several thousand, depending on the state. When a homeowner undertakes a small claims court action, the bank will at least be forced to defend its activity publicly (see chapter 21).

A state attorney general's office may be willing to pursue individual complaints against financial institutions, sometimes by pooling together many complaints. When sued by the attorneys general of several states, a major mortgage lender agreed to refund $100 million in excess escrow collections to thousands of homeowners.

Consumer organizations and consumer-oriented attorneys have undertaken successful challenges to banks in class actions.

Legislators are also quick to respond to the complaints of their constituents, and homeowners are perceived as voters with clout. Some banking problems—requiring a bank to accept the prepayment on the principal—can be corrected by passing new laws. Homeowners should let state legislators and federal representatives know about these concerns, contacting both the local legislators and the chairs of committees on banking practices.

COMPLAINT PROCEDURE

Financial institutions are regulated—some more effectively than others—either by a state agency or by a federal agency, depending on the type of institution.

If a homeowner has a complaint about a bank procedure or lending decision, the first step is to contact the bank's customer relations department. In many cases, a reconsideration may result in a change in the decision. For example, a homeowner who is denied refinancing could be offered private mortgage insurance to cover the additional risk that the bank was unwilling to take.

If satisfaction is not forthcoming from the bank itself, the homeowner should contact the appropriate regulatory agency and explain the problem clearly, attaching photocopies of the key documents or correspondence from the financial institution.

Every state has a state banking commissioner, superintendent of banks, commissioner of financial institutions, state comptroller, or department of finance. A consumer agency or the state attorney general's office can direct consumers to the appropriate agency.

State banks with Federal Deposit Insurance coverage are also monitored by the FDIC. Complaints can be sent to FDIC, Office of Consumer Affairs, 550 Seventeenth Street, N.W., Washington, DC 20429; 800-424-5488.

National banks are regulated by the Comptroller of the Currency, Department of Treasury, 250 E Street, S.W., Washington, DC 20219; 202-874-4820.

Savings and loan institutions and savings banks fall under the aegis of the federal government's Office of Thrift Supervision, also a division of the Department of the Treasury. Complaints can be sent to Office of Thrift Supervision, Consumer Affairs, 1700 G Street, N.W., Washington, DC 20552; 800-842-6929.

Several types of mortgages—Veterans Administration (VA), the Federal Housing Administration (FHA), and others—may have particular rules that apply to the procedures of the financial institution. Borrowers should not hesitate to contact the monitoring agency. Complaints about FHA loans can be made to the Department of Housing and Urban Development, Office of Single Family Housing, Room 9282, Washington, DC 20410; 202-708-3175. Complaints about VA loans can be made to Consumer Affairs Services, Department of Veterans Affairs, 810 Vermont Avenue, N.W., Washington, DC 20420; 202-535-8962. Documents provided at the time of the original closing should identify the appropriate agency.

In other cases, the financial institution acts under the authority of a public-private mortgaging association that buys the loan from the bank. These associations (for example, the Government National Mortgage Association or Ginnie Mae; the Federal National Mortgage Association, Fannie Mae) also have rules that the bank must follow in dealing with those loans. Homeowners should ask the bank what financing vehicle was used and how that financing agency can be contacted.

In addition, a voluntary association of banking members, the Mortgage Bankers Association of America, 1125 Fifteenth Street, N.W., 7th Floor, Washington, DC 20005; 202-861-1929, maintains information on banks and other financial institutions. The association has a private dispute resolution program.

Duplicate copies of complaint letters written to regulatory agencies should be sent to state or federal legislators. The additional scrutiny may encourage a prompt solution.

HANDLING FINANCIAL CONCERNS

Refinancing the original mortgage can provide benefits, but there can be many barriers. Costs are high, and, in some cases, stricter rules of eligibility are applied.

In terms of legal concerns, if borrowers run into obstacles with a financial institution, for redress they can contact the regulatory agencies that oversee the bank or financial institution, or the state attorney general. Borrowers should also consider contacting consumer organizations and state legislators to effect changes and get action.

14

Co-ownership, Personal Relations, and the Home

The ownership status of a home can be affected by the owner's personal relations, especially by marriage, divorce, death, cohabitation, or the split-up of cohabiting couples or other nonmarried joint owners. The effect of these events on the property depends on three things:

1. *The nature of the property ownership.* The titled ownership can be held in various ways—as a solo owner, as joint tenants with a right of survivorship, as tenants in common, or in some other form of legal ownership.
2. *State laws.* Case law, statutes, and procedures define the ownership of property in many ways and have particular ramifications on property division after divorce or on the death of an owner.
3. *Individual agreement or document.* A will, trust, prenuptial agreement, or other contractual arrangement about property

division can determine what will happen to the property. Cohabiting couples, who rarely have the benefit of state laws to protect them, can draw up an independent contract to safeguard their individual interests in the property.

Nature of Property Ownership

How the title to property is structured makes a difference when changes evolve in the owner's personal status. Especially when property is owned by two or more persons together, the nature of the ownership may determine whether and how the property will change hands.

There are several types of property ownership.

- Joint tenancy
- Tenancy in common
- Community property
- Tenancy by the entireties
- Sole ownership
- Trust

In this context, tenancy has nothing to do with a landlord-tenant situation, but is a historical legal term to describe the relationship among property owners.

The type of ownership interest is stated in the deed—for example, the property is deeded to "Pat and Kim as tenants in common." The form of ownership interest is changed only when a property transfer occurs, either by process of the law (as upon death) or by a transfer by one or both parties.

Generally, merely altering the deed does not change the type of ownership. If the owners of property wish to change the nature of their ownership interest, they do so by simulating the transfer of the property: the owners deed the property to a straw person who then retransfers the property back to the original title owners in the revised form of legal ownership. Some modern laws do not permit a change in the form of ownership without a straw person.

Joint tenancy is a way for two or more people to hold property. Its full name is *joint tenancy with a right of survivorship,* which is also a fair description of the rights that pass along with joint tenancy. People who own property in joint tenancy each own equal, undivided interests in the property. There is only one title, which lists the names of all joint owners. Each joint tenant has an equal right to live on the property. Under the right of survivorship, when one person dies, the property automatically passes to the other owner without the necessity of going through probate. No owner can pass the property on to a third person by will; the surviving tenant takes the property interest.

Explicit wording is needed to form a joint tenancy with the right of survivorship—without the language, the property is presumed to be owned as tenants in common. A joint tenancy can be created or ended by agreement of the owners. The sale of the property interest of one joint tenant destroys the joint tenancy and creates a tenancy-in-common between the remaining joint tenant and the new purchaser.

Joint tenancy is generally the form of ownership used by married couples. Sometimes joint tenancy is used when one party buys property for the benefit of another. A parent might pay the down payment on a home that is to be used and occupied by adult children. Those using the house can't sell it without the parent's involvement, but when the parent dies, the property can be transferred automatically to the children as the survivors under the right of survivorship. Likewise, if the children were to die first, property ownership would immediately transfer to the parents.

Tenancy in common is a form of ownership by two or more persons in which each owner has a divided interest in the whole. The share of ownership may be unequal. Essentially, the tenant in common owns a piece of a common pie, which can be sold individually or passed on after death to the owner's heir or other-named person.

Unrelated people who are buying a house together might use this type of ownership. When the language of the deed fails to state the type of ownership interest of two or more people, the law implies that a tenancy in common was created.

Community property is recognized in eight states as encompassing the property owned by a married couple (Arizona, California, Idaho, Louisiana, Nevada, New Mexico, Texas, and Washington; Wisconsin has a similar system with a different name). Each individual is considered to own half of the property. Unlike joint tenancy with a right of survivorship, upon death the ownership interests of the deceased spouse do not automatically go to the other party. The property interests can be passed by will to someone else. All property acquired during the marriage is considered community property, excepting that given to one spouse by gift or inheritance.

Tenancy by the entireties applies to married couples and is a recognized form of property ownership in about 20 states. The right of survivorship of one spouse to the ownership interests of the other spouse applies automatically in a tenancy by the entireties. By law, however, one spouse may be protected from the debts of the other spouse. Also, neither spouse can sell off the tenancy alone or cut off the rights of the other spouse.

Sole ownership applies to the single, individual property owner who owns all of the property and the rights associated with it. In the case of a person married at the time of purchase, the law may imply ownership in the other spouse, even though the title designates a single individual.

Trusts are used to place the legal title in a property in the name of a trustee, who is to use the property for the benefit of a third person, a beneficiary. The legal title to the property passes to the beneficiary on the death of the owner in the case of a testamentary trustee. The aim of most trusts is to avoid probate. A trust can also be operative while the property owner is alive if special rules are followed, and this is known as a *living trust.* An attorney can draft trust papers without too much cost or difficulty, but the specific language used in creating the trust needs to be precise.

DEATH

Upon the death of the owner or co-owner of the home, different scenarios can develop, depending on the manner of ownership, state intestacy laws, or the existence of a will.

If the home is owned by the deceased person and one other person through joint ownership with a right of survivorship, or with a spouse through tenancy by the entireties, the surviving owner automatically gains the deceased's property interest.

The surviving owner could transfer the title to the property by presenting the appropriate documents to the clerk of deeds or other official charged with this task.

The process is not inordinately complicated when the property involved is owned as joint tenants with a right of survivorship. The surviving homeowner, though, should complete a formal transfer soon after the joint owner's death.

Spouses who own their home as tenants by the entireties also are entitled to full title ownership upon the death of one of them. The portion of the property that is attributed to the deceased spouse may, however, be subject to estate taxes based on a percentage of the purchasing cost.

Spouses who own property in a community property state are not automatically entitled to a share of the property when one spouse dies. The deceased's share of the property is transferred to a new owner by will, if there is one, or by state intestacy laws, which define property inheritance in the absence of a will. The surviving spouse may very well be the person to whom the property is willed. In most community property states, intestacy laws provide that the spouse inherits the community property.

Some community property states no longer require spouses to go through the probate process. In most states, probate is necessary, and in some cases, it is preferred to cut off creditors' claims that are not filed within a statutory time limit. The portion of the community property owned by the deceased spouse is subject to estate taxes.

Property that is owned by people as tenants in common never has a right of survivorship attached to it. Upon death, the property is always transferred by the operation of a will or by state intestacy laws. Property held by tenants in common always goes through the probate process, and it is this, more than anything, that distinguishes it from joint ownership with a right of survivorship.

At times, the death of one property owner means that the property needs to be sold. All of the heirs may agree to this process or a court can order the property sold because there is no fair way to divide it among the heirs.

Selling real estate during probate involves a good deal of paperwork. Sometimes it is better to sell the real estate after the probate has concluded and the property ownership is transferred to one individual or group of individuals. This way, some of the costs may be avoided.

With a trust, the death of the property owner means that the property can be transferred to the named beneficiary by opera-

> In one case, a woman was survived by her second husband and children from two marriages, all of whom had an interest in land that she inherited from her first husband. The survivors disagreed about how to divide the property. The court felt the only fair approach was to sell the property and divide the proceeds.

tion of the trust and probate can be avoided. Conditions for a valid trust—testamentary or living—can be quite specific; local laws should be consulted.

When the property in question is a co-op, the person who inherits it may still have to qualify with the cooperative board. Unless the proprietary lease allows an automatic transfer of the property to an heir, the co-op board can refuse to transfer shares, in which case the property is returned to the deceased's estate for sale or other disposition.

MARRIAGE AND DIVORCE

A house is often the most valuable possession in a marriage. Along with financial value, it is sometimes filled with emotional attachments.

There is no one way that the division of property is handled upon divorce. The laws and the interpretation of them differ considerably from state to state, and in many cases, from county to county, or judge to judge. In a large number of cases, the disposition of a home is handled by an agreement between the parties that takes into account their needs, including their finances, jobs, children, particular housing concerns, and anticipated future circumstances.

The disposition of the house is handled simultaneously with other matters considered in a divorce, and negotiations over the property are part of a bigger picture. For example, one spouse may be awarded the right to live in a house until all minor children are 18, at which time the house will be sold and the proceeds disbursed based on a formula that considers taxes, child support, earnings, home improvements, investment, expenses, and other factors. At the same time, the other spouse is awarded the family car, the right to a vacation home 11 months out of 12, the obligation to pay a portion of the mortgage loan payments, and the right to a portion of the tax deductions arising from the ownership of the home.

In the community property states, all property acquired during the marriage is to be divided equally between the spouses. In the other states, property is divided by a rule of equitable distribution, or fair distribution under the circumstances. Although who is at fault in a divorce is no longer the all-encompassing concern it once was, in some equitable distribution states, a judge can consider whether one party was at fault when deciding how to divide the property. A judge also considers the assets and employability of the spouses, the length of the marriage, the monetary and nonmonetary contributions of each spouse, their expenses, and the custody of and needs of minor children. In one state—Mississippi—property is allocated to the spouse whose name is on the title, if only one spouse is named.

In both equitable distribution and community property states, the spouses can have separate property that they owned prior to the marriage or gained through inheritance. Separate property is retained by the spouse to whom it belongs, so long as it can be identified as separate property. A home owned by one party prior to the marriage is separate property. The proceeds of a home sold prior to the marriage can be separate property, too, if they remain so identified. A down payment made by one partner prior to the marriage can be considered separate property, to be returned to the spouse upon divorce. In order to be credited with the separate property, the contributing partner should keep clear records of the money, its transfers, and how it was used.

The best way to safeguard an interest in separate property is through a written prenuptial agreement. A prenuptial agreement will be upheld if both parties enter into it voluntarily and without coercion, and if prior to signing it both parties make a full and complete disclosure of all of their assets. The agreement must be in writing. An agreement that is obviously unfair will not be upheld. For example, through a prenuptial agreement, a person who owns an old family home could specify that the house ownership will be considered separate property, and that upon death, any ownership interest in the home will go not to the spouse, but to a person designated by will. If the parties divorce, the owner of the old family home can use the prenuptial agreement to make the case that the home should be considered separate property, not property of the marriage.

In some cases, parties who never formally married are considered married by common law. Fifteen jurisdictions* formally recognize people as married if they have lived together and held themselves out to the public as a married couple. If a couple is recognized as married under common law, their property is subject to being divided the same as a married couple's when they separate.

In some states that do not recognize common-law marriages, the courts have applied the same rules that are applied to married couples in dividing the property that a couple has accumulated. These are the so-called palimony cases. One party argues that, although unmarried and even though they had no cohabitation agreement (sometimes even if they did), the parties lived as a couple, serving each other's personal needs, and that the home represents a joint accumulation of assets. Under concepts of equity or fairness, some courts have divided the property between both individuals even though one person is the title owner.

PREPARATION FOR DIVISION OF PROPERTY BECAUSE OF DIVORCE

When a divorce becomes apparent and a house is involved, the parties are wise to engage attorneys, even if there are few other assets.

The first step is to gather all of the financial documents related to the house—title, mortgage, loan, insurance, bank statements.

The second step is to calculate the true costs and value of the home. The fair market value may need to be estimated by an appraiser or realtor. In addition, the parties may need to look at various formulations. For example, if the house is to be sold, an estimation of the net value may be needed—after presale repairs, closing costs, inspectors' fees, taxes, insurance, association dues, moving expenses, and moneys owed to the bank are calculated.

---

*Alabama, Colorado, District of Columbia, Georgia, Idaho, Iowa, Kansas, Montana, New Hampshire, Ohio, Oklahoma, Pennsylvania, Rhode Island, South Carolina, Texas.

The third step is to make a clear assessment of the pros and cons of keeping or selling the house and to work out the financial and pragmatic arrangements associated with it.

Once a decision is made about the property, documents transferring or specifying each party's interest are signed and filed with the appropriate authorities. As with all aspects of a divorce, the matter is heard and reviewed by a judge. The parties also need to agree upon tax status—who will pay, who will take deductions.

When the divorcing couple owns a cooperative apartment, and one wishes to stay in the unit, association boards may require a complete financial reevaluation before transferring the co-op shares from two names to one.

COHABITATION, JOINT NONMARRIED OWNERS, AND PROPERTY OWNERSHIP

When unrelated people buy property together, they need to think carefully about the best form of ownership. This includes friends, two unrelated families, business associates, cousins, unmarried heterosexual couples, and same-sex couples. For example, a joint tenancy with a right of survivorship creates the right in the surviving purchaser to own the full property. For same-sex couples who cannot participate in a legal marriage, this may be exactly the type of commitment desired. But it may not. A tenancy in common permits the co-owner to designate an heir—mother, brother, niece, or unrelated friend.

Property ownership formats don't contemplate all the problems co-owners can encounter. This is where a contract between the parties can help. For example, without an agreement, a joint owner could potentially defeat the other party's rights of survivorship by transferring the interest in the property to a third person. But if the parties agreed in a valid contract that, in contemplation and consideration of their intention to purchase the property as joint owners, neither would sell an individual property interest, the parties could have double protection.

Many situations that arise in nontraditional ownership might be aided by a contract. Suppose one family of a jointly purchased two-family house undergoes a divorce, a job transfer, or bankruptcy. Suppose two friends who bought a house to share as their primary residence have a major breach in their friendship. Suppose one partner of an unmarried couple dies without a will, resulting in the tenancy in common property being inherited by a parent or other relative?

Because the complications can be enormous, people purchasing property together who are not otherwise protected by state laws (as married couples are) should consider entering into a binding written contract to protect each person's interest in the property and to clarify how costs, maintenance, and valuation on sale of a partial interest will be calculated. This agreement should be entered into before or in conjunction with the purchase of a home. Both parties should consult with their own attorneys.

For couples living together, such contracts are often referred to as cohabitation agreements, and approximately half the states now recognize them. As with a prenuptial agreement, a cohabitation agreement may define both provisions related to jointly purchased property and other concerns, such as the separate ownership of property and provisions for financial support by one party for the other upon dissolution of the relationship. The contract must be entered into willingly and with full disclosure of the facts.

With reference to property to be held or purchased jointly, some of the things co-purchasers might cover in a written contract include:

- Amount of the down payment each party will make
- How much each party will contribute to the monthly mortgage loan payment, and how those contributions will be evaluated upon sale
- Who will be in primary contact with a lending institution and homeowner's association
- Who will pay property taxes and insurance
- Who will be entitled to income tax deductions for interest on the mortgage loan, or how they will be divided
- What ordinary maintenance is and how each party will contribute financially to it
- The types of receipts or financial information indicating expenses each party will maintain
- How the nonfinancial contributions to maintenance will be evaluated

- How major maintenance costs will be handled—for example, by the contributions of one party, by a determination at the time they occur, or by a joint maintenance account (not unlike that established by a cooperative or condominium)
- If a portion of the property is to be rented, how the income, expenses, and depreciation for the rental will be handled
- If a rental is part of the property, how the management responsibilities of one co-owner will be assessed
- If a portion of the property is used as a home office by one co-owner, how the deductions and resulting changes in tax benefits upon sale will be calculated
- If disputes about property ownership arise, how the parties will handle them—for example, entering good-faith mediation or arbitration prior to any legal action
- Providing joint access to papers, documents, and financial accounting, including a yearly review of accounts by co-owners, as a way of ensuring that one co-owner is not neglecting taxes, liens, or other items that could have a disastrous effect on the property
- Whether the parties will maintain disability insurance or other security devices to cover mortgage payments in the event of illness
- Granting one of the co-owners or some other individual the power of attorney to handle financial considerations should one owner become incapacitated
- Providing for survival ownership rights—for example, by will, especially if only one party is listed on ownership documents, and especially in situations involving cooperatives or condominiums, in which boards may raise objections to co-owner status
- Who will remain on the property if the parties can no longer live together, or the process by which such a decision will be made
- What will happen to a co-owner's financial share if one decides to leave—for example, giving the other co-owner the first option to purchase the share at an agreed-upon evaluation rate
- If one party chooses to buy out another party, what method of appraisal will be used

IMPORTANCE OF CO-OWNERSHIP AGREEMENTS

Purchasing property with someone else can offer enormous benefits, and in some cases is financially necessary to afford the purchase. Protecting that investment means discussing basic ownership questions and setting ground rules.

In many instances, the law of property is still lagging behind social and personal arrangements. Homeowners need to know what their rights are vis-à-vis another owner. The rights can be established by the very ownership documents to the property and by the laws existing in the state. When the laws are unclear or insufficient, co-owners should create their own agreements to clarify their property interests and rights.

15

Environmental Contaminants Inside the Home

Environmental concerns are not limited to distant sites with smokestacks—they now affect home and yard. On federal, state, and local levels, new laws are requiring the testing, disclosure, removal, and elimination of dangerous products. Homeowners need to be alert to product warnings, such as the banning of certain insecticides; new preventive laws, such as the establishment of radon testing; and new responsibilities, such as disclosing asbestos in the home upon sale in some communities.

ENVIRONMENTAL CONCERNS

The Environmental Protection Agency (EPA) is responsible for monitoring most environmental contaminants on a federal level. Ten regional EPA centers have information about hazards in those areas. In addition, state environmental agencies and health departments take action on indoor pollutants. Special state offices have been established to monitor certain environmental hazards, such as radon.

Following is a discussion of some of the pollutants that concern most people.

Lead Paint   Very hazardous if ingested by children, lead paint abatement programs are ongoing in communities throughout the nation. HUD has mandated that abatement take place in all of its housing.

Lead in Drinking Water   An excessive amount of lead in water can cause internal damage to the nervous system. Lead enters drinking water from lead pipes used prior to 1930, or from the lead solder that is used with copper pipes in newer homes. Special laboratories can test for lead. Plumbing replacement or treatment devices—such as the reverse osmosis units—can reduce lead.

Asbestos   Banned in 1980, asbestos is found in older homes wrapped around pipes, boilers, furnaces, and radiators, or as building insulation. Asbestos causes cancer and lung disease, and it is most dangerous when it is fraying, cracked, or decomposing, and when it is disturbed or being removed. Removal or abatement by encapsulation needs to be undertaken by qualified contractors.

Commercial and institutional buildings, including co-ops and condos, can be required to remove asbestos, particularly during building renovations.

The existence of asbestos in a home should be revealed prior to the sale, and disclosure is now required in a few states.

Radon   Radon is a radioactive gas that can cause lung cancer. Radon occurs naturally in the soil as a result of the breakdown of uranium and can seep into a home through cracks in basement floors, sump drains, openings around pipes and cinder blocks, or in water taken from a well.

Radon can be tested by commercial companies, lists of which are maintained by state health offices. Self-testing products may not be reliable; fraudulent companies have been known to provide false testing results. Some states are establishing free or low-cost radon testing programs.

If radon levels are high, the homeowner can install sub-slab ventilators or air-to-air exchangers, or seal cracks and cover open drains or exposed soil.

Formaldehyde   Used as a bonding agent in furniture, carpets, and building materials, formaldehyde can cause eye, nose, and throat irritation; incite asthmatic attacks, headaches, memory loss, depression, or fatigue; and increase chemical sensitivity.

The federal government as well as consumer organizations publish a number of pamphlets on environmental concerns.

Homebuyer's Guide to Environmental Hazards (available from the EPA Public Information Center, 201 M Street, S.W., Washington, DC 20460; [202] 382-2080).
The Inside Story: A Guide to Indoor Air Quality (EPA)
What You Should Know About Lead-Based Paint in Your Home (available from the Consumer Product Safety Commission, Washington, DC 20207)
Lead and Your Drinking Water (EPA)
Asbestos in the Home (CPSC)
A Citizen's Guide to Radon (EPA)
Radon Reduction Methods: A Homeowner's Guide (EPA)
Removal of Radon from Household Water (EPA)
Formaldehyde: Everything You Wanted to Know, But Were Afraid to Ask (available from the Consumer Federation of America, 1314 Fourteenth Street, N.W., Washington, DC 20005)

There are also toll-free hotlines to help the homeowner.

Product Safety hot line 800-638-CPSC
Safe Drinking Water 800-426-4791
Asbestos hot line 202-554-1404
Pesticides 800-858-PEST

Testing can be conducted for formaldehyde by city or state health agencies, often for free, and by private chemical laboratories. Self-test kits are also available. Excessive levels of formaldehyde can be treated by removing the products, increasing ventilation, or spraying a lab-prepared solution.

Formaldehyde emissions wear off with time; the greatest risks from the toxicity are posed in new building projects. Some states require disclosure of the levels of formaldehyde in materials and buildings, and HUD has established maximum levels of formaldehyde emission permitted in mobile homes.

Termiticides and Pesticides   Chemicals used to kill termites, insects, and rodents can cause cancer. Some pesticide chemicals were banned in 1988; others are allowed to be used only in limited situations.

Lawn Chemicals   Lawn chemicals can affect the nervous system. Some cities and states are beginning to regulate the use of lawn chemicals by requiring that neighbors be notified before lawn spraying takes place, that potential health hazards from the chemicals be disclosed, that signs be posted when chemicals have been sprayed, or by proposing to ban the use of lawn chemicals altogether.

Carbon Monoxide   Homes with attached garages, or co-ops or condos with garages, can suffer from carbon monoxide leakage.

LAWS AND REGULATIONS

There is no federal indoor air-pollution legislation nor are there federal government standards for indoor air pollution. Proposals for an Indoor Air Quality Act, calling for federal research, have not been passed by Congress.

Federal regulations have banned the use of certain chemicals known to be dangerous. The EPA is the watchdog agency for review and regulation of hazardous substances. HUD has set formaldehyde levels for mobile homes and is requiring asbestos removal on HUD-owned properties.

Some states have indoor air pollution laws, but the number of states and the reach of their laws are limited. Most laws are linked only to commercial, institutional, or government buildings, or to employers. Few apply to residential homes, although some apply to cooperative and condominium buildings.

For example, Minnesota requires builders to disclose the levels of urea formaldehyde. Wisconsin has also set levels for permissible exposure to formaldehyde. New Hampshire requires builders and sellers to comply with environmental standards set for radon and asbestos. New Hampshire and Maine have adopted standards for proper ventilation. Other states have developed regulatory programs to conduct testing in residences for radon, asbestos, or formaldehyde.

In isolated communities, local ordinances require disclosure notices when lawn chemicals are sprayed.

Building codes touch on some issues related to indoor air pollution, particularly those regulations that affect the heating, ventilating, and air-conditioning systems. Trade associations such as the American Society of Heating, Refrigerating and Air Conditioning Engineers are beginning to adopt model standards for ventilation.

LEGAL STRATEGIES

The law in this area is still uncharted; however, some avenues for legal solutions are emerging.

Contracts   A homeowner's best protection against indoor pollution is prevention. When new construction or remodeling is under way, homeowners can specify that nontoxic materials be used and seek out builders with environmental sensitivity. In addition, the builder can be required to include whole ventilation systems and provide proper drainage and sealing to protect against radon seepage.

Undisclosed Defect   Home buyers who have discovered radon or asbestos that was not disclosed to them prior to the sale have brought suits against the sellers (see chapter 2). Real estate brokers may also be held liable, and broker associations are increasingly advising members to secure and release environmental information, particularly about radon, asbestos, and lead paint. Some lenders require residential loan applications to include environmental reports, which are commonly used in approving commercial loans.

Home purchasers are also entitled to have access to the property to conduct necessary tests.

Breach of Warranty   The builder of a new home or a home remodeling contractor may face liability for the breach of an implied warranty of habitability if unsafe products are used in construction (see chapter 2). Cooperative and condominium associations faced with removing asbestos in converted buildings can look to developers or sponsors to cover the costs. Mobile-home owners may have claims if formaldehyde levels exceed government specifications.

> *If someone suffers injury or illness that can be traced to a particular product, the manufacturer could be liable for making products with excessively high levels of toxicity.*

Product Liability   If someone suffers injury or illness that can be traced to a particular product, the manufacturer could be liable for making products with excessively high levels of toxicity. Manufacturers could also be liable for injuries if they failed adequately to warn consumers about the dangers (see Product Liability in chapter 2). The person or company that installed or used the dangerous product could also be liable for injuries resulting from its use or failing to warn the injured person about the possible harms. In many indoor pollution cases, proving which product was involved and how it caused the harm or illness are difficult evidentiary obstacles.

Nuisance   A homeowner might have a legitimate claim that the airborne spillover from a neighbor's chemical spraying interferes with the use and enjoyment of the property or is a private nuisance (see chapter 10). A case could even be pressed in small claims court.

Negligence   Companies that spray pesticides or use other chemical products in the home could be liable for negligence if they do not handle the products properly, resulting in injuries or illnesses to residents. In one case in Texas, residents of apartment complexes who suffered ill-health were awarded money for the misapplication of a chlordane termiticide.

Consumer Agencies   Federal and state agencies are charged with environmental or health oversight. Many states have radon programs. In addition, reporting problems to these agencies adds to the record for future action.

FUTURE PROSPECTS

For future safety, federal, state, and local officials may be prompted to take new legal action on pollution in the home. Concerned homeowners are beginning to lobby for rules and regulations and contact legislators about environmental concerns.

Creative solutions—whether tax breaks for homeowners who remove asbestos or reduce radon, or requiring the wider use of disclosure of toxicity levels—can be proposed individually or in conjunction with citizens' groups.

Homeowners who directly encounter indoor air pollution problems, particularly if known hazards were undisclosed at the time of purchase, or if injuries were caused by negligence or by the preventable actions of product manufacturers, may have legal claims.

16

Takings of Private Property for Public Use

D espite the sanctity of private property, public projects such as roads may require the use of land that was not previously acquired by the government. Long ago, the concept of eminent domain developed—a superior power over land exercised by the government to fulfill public needs. Through this power, the government could condemn property and use it for a public purpose.

In writing the U.S. Constitution, the founders wanted to make sure that no person's property would be taken away unless the person was paid. The last clause in the Fifth Amendment of the Bill of Rights states that "private property" shall not "be taken for public use, without just compensation."

Known as the *taking* or the *just compensation* clause, this power has been exercised throughout American history. Eminent domain was instrumental in the building of railroads, schools, subways, highways, water delivery systems, sewage, navigable rivers, and parks. But this provision is not a figment of history. There are a flood of contemporary questions raised by the concept of eminent domain, and a huge number have to do with the power of government to issue regulations that restrict the use of private property.

What is a public use? A road is surely a public use, but what about urban renewal or economic development plans that include a shopping mall and a high-rise office tower? What about zoning or environmental regulations that don't physically take property away, but reduce the value of the property or the owner's use or enjoyment? Does a beachfront owner have a right to complain if a state government rules that no private housing can be built along the shore to protect the coastline? Does the noise from airplanes so reduce a home's worth that it amounts to a taking, so that the homeowner can rightly bring a claim against the government for inverse condemnation? When does a homeowner deserve compensation and how much compensation is just?

These questions are increasingly preoccupying neighborhood associations, planning boards, town halls, and courts, including the United States Supreme Court. They are central issues in controlling development, planning cities, and maintaining natural resources in the face of environmental degradation. The meaning of the taking clause is being reevaluated and new distinctions in the law may develop.

Eminent Domain

The power of eminent domain exists in the federal, state, and local government and, in some instances, in utility companies. A government may take property for a public use if the action has a rational relationship to a legitimate purpose or need.

When a government seeks to obtain private property, it initiates a condemnation proceeding. The amount of money to be paid to the property owner is determined by an offer, negotiation, or a trial by jury.

In some cases, homeowners feel that the value of their property has been wrecked by a government action, even when the government didn't formally take the property. The homeowner must then initiate a lawsuit, known as *inverse condemnation,* to demand payment from the government.

There are four important elements to eminent domain:

1.   a taking
2.   of property
3.   for public use
4.   requiring a payment of just compensation

TAKING

Taking of private property can occur when there is

- A government takeover of the property for conversion to some public use, such as building a school
- In many cases, an act of the government that physically affects the land, such as building a dam that causes flooding onto private land
- In a few cases, a regulation on land use that diminishes the value of the land, such as eliminating the use of the property under a zoning ordinance
- In limited circumstances, a requirement that the owner undertake a specific act in exchange for a right, such as requiring public access to a beach before the city grants a building permit
- In rare situations, the indirect action of the government, such as giving approval to a private developer's drainage plan that subsequently causes flooding to someone else's property

PROPERTY INTEREST

All or part of an owner's property rights can be taken—land, air, water, support, access, freedom from physical invasion, and freedom from intrusive interference. The taking can be complete, or it can be an easement or other partial use of the property. However, the government may take only that part of the property necessary to the completion of the project.

A partial use of the property can amount to a taking. When the government required property owners to permit cable television installations, it was taking an easement right.

Even a temporary taking can require just compensation. When a property owner was forbidden from using the land because of an interim flood control program, the court held that the owner should be compensated for the time during which the property could not be used. A shift in treatment of property can amount to a taking. Spot zoning of particular pieces of property can be a taking. The attempted elimination in a zoning scheme of a nonconforming sign that predated the zoning plan was a taking that required government compensation.

The taking might also involve incidental rights (see chapter 8). The government can take property by raising or lowering the level of a stream. The spillage of sewage onto private property from a municipal sewer plant could amount to a taking of the property. Wires over property or low-flying airplanes could constitute a taking of the airspace.

PUBLIC USE AND CONDEMNATION

Under the law, when private property is taken, it must be for public use. Public use has been broadly defined as a use that has a rational connection to some public purpose.

In practice, the question of public use arises when people object to their property being taken under the power of eminent domain. The owner of the property may question the project's purpose and its public use. If a public use is *not* found, the government cannot exercise the power of eminent domain.

|| *When private property is taken, it must be for public use.* ||

Unfortunately for homeowners, nearly every action of the government used as a rationale to condemn property has qualified as a proper public use. One reason is that a judge can always find that the homeowner is getting something in return for the loss of the property—money or just compensation.

Certain uses are unquestionably public uses. A highway, school, government building, and the like are clearly projects directly linked to government activity. Public use has been found when public health, safety, welfare, morals, transportation, river navigation, or air navigation are involved. Economic benefit has been considered a valid public goal. Environmental conservation is, at times, considered to fulfill a public purpose, as are esthetic goals. Even public convenience has been cited as a public purpose.

In some cases, property owners assert that the government has engaged in *excess condemnation,* that is, has blocked out a much larger area than is needed for the project in mind. In other cases, property owners question the definiteness of the project. Condemnation has taken place for a plan the government had vaguely in mind for some time in the future. In one case, a park to be built in the future was not considered a public use; in another case, it was.

Strong objections have been raised—and rejected—when the government condemns and buys property, then transfers it to another private individual. In urban renewal programs neighborhoods are cleared out and the property is passed on to private developers. The courts have held that the mere fact that the property will be transferred to a private owner does not mean that it is not for a public use.

The Supreme Court ruled in an urban renewal case that as long as the purpose the government had in mind was to benefit the public—such as ridding the city of slums and improving its appeal—then the project fit within a public use. Eminent domain was merely a tool to accomplish a legitimate government goal.

In this view, the power of eminent domain can be used even for commercial or industrial purposes. The economic benefits that would accrue to a city and public port authority from the building of two large office towers (the World Trade Center in New York City) were held to be a valid public purpose that could justify the condemnation of private property.

Public use was found where property was purchased by the government and sold to a car manufacturer that planned to build a manufacturing plant. The property in that case was not in poor condition. But the reviewing court held that improving the city's economic condition and providing jobs were valid public purposes for the exercise of eminent domain.

Public use was found when the state of Hawaii decided to use the power of eminent domain to break up the massive holdings of a small number of landowners by taking the property and transferring it to lessees. The plan was a valid way to loosen the domination of the real estate market, the court said.

JUST COMPENSATION

Most eminent domain cases that involve homeowners are centered around one question: How much money? Property owners are supposed to receive just compensation for the loss of their home. How much compensation is fair, and how should the value of the property be ascertained?

Homeowners, of course, want to be paid as much as possible for the taking of their property. Appraisal and value are the heart of condemnation proceedings. Indeed, the hearings tend to become a battle of the experts, each with a slew of figures and information to back up the determination of just compensation.

Just compensation is considered the fair market value of the property at the time of the taking. But for homeowners, the determination of just compensation is not so straightforward. Emotional attachment is not valued. In addition, the property owner is not entitled to the replacement cost of a new home, or to consequential damages, such as the cost of packing, moving, or a new mortgage.

CONDEMNATION PROCEEDING

Many homeowners contest the initial appraisal of the government and seek a greater amount in a condemnation hearing. Condemnation cases can be heard by a jury. Homeowners have a good chance of success with a well-presented case.

Even prior to a hearing, the property owners can negotiate with the government by getting and presenting independent appraisals about the fair market value.

When the condemnation is for only a portion of the property, the land owner may be able to negotiate nonmonetary conditions. In the taking of strips of land for an underground oil pipeline, homeowners were able to negotiate the replanting of trees along those portions of land that were taken.

In nearly all jurisdictions, homeowners can accept the compensation offered by the government and still have a hearing in court to try to get the higher amount that they believe is fair. Homeowners should consult an attorney who specializes in condemnation proceedings.

TEST OF MARKET VALUE

Fair market value means the value that a willing seller would pay a willing buyer. Estimations of fair market value inevitably contain a good amount of guesswork. The market value of the property is determined by basic appraisal tools. The most accepted way of demonstrating fair market value is by the prices obtained for comparable properties in the community. The homeowner's appraiser researches the real estate sales market and tries to fashion both comparability and community in ways that are most favorable to the homeowner. Sometimes homes are compared detail for detail in order to make an evaluation.

A less preferred method of appraisal is based on a depreciated-cost approach, which involves calculating the cost of building the house and subtracting from that the wear and tear or depreciation of the house and its parts. The value of the lot is added in.

The appraisal method that is *not* considered in eminent domain proceedings is replacement value. Fair market value is not assessed by the costs of buying or finding a substitute home, except in extremely rare cases of out-and-out injustice. Even when the property is virtually irreplaceable, such as camp land owned by a nonprofit corporation, the cost of replacement is not a permitted determination for just compensation.

The property owner is entitled to be compensated for the highest and best use of the land. Someone who owns a house in a semicommercial zone might be able to present evidence that its fair market value as a fast-food restaurant was the highest and best use, not its value as a mere residence.

When only a portion of the property is taken, the owner is entitled to ask for severance damages. Severance damages recognize that the owner has lost not only the exact property that the government has taken, but also stands to suffer a reduction in value to the remaining property.

In some instances of a partial taking, the government's position is that the property actually stands to benefit—for example, from a new highway or sewer system. The government may then try to reduce the award in order to reflect the beneficial use.

INDIRECT ACTIONS:
WHEN TAKING IS RAISED BY HOMEOWNERS

In inverse condemnation cases, the homeowner asserts that an action of the government has taken away the home's value, even though the government may not have had any real intention to take the property.

For example, when an airport is built nearby, the noise overhead from planes landing and taking off can be so overwhelming that it interferes with the homeowner's use and enjoyment of the property. The homeowner can sue the government, claiming that its building of the airport was, in effect, an action of taking the home.

The government, not wishing to have to compensate every property owner disturbed by aircraft, will deny that its action was a taking. Homeowners have had mixed results in airport disturbance cases.

A large number of inverse condemnation cases question restrictions placed on the property as a result of agency rulings and whether they amount to a taking. These are often called regulatory takings. In the majority of these cases, property owners have lost.

For example, zoning was clearly established as not amounting to a taking of property in the earliest challenges against it (see chapter 4). Requiring a subdivision to provide open land before its plan could be approved was not a taking. Placing limitations on the development or modification of landmark property was not a taking. The denial of a permit to fill wetlands property for development was not a taking.

The United States Supreme Court shifted its position on what constitutes a regulatory taking when environmental regulations prevented all property owners from using the land exactly as they desired. A property owner succeeded in arguing that environmental regulations that prohibited oceanfront building reduced the land's value and were a taking that demanded just compensation. New eminent domain challenges are bound to arise as a result.

When government actions are challenged as intruding on private property by physical trespass or by nuisance, the claims will be analyzed as presenting issues of eminent domain. These matters invariably are raised in inverse condemnation proceedings brought by the homeowner (see chapters 9 and 10).

In some cases, if a trespass or nuisance is found, the court agrees that the government has effectively condemned the land, particularly if a physical invasion can be shown, such as by flooding waters or overhead cables.

If the claim is of a nuisance interfering with the enjoyment of the property, courts balance the value of the public use with the harm suffered by the homeowner, using a more subjective and difficult test.

Slightly more than half the states avoid the problem of determining whether a trespass or a private nuisance claim has risen to the level of a taking. Instead, these states require the government to compensate landowners for property that is damaged as well as property that is taken. The federal government does not follow that rule.

PUBLIC USE AND INVERSE CONDEMNATION

The arguments that a project is not a public use in direct condemnation cases are reversed when property owners bring inverse condemnation proceedings. In inverse condemnation, the homeowner argues that the property has, in effect, been taken by some action, inaction, or negligence by the government. If the action involved—excessive noise from an airport—is not the result of the government activity, then the homeowner has no claim against the government. The only recourse is to attempt to get compensation from the private concerns involved on theories of nuisance or trespass.

Although public use has been defined very broadly for the purposes of direct condemnation, it has been given a much more limited interpretation in indirect takings or inverse condemnation cases. This is particularly true of situations in which the government is accused of having failed to act in some way. For example, the sewage or drainage system of a private developer does not constitute a public use sufficient to trigger the takings clause simply because the municipality approved a subdivision map or required the system as a condition of a development plan. If the government were more deeply involved—such as approving the actual plans for the system—the public purpose requirement might be met.

Presenting an Inverse Condemnation Case

In inverse condemnation cases, the homeowner sues the government and attempts to prove that its acts have so damaged the value of the property that a taking has, in fact, occurred. The owner then seeks compensation for the taking. In general, the rules on inverse condemnation are less clear-cut than those on direct condemnation.

There is a strong consensus that a property owner must try all other avenues of appeal before bringing a lawsuit based on inverse condemnation. For example, when a zoning regulation denies an owner a certain use of the property, the owner must first seek a variance from the zoning board of appeals (see chapter 4). If the owner goes into court instead, the court is likely to throw out the case, claiming that it is not ripe for a decision on inverse condemnation.

In an inverse condemnation action, the homeowner has to show that

- There are government actions involved and what they are
- The actions amounted to a taking of property
- The actions were for a public use (only if there is a public use is the homeowner entitled to compensation from an indirect taking)
- The harm to the homeowner was greater than the benefit to the public at large, or the regulation in question exceeded its public purpose
- Just compensation is warranted, and what it would be

Tests Applied in Inverse Condemnation and Regulatory Takings

The tests on whether a particular situation amounts to inverse condemnation are largely subjective. Courts seem to rule that when the regulations go too far in reaching their goals, the property owner is entitled to just compensation. A physical invasion may be considered going too far.

A common test applied in regulatory takings cases is whether the good to the public from the regulation outweighs the harm to the property owner. If the public good is greater, then there is no taking even if the property's value has been reduced as a result.

A different approach uses an economic analysis, weighing whether the property owner had a reasonable expectation of return from the property that has been stripped of value by the government's action.

LEGAL STRATEGIES IN TAKINGS CASES

The legal strategies in takings cases vary depending on whether the homeowner objects to the taking altogether or merely seeks to get the most money possible for the property. There are also differences between a condemnation hearing, which the government initiates, and an inverse condemnation, which the property owner initiates.

- The first step is preventive. Homeowners should be aware of public decision making and major public or private developments that could affect the property. Objecting at planning commission hearings or community board meetings to legislative or congressional representatives and in political forums may be the best way to stop a project from getting started.
- For certain federal projects, such as those falling under the Endangered Species Act, the agency must complete a *takings implication assessment,* or TIA. The TIA states the extent of anticipated property takings and the cost to the government. Homeowners can get a copy of the TIA by contacting a congressional representative, or by filing a Freedom of Information request. Some representatives want to extend the TIA process to all federal agencies.
- Homeowners, at times, can band together in a class action to contest a government plan and to seek an injunction stopping the project. Minority communities have begun to question whether certain regulatory actions are discriminatory, including zoning that prohibits affordable housing and especially the seem-

ingly disproportionate placement of waste dumps in proximity to minority communities.

• In direct condemnation, the homeowner can raise certain legal issues about public projects, including whether the project casts a wider net of takings than is necessary; whether the project is definite enough to warrant taking property; and whether the project serves a legitimate public purpose.

• If the taking comes as the result of a change in a zoning ordinance, city plan, or building regulation, an inverse condemnation claim is probably necessary. The homeowner should make an immediate challenge to the regulation to the appropriate administrative body. If a zoning question is raised, an appeal or a request for a variance to the zoning board of appeals should be made (see chapter 4).

• If the taking comes from a condemnation notice, the homeowner should remember that the government's offer of just compensation is by no means written in stone. The owner can obtain a qualified independent appraisal to set the fair market value. When only a portion of the property is being taken, the homeowner can negotiate for benefits aside from money—a fence or tree replantings.

• At a condemnation trial, the homeowner should present independent evidence and experts who can demonstrate the higher market value of the property. Homeowners should also present evidence of comparable sales. The owners and their neighbors can testify, as well.

• The real question often is: How much money is fair to compensate the owner for the loss? The homeowner is entitled to a trial by jury, and, in many cases, juries are more sympathetic to property owners than to the government.

• In an inverse condemnation case, the homeowner will have to initiate a lawsuit against the government and show that a taking occurred because of a government action.

• The technicalities justify the homeowner's contacting an attorney who specializes in condemnation proceedings. They often work on a contingency or percentage of the award basis.

FORFEITURE LAWS AND THE HOME

The government sometimes attempts to take property by asset forfeiture. Federal and some state and city laws permit the government to seek the forfeiture of property that is used in criminal activity, principally in the illegal drug trade. The ramifications of forfeiture are drastic.

The government seizes the property, ejects the owner, and sells the property. The property owner is not entitled to any compensation or any proceeds from the sale. In numerous cases, property owners have had asset forfeiture proceedings instituted against them when the criminal activity involved someone else, such as a tenant, guest, or relative.

Many constitutional and procedural questions are raised by forfeiture laws. Notification of a forfeiture action requires contacting an attorney immediately.

RAISING CONCERNS ABOUT GOVERNMENT TAKINGS OF PRIVATE PROPERTY

The power of eminent domain can be exercised by federal, state, and local governments, so long as just compensation is provided. Concerns about the taking of private property are raised in two situations: in condemnation actions brought by the government and in inverse condemnation proceedings brought by property owners who believe that a government action has so intruded on their property that it has had the effect of condemning it.

The government may exercise the right of eminent domain for any use rationally related to a public purpose. Public use is broadly defined to include health, welfare, safety, transportation, morals, environmental conservation, economic benefit, urban renewal, and esthetics, and it can exist even though the property will be transferred to another private owner.

Since takings of property intrude on the most basic private-property interest, homeowners who wish to fight eminent domain proceedings should organize early to try to prevent them. When the taking is inevitable, the focus shifts to obtaining the best dollar value or just compensation for the property. If the government has not formally taken the property through condemnation proceedings, but is affecting the value of the property by other actions, the homeowner must take the initiative and sue the government for compensation in inverse condemnation proceedings.

17

Homeowner's Associations, Condominium Associations, and Cooperative Boards

The advent of planned communities sent a constellation of new law into the world of home ownership. This new body of law relates to homeowner's associations, also known as community associations, property owner's associations, condominium owner's associations, or cooperative associations. Homeowner's associations affect subdivisions of single-family homes, tract homes, and condominium and cooperative housing. There are more than 150,000 homeowner's associations in the United States.

The homeowner's association, composed of all of the owners in the complex, can have an enormous impact on an individual property owner's use and enjoyment of the property. The purchasers of property in these communities are required to be members of the association—in fact, the mandatory membership is a defining feature of the organization. To purchase property in a complex governed by a homeowner's association is to agree to be bound by its procedures, rules, and regulations.

The central theme of homeowner's associations is to serve the common interest of all homeowners. The association is assigned oversight of the community regulations and the maintenance of common space. It also has the power to make decisions about changes to unit property and about house rules that can touch on owners' lives. Homeowners can find that their personal interest is often not consistent with the common interest. The results can be painful and the basis of a board battle or legal challenge.

The basis of authority, the legal latitude, and the exact functions of a homeowner's association vary depending on the design involved—a homeowner's association in a subdivision is different from a co-op board. In addition, each association has its own set of guidelines and rules. But there are also many similarities that connect them in terms of process and extent of their authority.

These homeowner's associations are distinct from community organizations and citizen action groups that involve entirely voluntary membership.

DEFINING THE HOMEOWNER'S ASSOCIATION

In effect, a homeowner's association is a form of private government. The homeowner could just as easily be moving into a little town as a condo or subdivision. People who in a different type of neighborhood would just be the folks next door, are now co-decision makers and co-enforcers of community restrictions.

Instead of a city council and a mayor, this community has a powerful board of directors with elected officers and a president. A violation of the rules need not entail a trial, but it can mean a fine that converts to a lien on the property or, potentially, a forced exit from the home.

Homeowner's associations have major legal responsibilities to oversee the property, maintain common grounds, apply financial oversight, and preserve peace and goodwill. Associations can be

Homeowner's associations have major legal responsibilities to oversee the property, maintain common grounds, apply financial oversight, and preserve peace and goodwill.

a united force in issues arising between developers and home buyers. Their efforts contribute to the stability of the individual units.

On the other hand, the associations can also wield significant control over day-to-day activities, with covenants, rules, or regulations that restrict remodeling, architectural or environmental changes, activities, and use. The rules are designed to preserve property values by sustaining neighborhood qualities and to enhance everyone's right to quiet enjoyment of the property by minimizing disruptions and disturbances. The rules and regulations can be basic—the property can be used only for residential purposes—or they can be extensive, even archaic—all window dressings must be white, pets must be registered, piano playing is limited to soloists between certain hours.

Membership in the association entitles the members to use common facilities, such as a laundry room, pool, or yard. They may vote for board members, attend meetings, and also take an active role in operating the community by running for office or participating on a committee.

CREATION OF A HOMEOWNER'S ASSOCIATION

There are four distinct legal steps that must exist to create the working homeowner's association:

1.   Documents establish property ownership, such as the deed, declaration of condominium, or prospectus or shares in a cooperative.

2.   A clause, such as a covenant in a deed or statement in the declaration or prospectus, authorizes the association to handle certain affairs and properties and binds the unit owner to be a member.

3.   An actual operational association carries out this role and has articles of incorporation and bylaws describing its operating rules.

4.   Documents, such as a code of regulations or proprietary lease for a cooperative, define the relationship between the unit owner and the association, articulating the rights and responsibilities of unit owners, including penalties to which they may be subjected.

GENERAL ROLE OF HOMEOWNER'S ASSOCIATIONS

The duties and responsibilities of homeowner's associations are set out in several documents, including the deed or declaration, charter, articles of incorporation, bylaws, and rules.

Associations are not-for-profit corporations and must follow all the regular procedures of such organizations. Members elect a board, usually five to nine people, which has the major responsibility for handling association affairs. Many boards, in turn, hire management firms.

The homeowner's association is the legal owner of and is responsible for the care and management of all common areas of the building or complex. In the case of a cooperative or condominium, the association also has ownership control over the building containing the living units. A cooperative association is responsible for paying the mortgage, taxes, and insurance.

To finance all of this, fees are collected from each unit owner. The board manages books and budgets.

The board is responsible for its own legal and financial affairs. It must manage the property and the resources of the association prudently and using good business sense, and report back to the members or unit owners.

The association also has the responsibility to enforce rules and regulations that apply to each unit owner and, in some cases, to mediate disputes among them.

LEGAL ATTITUDE TOWARD HOMEOWNER'S ASSOCIATIONS

In general, courts have been extremely willing to endorse the actions of homeowner's associations. Association boards are given latitude and discretion to make decisions and to act on them.

When homeowners have disagreements with actions of the board, especially in situations involving undeniable rules, such as the payment of dues, the courts commonly side with the association. Judges often feel that, in purchasing the property, the homeowner voluntarily agrees to abide by the rules and regulations of the association. Although property ownership is valued strongly, the common good that the homeowner's association represents is valued above the individual's desires. Unless there is an overpowering reason to find otherwise, the homeowner must live with the rules and accept the common scheme.

There are, of course, important exceptions. Boards of homeowner's associations are not allowed to take actions that disregard their own rules, are arbitrary, are discriminatory or illegal, or ignore fiscal or other central responsibilities.

POWER AND RESPONSIBILITIES OF THE HOMEOWNER'S ASSOCIATION

The board members of a homeowner's association are elected by association members for a term of office. Limitations can be placed on who may become a board member—some associations are limited to owners who live on the property, as opposed to tenants or owners who live elsewhere and have rented out their property. Sometimes board membership is expanded, so that nonresident professionals, such as the managing agent or attorney, can also sit on the board.

In broad terms, the boards of associations are charged with many responsibilities to

- Collect dues
- Set assessments from members
- Place a lien on the property to enforce dues or assessment collection
- Make and enforce rules for the use of common property
- Make and enforce rules, within some limits, for the use of individual living units, including changes to the property, sales, and restrictions on resident activity
- Spend moneys and write checks on behalf of the association
- Prepare and maintain budgets for the association, including plans for reserve funds, projected expenditures, assessments and fee collections, and scrutinize all financial reports
- File appropriate government documents, including local, state, and federal tax returns, building permits, and special permits such as for elevators, boilers, and pools
- Keep an adequate reserve fund to meet emergency and special needs of the association
- Take out loans on behalf of the association

- Hire such outside assistance as is necessary to fulfill its role—whether managers, accountants, lawyers, or contractors; hire and supervise contractors or complex employees
- Represent the association in association-wide matters, such as in community meetings, developer dealings, appeals of tax assessments, or contacts with government officials
- In some cases, grant variances or modifications to the existing rules or regulations
- Oversee the architectural and environmental integrity of the complex
- Inspect and maintain common property, including grounds, facilities, utilities; and in condominiums and cooperatives, structural systems such as plumbing, heating, electrical, exterior, roof, and elevator
- Regulate owner sublets and rentals, and regulate and exercise control over the sale of the units to assure that the original conditions of the complex are met and included in all documents, and also exercise the right to approve or reject purchasers
- Communicate with members about board activities, meetings, rules, regulations, fiscal standing, and any proposed or pending assessment
- Maintain adequate insurance on the property, including the bonding and insuring of board officers, fire insurance, title insurance, and liability insurance
- Prevent injury to persons living on or visiting the property
- Oversee any services provided by the complex, whether maintenance, education, child care, health care, social programming, or cultural events; oversee security concerns, traffic lights, and quality-of-life issues
- In some cases, mediate disputes among homeowners and members
- Attend board and association meetings, be informed and knowledgeable about association business
- Act at all times in a professional and responsible manner as an association fiduciary, use good business judgment, fol-

If the board fails to fulfill its duties, board members can, in some cases, be held personally liable.

low the rules and procedures of the association's documents and public laws, act promptly and with diligence, act with equanimity and fairness toward all members of the association, refrain from any acts of discrimination, refrain from arbitrary or capricious decision making, and refrain from any self-dealing or promotion of self-interest

SUBDIVISIONS AND ASSOCIATIONS
ESTABLISHED BY COVENANTS IN THE DEED

A subdivision is a neighborhood of individual plots carved or divided from one large block of land. Developers usually plan, build, and sell the homes in the subdivision. The developer also sets up the homeowner's association as a part of the plan, and usually controls the initial board. As the units are sold, the association is gradually turned over to the real homeowners' board.

Forty years after a subdivision was established with covenants in each deed restricting the property to residential use only, the community had changed substantially and the developer wanted to add a supermarket. The court ruled that the covenants prohibited that despite changes in the surrounding area.

Homeowners in a subdivision get a deed to the property, with the full ownership of the house and land. Common grounds—streets, playgrounds, recreational sites—are deeded to the homeowner's association for use by members. Every homeowner is required, by a covenant in the deed, to be a member of the association. Homeowners get one vote in the association, regardless of the size of their lots. The association is also controlled by articles of incorporation and its bylaws.

The fact that the homeowner's association is set up by a covenant in all of the deeds, sometimes known as *covenants, conditions, and restrictions* or CC&Rs, has bearing on the situation of a subdivision owner. A covenant—or agreement—can be placed in a deed by a landowner who divides off portions of a main block of property. A covenant is said to run with the land, so that the same restriction applies no matter who owns the property.

Like the land, a covenant can last forever. When faced with a homeowner dispute arising from a covenant, the courts almost always uphold the covenant, even when it seems unreasonable, ridiculous, or outmoded.

A covenant that is illegal as a matter of law or policy, or that discriminates, will not be enforced. Covenants that attempt to prohibit sales or rentals to minorities are unenforceable. In one case, a court held that a restrictive covenant limiting property use to single-family dwellings should not be enforced as a matter of public policy when it was used to try to prevent a group home for retarded children.

The homeowner's association is created by and charged with enforcement of the covenants. Some developers have tried to anticipate that needs of homeowners will change and put a provision in the deed permitting a vote of two-thirds of the owners to alter the covenants.

Even when a covenant can be changed, the change will not come easily. An architectural committee or board cannot casually waive a provision that came about through the covenant.

Another peculiarity of the covenant form is that it can be enforced not only by the homeowner's association, but by the original landowner or developer, and by any other person who took the land with a similar covenant. Neighbor A could sue neighbor B to enforce a covenant, even though the association decides not to take action.

When one homeowner in a subdivision built a 15-foot-by-15-foot shed on the property, a neighbor sued to have it removed, based on a covenant that prohibited property owners from adding new permanent structures to the property. The court ruled that the covenant controlled, and the shed had to be removed.

CONDOMINIUMS AND JOINT OWNERSHIP

A condominium is an individual unit that exists as part of a larger project. The unit can be an apartment, a town house, even an office or a boat. A condominium refers to a particular species of ownership, not the actual building.

The condominium owner gets a deed to the individual living unit. The ownership of all common space, the land, and even the buildings themselves (shell and major structural systems) are owned jointly by all of the unit owners. Condo owners have assigned percentages of ownership in the common areas based on the size of their units, the value of the unit, or, at times, on a per unit basis. The owner's mortgage loan payment covers a portion of the building mortgage loan and building real estate taxes.

The condo owner owns the floor, the ceiling, the four walls of the unit, and all the space in between, but not the halls, the roof, or the land. Unlike a tenant, the condo owner is responsible for the costs of interior repairs, while the association has an easement interest in buildingwide systems that exist from apartment to apartment. A broken toilet is the responsibility of the unit owner; a leaking pipe in the walls is the responsibility of the association.

The condominium documents make each homeowner a member of the association. The key document in terms of creating a condominium owner's association is the *declaration* or *declaration of condominium,* which is required by state law. The declaration contains the rights and responsibilities of owners within the association and outlines the method of operation for the association. The unit owner's deed states that the owner takes the property subject to the declaration, and assigns the percentage of ownership that the unit will have. The declaration is recorded in land records like a deed and, like a covenant, it runs with the land.

The developer of a condominium project is known as the *declarant.* As with the subdivision board, the declarant usually controls the initial board until the units in the condo are sold.

The association is responsible for the physical maintenance of the outside structures of the buildings, along with major systems, such as plumbing, heating, and wiring. Maintaining and upgrading these systems can be costly, and the association must collect a maintenance fee from condo owners and maintain an adequate reserve fund to cover emergencies or major capital expenditures, such as replacing a boiler that explodes. In contrast, the subdivision association is responsible only for maintaining common buildings and common grounds.

Some of the major disagreements between individual owners and the condo association board come down to who will pay for what. If first-floor owner A has a leak, is it because of the negligence of second-floor owner B, right above, in which case B would have to compensate A? Or is it because the roof is leaking, in which case the association is liable to both A and B?

The interlocking nature of condo ownership means that what happens inside one unit can easily affect what happens in the unit next door. For this reason, condominium associations have house rules that affect quality-of-life concerns.

There are many variations on condo ownership, all with a homeowner's association, including:

- *Condo building.* A building in which all of the units or apartments are owned individually by condo owners.
- *Fee simple town house condominium.* The unit owner also owns the land under the town house, while common areas are still under joint ownership.
- *Time-share condos.* Each purchaser has an ownership interest in the property, but has the right to occupy the unit or to use the common areas only during a designated period each year. Problems can arise within the unit ownership about responsibility with maintenance—who caused what?—and in forming a reasonable connection with the condo association's work in general.
- *Lifecare housing.* Residents are limited to senior citizens who for a large fee above their mortgage loan payment can get specialized services, such as meals, nursing care, housecleaning, and other benefits. Questions about the exclusion of children in seniors-only complexes have been raised. In the majority of cases, the right to restrict children has been upheld.

COOPERATIVES AND SHARE OWNERSHIP

Cooperative ownership differs in many important respects from the ownership of a condominium.

Co-op owners do not own any real estate, but only shares in a corporation that owns real estate. The individual owner does not get a deed. The only deed is to a building of individual apartments, which is owned and held by the cooperative corporation.

The unit purchasers get a proprietary lease to the unit, designating them as the proprietor of the apartment, with exclusive control over it. In the share ownership documents, the co-op owner is made a member of the homeowner's association. Shares are keyed to the size and location of the unit, and votes in the association are determined by the number of shares an owner has.

Co-op owners do not own any real estate, but only shares in a corporation that owns real estate.

State laws authorize and establish the homeowner's association in the cooperative and often set guidelines for it. The association must have a charter, articles of incorporation, and bylaws. Conditions the cooperative owner must follow are further stated in the prospectus, the proprietary lease, the cooperative corporation's code of regulations, and house or community rules.

In the initial stages of development or conversion from a rental property to a cooperative ownership property, the board is dominated by the sponsor.

The cooperative building is owned by the association and consequently is jointly owned by all the shareholders. The association pays the mortgage, tax, and insurance. Cooperative shareowners pay large fees to cover those costs, usually amounting to about half the monthly maintenance fee.

Even more so than in a building condominium, the interests of cooperative shareowners are uniquely linked to one another. Keeping an adequate reserve account for emergency building repairs and capital needs is critical. Decisions by the board or association about buildingwide repairs or amenities affect each owner, since the result may be an assessment or increased maintenance fee for each share.

As with condominiums, quality-of-life issues, spelled out in the rules and regulations, become of enormous importance since cooperative owners all live in one building.

VOLUNTARY ASSOCIATIONS

Voluntary citizen's associations participate in civic affairs, conduct neighborhood improvement campaigns, organize social events and activities, undertake community patrols or hire security forces, lobby for their needs, and sometimes bring lawsuits to press united concerns. In addition, residents of some communities may be eligible to become members of a golf course or country club. All of these associations are very different from those that have mandatory membership as a condition of property ownership.

Participation of Developer or Sponsor

Early on in the life of the complex, the developer or sponsor still owns the major portion of the property. In a very literal sense, the developer or sponsor has control of the homeowner's association.

This can raise concerns later. The developer wants to finish off the project and is not necessarily interested in long-term capital improvements. The goal of the developer is to sell the remaining units, and one technique for accomplishing that is to keep the maintenance fees of the homeowner's association low.

When homeowners later take over the majority on the board, they may find that maintenance tasks have piled up, but the money to deal with them has not. In trying to keep the fees low, developers or sponsors may intentionally underfund the reserve for major expenditures.

If an emergency arises, homeowners with insufficient reserves face difficult decisions—raising the monthly fee to the members, making a special assessment, postponing the expenditure, or taking out a loan.

In other cases, the association's coffers are not full at the outset because the sponsor has not been paying fees for the unoccupied

---

One condominium that was left without sufficient funds by the developer took the worst course. To save money, the association turned off security lights at a time when crime was rising and more lighting was needed. Despite repeated requests from members, the board delayed. When a woman was assaulted, she sued the board for damages.

or unsold units. Every unit is supposed to pay fees, even unsold ones, which still belong to the sponsor. If homeowners take over the association and find a deficit or other neglect of duties, they may have to seek compensation from the initial board or the developer. Often lawsuits follow, and in more than one case, the developer has gone out of business, leaving the association with a shortage.

The homeowner's association is also obligated to follow up on problems created by the developer or sponsor because of shoddy work or product failure. The association often represents homeowners when problems arise for which the developer should be responsible. In some cases, the state attorney general's office, which may be responsible for the registration and oversight of developments, can assist the homeowner's association.

Rules and Regulations

Day-to-day life of homeowners is most directly affected by the rules and regulations made and enforced by the homeowner's association.

The rules and regulations can be extensive and make complexes something of a controlled environment—many of the nuisances of other neighborhoods are eliminated or diminished. On the other hand, the homeowner's freedom is curtailed. Clashes can arise between individual needs and community regulations.

In general, the rule of nondisruption prevails, in which discomfort of any homeowner is appeased. The area of pets is a vivid example. Some small number of people have a problem with dogs, while a small percentage own dogs. Yet homeowner's associations have increasingly sought ways to ban a person's best friend. The association tends to respond to the squeaky wheel that complains, but may be less responsive to the minority that stands to benefit.

Rules and regulations are subject to amendment and change, which can upset any homeowner who relied on them at the time of purchase. Courts are beginning to scrutinize how the rules were adopted and whether a rule has a retroactive application that is unfair—for example, banning pets when many homeowners have them already.

The important issues covered in the rules and regulations fall into five broad areas:

1. Zoninglike issues, such as restrictions on expansion of buildings, parking, and business use of the property; permits for construction; architectural, environmental, and esthetic concerns, such as paint colors and type of landscaping that are permitted; exclusion of certain items, such as satellite dishes
2. Easements for other owners, including preservation of air, light, and view for each property; and protections to common property, such as lakes and rivers
3. Protection from common private nuisances, including restrictions on noise, trash, pollution, use of chemicals; and the affirmative obligation to maintain unit property by cutting grass and preventing eyesores (see chapter 10)
4. Control over and maintenance of the character of the community, including limitations on sale and rental without board approval
5. Quality-of-life issues, such as age of residents, pets, and the definition of a family

COMMON PROBLEMS

There are a number of recurring issues concerning the rules and regulations of homeowner's associations.

Architectural Restrictions   One of the key functions of the homeowner's association is to oversee architectural and environmental restrictions. These are particularly important to owners of single-family residences in subdivisions, who may desire to fashion their property to their own tastes. The role of the association is to preserve and enhance the property by exercising some control.

An architectural and environmental control committee is usually empowered to hear requests and make recommendations to the board. One major justification for the architectural review is that lenders demand it, to make sure that the property value is sustained.

Some architectural matters may be out of the control of the

committee because they were established in the covenants or declaration. The covenant may prohibit any permanent buildings being added to the property. The committee would not be empowered to waive that restriction and, in fact, could be liable to other homeowners if it did.

But some restrictions are left open-ended. If a homeowner wants to add a room, the plans may need approval by the board to assure that they fit within existing community standards. The rules may insist on certain materials, or prohibit other materials; may require certain colors in painting; a certain type of roof tiling; a particular style of lettering for address numbers; a style of mailbox; a ban on all fences, or a limit on the height and material of fences. Other rules may establish the exact landscaping, grass, and trees.

In condo or co-op buildings, homeowners are often prevented from making structural changes, such as removing a wall or adding a door, without board approval. The times, hours, and months when interior construction or remodeling can be undertaken may be restricted.

Because architectural changes are often based on personal esthetics, the review process can be contentious. When challenged, the role and decisions of architectural review committees have been sustained by courts so long as they act reasonably and in good faith. However, these committees are required to have mechanisms and procedures for establishing and reviewing architectural standards and homeowner requests.

When a homeowner was ordered to root up eight date palm trees planted in contravention to a rule that prohibited any plantings without permission, the court said that the association had failed to follow procedures and guidelines in enforcing the rules and had provided insufficient evidence of administrative review. The court in that case reversed the association's order.

Family Challenges are often raised when individual unit owners are restricted from having certain types of family relationships.

Homeowner's associations have been largely successful in defending no-children rules and regulations in senior communities. But associations have gotten into trouble when they try to restrict children below a certain age, such as children under 12. In one case, a court held that that was an unreasonable rule, since there is little difference between an 11-year-old and a 12-year-old.

Courts have also held that group homes for the retarded cannot be banned, as a matter of public policy. Associations in some cities have been prevented from discriminating against gay couples.

By and large, courts uphold association rules so long as they meet a standard of reasonableness, and most are found to do so. As in the zoning area, the definition of "family" will continue to be reevaluated in future matters.

Pets   A variety of restrictions have been placed on pets by homeowner's associations—requiring leashing even of cats; requiring pet cleanup; limiting the size of pets; prohibiting some pets such as pit bulldogs; limiting the number of pets; limiting the total weight of all pets in a household; and banishing the creatures altogether.

One area of current conflict is pet amortization, by which some associations amended their early rules that allowed pets to adopt new rules that prohibit pets. Since they could not require homeowners who already had pets to get rid of them, some pets were grandfathered (or "granddogged") in. But once that pet dies, that's it; the owner may not replace it. To regulate this situation, homeowners have been required to register their pets, along with physical descriptions and ages of the animals.

Vehicles   Homeowner's associations are empowered to make traffic rules, control parking, and limit the number and type of vehicles that may be parked on the premises. Some associations prohibit trucks or commercial vehicles from being parked overnight on the property. Courts have been quick to uphold parking restrictions, most of which are part of the deed and documents delivered to each unit owner.

Right to Rent or Sublet   A homeowner may have to get approval to rent or sublet the unit. Associations may refuse to allow homeowners the right to rent, or, alternatively, may levy a surcharge on the unit on the theory that a renter will cause more wear and tear to the common facilities than an owner who has a vested interest.

Also, resident and nonresident homeowners can be treated differently, even in assessments of fees or the right to serve on the board. Courts have held that resident status is not a prohibited basis of discrimination for a private homeowner's association.

Courts generally have upheld the provisions inhibiting or prohibiting rentals. Some associations, recognizing the hardship on an owner who is transferred or facing a tough sales market, have amended these rules, feeling that an empty unit detracts from neighborhood security.

Approval of Purchaser   Homeowner's associations have the right to approve the purchaser of a unit and, in some cases, the right of first refusal, meaning that they can buy the unit at the same price as a bidder and the bidder has to yield.

The right to approve a purchaser is especially rigorous in the cooperative situation, in which boards are known to conduct lengthy interviews. Yet because of the financial interdependence of a condominium or cooperative, courts have granted association boards extraordinary flexibility in deciding whether to reject a purchaser.

As long as the association has not discriminated on some prohibited basis—race, religion, ethnicity, color, gender, and in some cases, sexual identity—the board can reject prospective purchasers. The board need only give a fair hearing to the prospective purchaser and make a decision that is not malicious.

The board is also entitled to review all the purchasing documents prior to closing. This allows the board to be assured that the covenants, restrictions, and declarations that establish the association are properly included.

Responsibility for Repairs   A frequent problem in co-ops and condos arises over the responsibility for repairs affecting an individual unit in a multiple-unit building. The cause of structural problems can be difficult to ascertain, leading to conflicting determinations of legal responsibility between the unit owner, cooperative association, neighboring owner, or other.

For example, if a unit owner discovers significant cracks or holes in the walls, they could be the result of a leak in the roof. As part of the building structure, the building association is responsible. Or, they could be the result of an unusual impact inside the apartment—a bookcase bolted to a wall improperly or the fall of a guest, for which the unit owner is responsible. Or, they could be the result of the bathtub next door overflowing, for which the other unit owner is responsible. Finally, they could have been caused by outside entities—shoddy contractors hired by the sponsor or prior owner, or drilling in the street.

Repair problems go to the heart of legal responsibilities in a cooperative or condominium. The association is responsible for structural problems and systems, defined as everything inside the walls, the structure holding up and covering the building, and common space; the unit owner is responsible for problems inside the four walls. The original ownership documents speak specifically to the division of ownership responsibility.

In many instances, homeowners believe that the association should bear responsibility, and yet it declines to do so. In these situations, the unit owner must attempt to trace the repair problem to its source by getting a detailed, written opinion from an inspector, contractor, or repair person.

In the case of the cracks in the walls, the inspector should note the extent of the cracks, the type of investigation into the source, the cause or likely cause, the types of repairs that are necessary, and the cost. In addition, the unit owner should photograph the problem, and work to persuade the appropriate responsible party to pay for the repairs. If the association assumes liability for the damage, it is probably obligated to pay only the actual costs of repair. Damage to clothing or furniture might be covered. Only in the rare case will an association reimburse other consequential costs, such as lost rental income or substitute housing.

Building insurance might cover certain repairs, and the unit owner should try to check the policy protections.

When another unit owner has caused the problem, the association does not take action in most situations. The homeowner needs to contact the neighbor directly for reimbursement.

Damage caused by another unit may be covered by the insurance policy of either or both units.

If the problem is within the unit, the unit owner is liable for damages. Homeowner's insurance may cover some damages—for example, if an appliance explodes.

Maintenance problems can become particularly ticklish in the time-share condo. All of the owners are responsible for maintenance costs, particularly when they cannot be traced to the negligence or deliberate acts of any individual participating in the time-share.

ENFORCEMENT OF RULES AND REGULATIONS

How rules and regulations are enforced varies, based on the association's design. There is no standard procedure.

One thing that all associations do have, however, is the right to place a lien on a unit owner's property for the nonpayment of dues, fees, assessments, or fines; and, generally, to hold the unit owner personally liable, as well. If so inclined, the homeowner's association could initiate proceedings to foreclose on the property for default for failure to pay dues (see chapter 12).

The placement of a lien is the final stage in the enforcement process. Prior to that, a homeowner is likely to get an informal call or letter from the board or management agent, stating the violation. Next, the board sends a letter, asking that the situation be corrected.

Sometimes a homeowner can request a hearing or an opportunity to speak to the board or to present a defense. But there is no legal requirement for homeowner's associations to afford due process to members in the same way that a court or public agency must. The association might try to mediate a solution, particularly when the issue at hand involves a complaint about a rules violation made by one neighbor against another.

The association could levy a fine or a use fee. A homeowner may also be required to correct the situation, such as tearing down aluminum siding prohibited by association rules. Vehicles could be towed if parking rules were violated. In addition, privileges can be taken away, such as the right to use the community pool or to park.

In some cases, a homeowner can be taken to court to enforce the penalty or may choose to go to court to stop the homeowner's association action. In general, courts have been sympathetic to the association's point of view.

HOMEOWNER CHALLENGES

Homeowner's associations have been given considerable latitude in enforcing their rules and regulations. As private associations, courts have ruled that the content of association rules is wide open, and that the associations may regulate areas that might not be subject to regulation by public government.

Procedural failure is the one area in which a homeowner is most likely to be successful in a legal challenge to a homeowner's association decision. Courts are clear that associations must closely follow the procedures set out in their own rules and regulations. Failure to do so may invalidate the decision.

Homeowner's associations are also bound to follow state laws on corporation procedures (since they are nonprofit corporations) and, where appropriate, those on homeowner's association procedure. Other public laws that contradict the board's decision may need to be heeded.

In addition, a standard of reasonableness will be applied to all of the actions of the board.

If confronted with a decision that seems unfair or unwarranted, a homeowner should investigate the procedural basis. That involves finding the answers to a series of questions:

- Who made the decision and how was that person empowered to do so?
- Was the decision made by the appropriate entity, for example, by a vote of the association as a whole as opposed to the board alone?
- If a vote, was it passed by the required number and percentage of votes?
- Did only qualified persons vote?
- What notes or minutes recite the decision and the reasons for it?
- What association documents, rules, regulations, or bylaws provide the authority for the decision?
- What evidence was gathered by the decision maker prior to making the decision?
- What notice was provided to members, either as a group or individually?
- Was an opportunity to be heard provided, and, if not, should one have been permitted either by board rules or general policy considerations?
- What justification was provided for the decision's intent, scope, and reasonableness?
- How and when were the standards at issue made or promulgated, and were the appropriate procedures followed in doing so?

- What contradictory decisions have been made in similar situations?
- What public laws authorize the decision?
- What public laws contradict or supersede the decision?
- What limits are placed on the board's authority under state laws permitting condo or co-op associations, or by decisions of judges that affect the reach of homeowner's association decision making?

If the homeowner finds that the procedures were not followed in any significant way, it may be possible to challenge the decision. The challenge needs to go to the board and, if necessary, could be raised in court. The point is that boards are more likely to be scrutinized about the way a decision is made than whether it is an appropriate subject contentwise.

FISCAL CONCERNS

Value of the property and the cost of assessments are enormously important. Especially in condominiums and cooperatives, maintenance fees can become a major budget item to unit owners. When the assessments are increased, the owner naturally may become concerned.

Fiscal responsibility is one of the key charges of the association's board.

Fiscal responsibility is one of the key charges of the association's board. The board members are fiduciaries for the association and are entrusted with making prudent decisions, based on research, knowledge, and good business judgment.

There are three areas that send off fireworks in the fiscal area: mismanagement, poor planning, and fraud or self-dealing.

Although a manager or an accountant may prepare plans and statements, the board is ultimately responsible for all fiscal decisions. If fraud occurs, board members could be held personally liable as well as criminally responsible.

If homeowners have concerns about the fiscal integrity of

board members, they have a right to see the association's reports and documents. If the concerns are well founded, the homeowner could raise the issue with the board members and with insurers of the board members. A public agency, such as the state attorney general's office, may be empowered to investigate complaints.

Homeowners might consider also amassing a voting campaign to replace the directors. If the problems are serious, homeowners could take the association or board members to court.

LEGAL STRATEGIES OF HOMEOWNERS IN ASSOCIATION DISPUTES

When a unit owner disagrees with the decision of an association board, the claim can be pursued with several action steps:

1. Raise the issue informally with a board member.
2. Follow up with a letter to the board.
3. Discuss the problem with other unit owners and seek their support.
4. Ask for documents concerning the matter from the board or manager.
5. Attend a board meeting and present the complaint or issue in a calm, documented way. Ask for a specific date or time frame for a response from the board.
6. Negotiate with the board.
7. Seek a solution by mediator or arbitrator who can hear both sides of the issue and make a decision.
8. Raise the issue at the annual meeting of the membership.
9. Run a slate of candidates to oppose the existing board.
10. File a complaint with a government agency, such as the attorney general's office, or seek a remedy in court.

DEALING WITH THE HOMEOWNER'S ASSOCIATION

The body of law that affects homeowner's associations is new and developing, as the number of associations grows dramatically throughout the country. As an association in which membership is required by the terms of the deed, proprietary lease, or other documents, the association is granted broad authority over decisions affecting the housing complex or building. Homeowner's associations are common in subdivisions and planned communities, and are necessary components of condominiums and cooperatives.

A homeowner's association is generally responsible for collecting dues and making disbursements, maintaining the common space, and making and enforcing rules about the common space and about individual-unit ownership. The board of a homeowner's association is granted enormous power to make decisions.

Since homeowners have agreed to be subjected to the rules and decisions of the homeowner's association, courts normally uphold its rules and decisions. The few exceptions have been when the decisions were arbitrary, capricious, illegal, in derogation of duty, failed to employ a standard of reasonableness, or failed to follow established internal procedures.

Homeowners who have a problem with association decisions or rules should raise the issue with the board, attempt to negotiate, and can, if necessary, sue in civil court.

18

Working
at Home

The use of a home for work touches on two central legal concerns: zoning and occupancy rules, and federal income tax laws. In some cases, the homeowner who works from home is affected by other rules and regulations. For example, the operator of a medical office or a day-care center may have to comply with the physical requirements established by state and local health and welfare laws.

ZONING AND NEIGHBORHOOD RESTRICTIONS

Local zoning ordinances commonly place limits on the operation of a business in the home. This is especially true in areas that are zoned for single-family residences. Depending on the type of work or business, communities may ignore some of these ordinances—sometimes for no other reason than that many people who work at home are hidden from public scrutiny. Often, concerns arise only when neighbors lodge an official complaint.

In many subdivisions, co-ops, or condominiums, the rules and regulations of a homeowner's association prohibit home businesses.

Compliance with local laws or insurance rules may be particularly important when the work involves frequent visitors or clients, advertising, or the delivery of products. In addition, when services are involved that require special permits or licenses—such as the care of children, the elderly, medical patients, or the preparation of food—there is increased government scrutiny.

Some residential zoning schemes do permit the operation of home businesses. But there may be limits on the types of work for which the home can be used, as well as the amount of space in the home that can be used for business purposes. Zoning in mixed residential-business zones usually broadens the definition of acceptable businesses in the zone, but use limits may still demand that the work is consistent with the character of the neighborhood (see chapter 4).

Where business use is permitted, there may be other zoning or neighborhood limitations that may prohibit signs, require off-street parking, or prohibit the overnight parking of trucks or commercial vehicles.

Before setting up operations, the homeowner's safest course is to check the zoning laws that apply. The mere fact that a prior owner used the home for a business use may not be conclusive—for example, if the type of business was different, the prior owner had a nonconforming use of the property that predated the adoption of a zoning plan, or if the prior owner had a variance that applied only to the use by that owner.

In some circumstances in which the zoning is unfavorable, a homeowner can seek a zoning variance (see chapter 4). The number of people working at home has expanded so greatly that many communities have been forced to revise and update their zoning laws to reflect the times.

Operations that are illegal under any circumstances—running a gambling club or selling products not authorized by law—can subject a homeowner to criminal penalties, and in the most severe circumstances could endanger the property itself under forfeiture laws (see chapter 16).

Nuisance

The business use of property might raise questions of a nuisance. Even if a business is permitted under zoning laws, neighbors might have valid objections if it is noxious, inconsistent with the neighborhood, or interferes with their enjoyment of the property.

A business use of the property might be permitted in a residential area. But if the business is a recording studio that blasts music into the neighborhood, draws multiple late-night visitors, and involves trucks loading and unloading recording equipment in early morning hours, neighbors may complain that it is a nuisance. Or if the business is a home chemical plant that creates a reasonable fear of explosion or sends the fumes of toxic chemicals into the neighbors' windows, a nuisance claim could develop.

Permits and Licenses

The home business may need a special certificate of occupancy or building permit from a local building authority. This depends largely on the type of business. The building authority may require alterations to the facility or grounds, as well—fire exit, wheelchair ramp, fire alarm, parking spaces, or walkways.

Certain business uses are regulated by other agencies. A health department may have authority to review a doctor's office to see that medicine is kept in a locked container and waste is properly discarded. A kitchen used as a baking outlet for Pa's Pies may have to fit certain requirements.

Day-care centers for children, the elderly, or the disabled are regulated in many communities, and some of these regulations are specific. The hours of operation, number of persons cared for, size of the yard, and type of available play equipment for children all might be mandated before a permit will be granted.

In addition, in many communities, the home-business operator needs to get a small business license and pay a business tax or fee.

Insurance

Standard homeowner's insurance does not cover business use of residential property (see chapter 1).

Prior to opening a business that brings visitors or clients to the home, additional liability coverage may be necessary. Homeowner's insurance could refuse to cover injuries suffered by visitors to a business operation unless special coverage is in effect. One slip or trip, and the homeowner could be faced with a liability claim.

If the business involves a significant investment in equipment, the homeowner should make certain that casualty insurance will cover business equipment and is sufficient to meet a loss. Standard casualty coverage does not include business-related personal property.

Qualifying for Special Federal Income Tax Treatment

Under federal income tax laws, homeowners may be able to take tax deductions for the expense of operating a home office.

To qualify for federal income tax deductions, the home-office space must be used exclusively and regularly for business purposes. The space also must be used as a principal place of business or as a place to meet customers, clients, or patients in the course of doing business.

In essence, with the exception of day-care and inventory storage spaces, the business space must be a separate room used for one purpose: the business. A separate unattached structure on the property—studio, garage, or barn—can also qualify for the deductions.

The business in the space must be conducted regularly, but it need not be full-time or the sole source of income for the homeowner. The homeowner could have one job and a business on the side. The police officer who operates a vitamin sales company from home qualifies; the teacher who has a recording company qualifies, too. The hobbyist or an occasional dabbler in business ventures does not qualify, even if some income is earned.

The home space must also be the business's main center of operation. In some cases, the owners of stores who had offices at home did not qualify for the business deduction, because, the IRS said, the principal business location was the store.

Recently, the U.S. Supreme Court ruled that a taxpayer who worked as an anesthesiologist could not take a home office deduction. The anesthesiologist worked at three hospitals, none of which provided him with office space, for 30 to 35 hours a week. He spent 2 to 3 hours daily in his home office, a spare bedroom, studying, bookkeeping, billing, and preparing for operations. The Court found that his treatment of patients was his most important activity. And since he treated patients at the three hospitals, rather than at home, he was not entitled to the home office deduction.

If a homeowner works for someone else but uses an office at home, the use of the office must be for the employer's convenience. Alternatively, the homeowner can deduct expenses if the employer pays rent. An employee who keeps a home work space simply because it is handy is not entitled to tax deductions.

On the other hand, an employee who earns money on the side from independent work contracts can take the deductions if the home space otherwise qualifies as the regular, exclusive, and principal location for the side business.

In the 1991 tax reporting year, Form 8829 was introduced for homeowners using a portion of the home for business purposes. This form is an addition to Schedule C, required to report the profit or loss from a business. Form 8829 requires the homeowner to measure the total square feet of the home and the square feet set aside for business use, and to calculate the exact percentage of the home used for business purposes.

LICENSED CARE

A separate set of rules applies to homeowners who operate a licensed day-care facility for children, the elderly, or the disabled. In these cases, the business use of the space need not be exclusive. In the daytime the living room is a nursery and at night, it is a living room. The day-care center operator can still take the business use deductions, but must calculate them on a time-space formula.

FEDERAL INCOME TAX DEDUCTIONS

Deductions for the use of a home office may not exceed the gross income the business earns. This recent restriction is intended to eliminate those persons who had a sham office solely for the purpose of qualifying for tax deductions.

Homeowners who operate a qualifying business from home can deduct certain business expenses from their income. Direct expenses, such as the actual costs of constructing the business space, can be fully deducted. Indirect expenses that are related to the operation of the home (and the business space as a part of it) also can be deducted, but only in proportion to the business space used.

Indirect expenses that are eligible for a proportional deduction include real estate taxes; utilities and services (including gas, electric, trash removal, cleaning); business telephone calls or lines; insurance; repairs; security systems; losses from fire, theft, or other casualties; and deductible mortgage loan interest. In addition, depreciation is available on permanent improvements to the home, or on capital expenditures such as furniture, and the home itself. Depreciation cannot be applied to the land.

EFFECTS ON FEDERAL INCOME TAX FROM SALE OF HOME WITH BUSINESS USE

When homeowners sell a home with a business use, they can consider that two sales have occurred—the sale of the portion of the property that has been used solely as a residence and the sale of the property that has been used solely for business.

The homeowner does not have to pay income tax on the gain from the sale of the residential portion of the property if it is reinvested in a new home within two years of the sale of the old home (see chapters 11 and 20). The portion of the property allocated to a business does not fall under the reinvestment rule. The homeowner must pay income tax on the gain on that part of the home. The proportion is determined in the same way that it is in calculating deductions—with the business use being designated a certain percentage of the whole.

The homeowner must pay the tax on the portion of the gain allocated to the business in the year in which the home is sold. Unlike the residential portion, the tax payment cannot be postponed or deferred.

There is a glimmer of possibility, though, of avoiding tax on the gain. This need be paid only if the homeowner deducted expenses for the business use of the home in the year that the property is sold. If the business use was abandoned prior to the sale, or if the homeowner does not claim deductions for business use during the year of the sale, all of the property can be treated as a home, and the complete gain can be reinvested in a new home. The payment of the tax can also be postponed until the time period for reinvestment has elapsed. The homeowner should consult with a qualified accountant first.

The business use of the property also can affect the calculation of the adjusted basis of the old home, if the homeowner has deducted depreciation costs during the time of the ownership. Establishing the adjusted basis of the old home is the first step toward calculating the gain realized on the sale. Depreciation allowed in any year for the business use of a home is subtracted from the original purchase price, to create an adjusted basis. When the adjusted basis is lowered, the gain on the sale is increased. It is the gain, of course, which is subject to income tax.

OLDER CITIZEN'S EXCLUSION AND SALE OF HOME WITH BUSINESS USE

Ordinarily, a homeowner who is 55 years or older is entitled to a once-in-a-lifetime exclusion of up to $125,000 in gain on the sale of residential property. It does not have to be reported as income on the homeowner's federal return (see chapters 11 and 20). This exclusion applies only to residential property; income tax has to be paid on any gain that is allocated to the portion of the property used for business.

The IRS provides opportunities for older citizens with a business in the home to qualify for the full exclusion. The business use is merged into the residential use for the purposes of the $125,000 exclusion *if* there has been a business use for fewer than two of the five years preceding the date of the sale. The homeowner could end the business use three years before the anticipated sale and qualify for the exclusion on the whole property. Homeowners should consult with a qualified accountant.

Even if the business use doesn't have to be reported as a gain, depreciation taken during the years of a business is used to calculate an adjusted basis for the old home (as calculated with the residential reinvestment exclusion).

RECORD KEEPING

Record keeping is especially necessary for the homeowner who uses a portion of the home for a business. In particular, because of the specialized tax concerns on sale of the home, homeowners should keep all tax records and backup material, as well as clear records of depreciation and capital-improvement claims and the information on which these amounts are based.

ENJOYING THE BENEFITS OF THE HOME WORK SPACE

The business use of a home can enhance a homeowner's enjoyment of the property by permitting the owner to earn an income at home and by placing the homeowner in a position to take advantage of federal income tax deductions.

Before using the home for a business purpose, homeowners should investigate factors that will affect the property: zoning, neighborhood association rules, neighbor demands, and the requirements of local licensing bodies.

19

Leasing
a Portion
of a Home

In renting out a second unit, an apartment or room, the homeowner takes on new obligations. As a landlord, the homeowner must conform to laws about rental property, including
zoning regulations, rules on lease clauses, building code requirements, and the application of antidiscrimination or other laws.
These laws vary from city to city; by and large, local ordinances
will dictate the owner's actions.

In nearly every location, though, the homeowner is responsible
for providing tenants with safe and reasonably well-maintained
quarters and for observing the tenant's privacy.

Landlords get benefits from the rental of property. In addition
to the rental income, federal income tax laws can be used advan-
tageously (see chapter 11).

THE HOMEOWNER AS LANDLORD

Nearly every city has many laws that apply to rental situations. However, not all of these laws apply to owners with a limited number of units. Many of the toughest laws specifically exclude owner-occupied housing. In other cases, the laws exclude buildings with two, three, or four units.

This means that the homeowner who rents a portion of the property may be held to less strict standards of operation than the owner of an apartment complex or a high-rise building. This does not mean, though, that homeowners can do anything they like in managing the rental property. Certain minimum standards have to be met, and those minimums are more stringent than for homeowners living on the property with no tenants. The mere fact of renting out property for income imposes certain obligations on the landlord.

ZONING REQUIREMENTS

In order to lease a portion of the property, the home must be in a zone that permits rentals or multiunit buildings.

In order to lease a portion of the property, the home must be in a zone that permits rentals or multiunit buildings. The most limited residential zones—those permitting only single-family homes—would not permit an owner to rent a portion of the property. Zoning laws can also restrict the types of people who may become tenants—for example, a large group of unrelated persons, such as students, may be prohibited from living in a certain zone.

Since zoning laws vary enormously, the homeowner with rental property must scrutinize the local laws.

BUILDING, HEALTH, AND FIRE CODES

Cities and states have building codes, health codes, and fire codes, which affect rental properties. These codes might require the rental unit to have a separate bathroom, a separate entrance, fire escape doors, smoke detectors, a separate parking space, and so on.

Bedrooms in a rental unit may be required to be of a certain size and have a minimum number of windows or access to outside light and air. Working kitchen appliances may be required, and specific provisions may be necessary, such as outer door locks or window guards to prevent young children from falling out.

The general areas in building and health code laws that apply to rental units include

- Plumbing
- Electrical
- Hot and cold running water
- Heating
- Garbage disposal
- Sewage
- Windows and doors
- Adequate fire escape routes
- Security
- Postal box

Although some state and city laws may not apply to owner-occupied multifamily units, the owner will be required to meet standards of habitability (see following), and the effect might be the same.

CONDOMINIUMS, COOPERATIVES, AND SUBDIVISIONS

Rentals may be more restricted in condominiums, cooperatives, or subdivisions (see chapter 17).

Cooperatives frequently restrict the rental of units, even when the unit owner has been relocated to another city or wishes to share the space with a roommate. As long as these rules are laid out clearly at the time of purchase and are followed uniformly, the owner must abide by them.

Some co-ops and condos that do permit owners to rent the unit charge a onetime fee, sometimes known as a sublet fee or flip charge. The reasoning is that a tenant will be less conscientious about maintenance of the common areas than the unit owner, and the fee is to cover any extra repairs. Of course, it also discourages renting and provides additional income for the co-op or condo.

Condo, cooperative, and subdivision owners who rent out all or part of a unit are landlords, and all the usual rules apply—about repairs, notices, evictions, and even following special city rules such as installing window guards if young children are in the unit.

TENANT'S RIGHTS

The flip side of an owner's responsibility is a tenant's rights. A tenant is entitled to expect

- The apartment to be maintained in good condition
- Premises free from defects and dangerous conditions
- Quiet enjoyment of the premises without interference from the owner
- Privacy

STATE AND CITY LAWS ON OWNER RIGHTS AND RESPONSIBILITIES

Rental laws can set specific guidelines regarding the rights and responsibilities of owners and tenants. These laws vary considerably from city to city, but nearly everywhere they have grown enormously as legislatures seek to protect consumer-tenants.

The laws establishing owner responsibilities may exclude the owner with a limited number of rental units. City housing offices, local real estate associations, and even tenant organizations may provide booklets or materials on the duties of owners in the area.

Common areas on which these laws touch include:

- security deposits
- lease clauses
- termination
- tenant property storage
- repair costs of tenants
- rent increases
- privacy

ORAL AGREEMENT TO RENT

The rental of a unit can be established by a lease or by oral agreement. A very small number of states require residential rentals, or tenancies, to be in writing. A lease for longer than a year is only enforceable if it is in writing. Even if the rental agreement is verbal, the homeowner and the tenant still have legal responsibilities.

A verbal rental agreement is usually of a type known as *tenancy at will*. The landlord agrees to rent the unit for a fixed price, and the tenant pays that amount. A tenancy at will can be month to month or week to week, and it stays in force as long as both parties continue to consent—the landlord by doing nothing to terminate the situation, the tenant by paying the rent.

In order to terminate an oral tenancy at will, the landlord must usually give adequate notice, at least equal to one rental period. Although the rental agreement is verbal, the termination notice should be in writing. Often local and state laws require a written termination notice.

WRITTEN LEASE

A lease is a contractual agreement that contains the terms of the rental. Occasionally, courts will enforce verbal side agreements in residential rentals, but, for the most part, only written clauses are enforced. In many cities, local laws require certain provisions to be included in the lease, but beyond that, owners can shape the contract to meet their needs.

For example, the landlord could include a clause in the lease that no radios can be played after 11:00 P.M. Since there is no law that protects a tenant's right to play a radio, and if the tenant agreed by signing this lease, this would be a valid clause.

Lease forms are available from owner organizations, tenant organizations, and legal stationery shops. In order to assure that it is correct and up-to-date, the landlord should have a lawyer review a lease form prior to utilizing it.

The types of clauses that a lease normally covers include:

1. *Identification.* Name of the tenant, name of the owner, address of the property.
2. *Length of the lease.* How long the tenant will rent the property, including the first and last dates of occupancy.

3. *Rent.* Including any specific information as to where and how often it is to be paid; how it is to be paid, such as by check, delivered by hand to the owner; any penalties for late payment; and a clause that states that acceptance of late payment at any time does not relieve the tenant of the duty for timely payment at all other times. (Some local ordinances also limit the amount or imposition of late penalties.)

4. *Security deposit.* Including amount; an explanation of under what circumstances the deposit will be kept—for example, for damage to the property; the interest that will be paid on the security deposit; and the period of time after the tenant departs in which the owner will return or account for the deposit.

5. *Space.* Including identification of the unit, parking space, and any common space to which the tenant has access, such as laundry room or storage space; and any property that is not available to the tenant, whether a garage, backyard swimming pool, basement, or yard.

6. *Use limitations.* Including type of use, such as for residential purposes or the number of persons who are to be in residence.

7. *Right of entry.* Including when and how the landlord may gain entry to the apartment, such as with permission, or 24 hours after a written notice for repairs is presented to the tenant, or to show the apartment to a buyer or new tenant, or in the event of an emergency.

8. *Maintenance.* Including who is responsible for repairs on the property, how the tenant is to notify the landlord of repair problems, and when the tenant will be responsible for the repair or cost of repair, such as by damaging the property.

9. *Utilities.* Including who is responsible for what utility charges.

10. *Alterations.* Including whether the tenant can make any alterations to the property, and if so, how to obtain authorization.

11. *Subletting.* Including whether the tenant may sublet the unit and if so, how to get permission, and whether there is a sublet fee.

12. *Rules.* Including special rules of the house, such as access to the kitchen for a boarder; pets; keeping of equipment outside—bicycles, motorcycles, junk cars; notice of absence for more than a week; limitations on guests or hours for boarders;

requirements of entrance for exterminators or other special services; limitations on noise or music; and so on.

13. *Applicable laws.* A simple statement that both owner and tenant will comply with all applicable laws.

14. *Right to noninterference.* Including a statement about the right of the tenant to peaceful enjoyment of the property without unnecessary interference, sometimes known as quiet enjoyment; and what a tenant should do if this peace is disrupted.

15. *Special tenant responsibilities.* Other tenant obligations, such as to cut the lawn or shovel a sidewalk, if applicable.

16. *Payment.* A statement that money (or consideration) has been passed from the tenant to the landlord in exchange for the promises contained in the lease.

17. *Changes.* Any changes to the lease must be in writing.

18. *Severability.* If any clause in the lease violates a law, the rest of the lease will remain valid.

19. *Signature.* Both parties must sign and date the agreement; any alterations in other provisions should be initialed by each party, and each party gets a copy.

The landlord should make certain that any other legal or relevant concerns that the landlord or the tenant have are discussed and included in the lease. Communicating special concerns to avoid later misunderstandings is especially important for an owner who also lives on the premises. For example, the landlord might have a no-smoking rule or the tenant might request permission to set up an exercycle in the basement.

Any changes or alterations to the lease should be put in writing, with the date, and signed by both parties. An amendment to the lease should note that all other terms of the lease will remain in full force and effect.

FAIR HOUSING

Federal fair housing laws prohibit discrimination based on race, sex, religion, ethnicity, skin color, or physical disability in selecting a tenant. The federal fair housing laws do not apply to small owner-occupied units, but many state and local regulations of a similar type do.

City and state regulations may also prohibit discrimination against a person because of sexual orientation, marital status, or age. Other states prohibit discrimination because of children, or against college students, welfare recipients, or other classifications of persons.

The penalty for violating fair housing laws can require the homeowner to pay a fine to the person who suffered from discrimination. The owner can also be subjected to an arduous legal procedure.

PRIVACY

An owner is required to respect a tenant's privacy. Many states have specific laws governing when and how an owner may enter a rental unit. Privacy means that the owner does not have free or unlimited access to rented premises. Landlords are generally permitted to enter the tenant's area only after providing reasonable notice or for limited purposes, such as to make repairs or to show the rental to prospective purchasers or new tenants.

HABITABILITY

The requirement that a rental unit be habitable is established in almost all locations, either by local laws or by an implied right of habitability (see chapter 2).

The right of habitability is read into every rental, whether or not it is expressly stated. Even in those locations where owner-occupied units are exempt from certain rental laws or building code requirements for rental units, the obligation of providing a habitable space can still be required.

Although there is no absolute standard of habitability, the term means that at the very least all the basic systems of an apartment must be intact: plumbing, heating, water, electricity, and supplied appliances. In some locations, habitability means that the unit is in full compliance with the local building code, which can include a number of minor details, such as the number of electrical outlets per room or the temperature of the hot water.

Habitability could become an issue for an owner in several ways:

- The unit fails to meet the inspection of a building code officer who authorizes a certificate of occupancy.

- The tenant reports uninhabitable conditions to a building code enforcement unit, fire department, or other regulatory agency.
- Someone is injured on the property because of an uncorrected condition related to habitability.
- The tenant fails to pay the rent and claims as a defense that the unit is not habitable (and, therefore, not worth the rent).
- The tenant makes a repair and seeks reimbursement from the owner under a repair and deduct law, by presenting a bill to the owner, or by applying to a rent-regulating agency.

MAINTENANCE AND DEFECTIVE CONDITIONS

A landlord may also have an obligation to correct defective conditions on the property. This can be the same as habitability, depending on how broadly habitability is defined.

The question of defective conditions on the property sometimes can be raised as a tenant's defense to nonpayment of rent. Property defects also become a concern if someone is injured (see chapter 7).

The landlord has obligations with respect to defects:

1. To inspect the property prior to the rental to make certain there are no dangerous or defective conditions
2. To repair defects
3. To warn tenants about defective conditions that are not repaired
4. To respond to tenant reports of latent or new defects, by taking corrective action

MAINTENANCE OF COMMON PROPERTY

An owner is fully responsible for the maintenance of all common or shared property—stairways, foyers, exterior doors, parking lots, sidewalks, laundry facilities. This obligation will apply even to owner-occupied premises in locations in which such owners are exempted from other local laws.

The most serious problems with the maintenance of common property usually arise if a person is injured (see chapter 7). If the injury resulted from the failure to take care of common property, the owner may be held responsible for the injury.

With regard to common spaces, the owner is held to stringent standards, and needs to take active steps to be informed about the condition of common space by inspecting it and taking corrective action when problems arise.

Repair and Deduct

Some localities give tenants the right to make certain apartment repairs and to deduct the cost of the repairs from the rent. These repair and deduct laws generally require the tenant to notify the owner and give the owner a reasonable opportunity to repair the damage. In other locations, tenants can apply to a housing board or rent regulation agency for the costs of repairs they have made.

Unjustified Complaints About Conditions

Claims about habitability, defects, or problems in common areas can usually be prevented by the owner's keeping the rental unit in good condition, making repairs promptly, and assuring that no dangerous or defective conditions exist. Owners actually may be faced with keeping the rental unit in better condition than their own living space.

• The owner should take protective measures against unjustified complaints that the space is not habitable by taking photographs of the apartment when it is rented out, possibly with a witness who can verify the date of the photos.

• The landlord can present the tenant with an apartment inspection report, in which the tenant can check off the condition of each item on the property. The report might list plumbing, appliances, and window locks.

• The landlord should insert a clause in the lease in which the tenant agrees to notify the landlord in writing and at once of any problems that affect habitability. Even though the notification requires the landlord to take corrective action, the landlord wants to provide every opportunity for notification. That way, the tenant cannot assert later that the property was not habitable and that the landlord failed to respond to legitimate complaints.

• Some owners insert a clause in the lease—where permitted by state law—that the first $50 or $100 of a repair will be the responsibility of the tenant. With this provision, some tenants are encouraged to be gentle with the property.

RENT INCREASES

The rent cannot be raised during the period that the lease is in effect. A lease is a binding contract.

The rent cannot be raised during the period that the lease is in effect. A lease is a binding contract.

Beyond that, some cities or states have laws that prohibit landlords from arbitrarily raising the rent at the end of the lease. Under rent control laws, a landlord may be limited to raising the rent by a certain percentage in a year.

The landlord may be required to give adequate notice of a rental increase or to register the rent with a city rent control board.

TERMINATION

The rental can end in several ways. One is by voluntary termination, in which the tenant decides to move out at the end of the rental period and notifies the landlord. The landlord accepts and the tenancy is ended.

An involuntary termination occurs when the landlord decides to end the rental without the consent of the tenant. This may occur simply after notifying the tenant in writing, 30 days prior to the end of the lease or tenancy, that the rental will be terminated.

Some city or state laws require that a termination notice be provided further in advance than one rental period. In areas with extensive rent control laws, a landlord may be prohibited from refusing to offer the tenant a new lease without good cause. Good cause is defined by local rules. In some areas, the mere fact that the landlord wants to live in the apartment is good cause. In most cities, a landlord can ask a tenant to leave at the end of a lease without providing any reason or cause.

EVICTION

When the tenant does not pay rent, violates provisions of the lease, or refuses to leave after the lease is terminated, the owner may have to begin eviction proceedings.

Eviction proceedings differ from state to state. It is important that the landlord follow the exact procedures in the jurisdiction or the eviction can be rejected. In the worst case, the landlord may be liable for tenant harassment.

It is never acceptable to eject a tenant bodily. An owner may not turn off the utilities, lock the tenant out of the apartment, physically assault or mentally harass the tenant, or remove the tenant's belongings. A landlord can be subjected to substantial penalties and fines and, in some cases, may be committing a crime.

In order to evict a tenant, in most states the first step is to serve the tenant with a demand notice. The notice informs the tenant that the rent is overdue or that a provision of the lease has been violated, and it demands that the tenant pay the rent or follow the lease, or else vacate the premises.

This notice to pay or quit has a time period in which the tenant may comply and before further action can be taken. If the tenant pays the money or corrects the condition that led to the breach of lease, the matter is ended. If the tenant does not comply, formal eviction is necessary.

An eviction is a legal proceeding in which the landlord gets official authorization from a court to have a tenant removed from the premises. An eviction is really a civil lawsuit in which the owner demands back the possession of the premises. It is sometimes called an *unlawful detainer,* meaning that the tenant has illegally stayed on the property beyond the time period or conditions to which the landlord has consented.

As in any civil lawsuit, the first step is service of a notice of the unlawful detainer or eviction proceeding. The tenant must be given the information in writing, and it must be served by a process server, who then signs and files a certificate of service. In some states, the notice can be mailed or served by other means. The landlord should keep the proof of service in any case.

The eviction notice gives the tenant a date for a court hearing on the matter. In large cities, a special housing court or housing judge may hear these cases.

When the eviction is a result of overdue rent, the amount of rent due is stated. In most cases, if the tenant pays the amount, the proceeding is ended. Sometimes the costs of starting the termination proceeding can be added in.

In most states, the parties can appear in court without an attorney. But, if no attorney is used, the owner must be fully prepared. The owner will carry the burden of proof about why the eviction should be allowed.

Prior to appearing in court, the owner should organize all material pertinent to the rental, including

- A copy of the lease
- A copy of the notice to pay or quit
- A copy of the eviction or unlawful detainer notice and the certificate of the service of process
- Copies of any correspondence between landlord and tenant
- Copies of any receipts the landlord gave to the tenant and any checks the tenant gave the landlord, with particular attention to any checks returned for insufficient funds
- A copy of an accounting sheet showing the payments from the tenant
- Copies of the inspection report signed by the tenant and any photographs of the unit
- A photocopy of the deed or mortgage showing that the owner is, in fact, the owner of the unit
- A typewritten chronology of the tenant's rental history: when the unit was first rented, when it was rerented, the dates of rent payments missed by the tenant (or other breaches of the lease), the dates of notices sent to the tenant

If the tenant does not appear in court, the landlord can win by default and obtain a notice to vacate, by which the tenant is ordered to leave the premises.

If the tenant does appear, both parties present their cases. After the owner presents the reasons why the tenant should be ordered to vacate, the tenant or tenant's attorney can offer defenses and reasons why an eviction is not appropriate.

Some defenses the tenant might raise are that the rent was in fact paid; the tenant offered to pay the rent, but it was not accepted; the landlord calculated the rent improperly; the notices were not served properly, or failed to follow other requirements in the law; the apartment has not been maintained in good condition; the landlord has acted maliciously or illegally—removing the tenant's property, harassing the tenant, or acting in a discriminatory fashion.

The tenant might also make a plea for special consideration, or an *equitable defense,* for example, that rent is overdue because of illness or unemployment. Most equitable defenses are rejected by judges, although the judge may try to work out a settlement or give the tenant an extension to seek the assistance of a social services agency.

After the tenant presents defenses, the landlord or landlord's attorney can respond briefly.

After hearing both sides, the judge issues an order. In some cases, judges don't announce the order in the court, but will send it by mail.

If the landlord is successful (or if the tenant defaults), the court issues a writ of execution, permitting the sheriff to require the tenant to leave. If the tenant does not leave voluntarily after the order is issued, the sheriff can physically remove the tenant. A landlord should not attempt to take these actions.

A landlord can also win an order for back rent and other costs, although collecting the money is not always easy.

NEGOTIATING A SETTLEMENT

Before the court date in an eviction proceeding (and sometimes during or afterward), landlord and tenant may negotiate a solution. The tenant may have unexpected financial difficulties but offer to make the amount up over a period of months. The landlord may offer to reduce the rent for one month if the tenant is on time with the rent for the next month. A landlord can even offer to pay the tenant to move out and end the matter.

If the parties reach a settlement, they should put it in writing. This document should state: (1) that the agreement is being entered as a settlement of a disagreement between the owner and the tenant; (2) that the tenant is overdue in rent or has breached the terms of the lease; (3) that the owner demanded payment or other compliance with the lease; (4) that the owner and tenant have come to an amicable and voluntary resolution of the matter; (5) the exact terms of the agreement—for example, that the owner agrees to forgo half of one month's rent; (6) that the owner agrees to drop the action and what the tenant will pay or do; (7) that if the agreement is not kept, the owner has all the rights to proceed under the law; and (8) that the terms of the original lease remain in effect. The agreement should be signed and dated by both parties, possibly with a witness or before a notary. An attorney could draft this agreement.

SECURITY DEPOSITS

Many states have laws regulating the collection, maintenance, and return of security deposits. The owner must handle security deposits carefully. Failure to do so can result in significant penalties.

Security deposit laws are designed in several ways. For example, the laws may restrict the amount an owner can collect for a security deposit to one month's rent. The laws might require that the deposit be held in a separate escrow account during the period of the tenancy and specify the amount of interest that it must earn. The owner may be required to send the tenant periodic notices about how much interest has accumulated or send a check for the actual interest. The return of a security deposit must be handled meticulously. The owner can keep a security deposit only if there is actual damage to the apartment. Any property is expected to suffer from normal wear and tear, and the owner cannot use the security deposit for those costs. A hole in a wall, a broken window, or a missing cabinet door are damages, and the owner is entitled to use the security deposit to pay for repair and replacement.

If the apartment has been damaged, the landlord should take photographs of the damage prior to repairing it or retaining any portion of the security deposit.

Owners may feel entitled to charge a tenant a cleaning fee after the tenant has left; however, in some states, the law specifies that security deposits may not be used in this way.

Rules covering the return of security deposits can be demanding. An owner can end up paying a penalty up to three times the amount of the deposit for failing to return it on time. The tenant is entitled to an explanation of what was kept and why. The owner must be able to document any expenditures for repairs.

TENANT PROPERTY STORAGE

When tenants vacate, abandon, or are evicted from an apartment, many leave property behind. Local laws, known as *bailment* laws, may require storage of this property in a certain manner and for a certain period of time.

Some owners want to lay claim to this property as compensation for unpaid rent or damage. State laws often have strict guidelines limiting when and how owners may claim or sell a tenant's property, even if it is left on the scene.

Owners should be cautious about taking any action to dispose of a tenant's property without first investigating local laws.

INSURANCE

Prior to renting out a unit, the owner must make certain that adequate insurance is in effect.

Prior to renting out a unit, the owner must make certain that adequate insurance is in effect. Insurance companies have special rental policies or riders to homeowner's insurance to cover any catastrophe that befalls a tenant or guest of a tenant. Some policies can also protect the owner in the event of severe tenant complaints (see chapter 1).

Owners who live on the property may be able to get insurance that covers a tenant's property in the event of a fire or other accident. If the tenant's property is not covered, the tenants should be informed so that they can get renters' policies, if desired.

TAX IMPLICATIONS

In most states, residential property with a rental unit is assessed differently from a single-family residence in calculating property tax (see chapter 11). Because of the peculiar nature of tax assessments, the differential assessment does not always mean a higher tax rate—but that is the likely scenario. A homeowner who adds a rental unit to a single-family residence should expect an adjustment in the property tax.

Landlords are also treated differently under federal income tax laws (see chapter 11), as described in the following discussion.

Income   Rental income is reported on Schedule E, Supplemental Income Schedule for rental income.

Rental Maintenance Expenses   The homeowner may deduct the full costs of repairs and improvements directly connected to the rental unit, such as polishing the floors or adding new windows.

Property Maintenance Expenses   Owners who rent a portion of the property may deduct a prorated portion of the costs of improvements to the property as a whole, such as painting the whole house or asphalting a driveway.

Business Expenses   As a business operator, the homeowner may deduct the costs of related expenses, such as legal fees, costs associated with billing, banking, insurance, or advertising.

Depreciation   Depreciation applies only to the rental portion of the property. For tax purposes, the rental portion of the property is treated like a car or other item that wears out and has a limited useful life. Each year, the value of the property is presumed to go down, and the homeowner can deduct that portion of the depreciation cost (or loss) from taxable income.

This is a significant bonus, because in all likelihood the value of the property is actually going up. Deducting the depreciated cost can mean big savings.

Depreciation is reported on Form 4562. IRS Publication 946 details how to begin depreciating the property.

Loss   A homeowner can claim a limited loss from the rental of property if the expenses related to the maintenance of the property and depreciation are greater than the rental income. A loss benefits a taxpayer with other income, because the loss is subtracted from the total income, resulting in a lowered income tax.

The loss allowed to be claimed from rental property may be limited—for the 1991 reporting year, a couple with an outside adjustable gross income of under $100,000 could claim a loss of $25,000. People with outside incomes between $100,000 and $150,000 can take a smaller proportion of losses, and persons with higher incomes cannot use a rental loss to reduce ordinary income.

Owner-occupied rental property or rental property owned by senior citizens may be treated differently from other rental units.

Tax rules are always subject to change. Consult a qualified accountant.

RECORD KEEPING

Renting a room or an apartment is a business, and an owner should establish simple business systems.

To simplify matters, the landlord should open a separate bank account for the rental business. In many states, an owner with rental property is required to have a separate escrow account for security deposits.

The owner should keep full and complete records on all aspects of the rental.

• *Receipts for all home maintenance expenses* relating either to the apartment unit or to the structural aspects of the building that affect the rental unit (a heating system in a two-family home), including materials, wages, fixtures for the apartment.

• *Receipts for related expenses,* such as attorney fees, photocopying, advertising costs, accounting expenses, fees for association memberships or materials.

• *General tenant information,* including notices of advertisements, applications, credit references.

• *Specific tenant information,* including the lease, security deposit information, a signed inspection form, any letters from or to the tenant, copies of checks from the tenant, copies of receipts, chronology of apartment use and repairs, a checklist of annual notices (such as on the security deposit) and when they were sent.

- *General property information:* tax and mortgage information; utility charges; accounting and banking materials; photographs of the condition of the unit.

Some associations of owners, tenant organizations, legal aid societies, the state attorney general's office, the court system, or consumer service organizations have materials and newsletters that can keep landlords updated on the law.

20

Selling
the Home

Probably no area of the law of home ownership is changing as rapidly as the responsibility of a seller. The complexities of the real estate transfer, added to the high stakes involved for both the buyer and seller, can cause enormous difficulties. Improper handling can result in problems that last well beyond the sale.

The greatest changes have occurred in the information a seller is required to disclose to a buyer about the condition of the property. Multiple inspections may be necessary by various experts. Home warranties, providing certain guarantees to the buyer, are increasing in popularity.

Other legal concerns for the seller include contract provisions, advertising, discrimination, broker responsibility, title imperfections, and financial terms. Homeowners should enter the real estate sales market with patience and caution.

DISCLOSURE

The rules of real estate sales have moved away from the old ethos that left it entirely up to the buyer to discover defects with the property. If the buyer failed to notice a problem, the seller was off the hook.

That is changing. Increasingly, sellers are required to disclose problems with the property, and if they fail to disclose a material defect, buyers may have a claim against them (see chapter 2). The theory is that the seller has lived on the property, knows the property, and is in the best position to report its condition to the innocent, unknowing buyer. Not all states have accepted this new view, and many still hold to "buyer beware." But the trend is pointed toward greater seller responsibility.

At a mininum, a seller may not give false information and may not hide, disguise, or mask a serious problem. In addition, *if asked,* the seller or broker must answer truthfully.

In many locations, the seller's obligations go far beyond this. One recent reform, reflected in new laws in several states, requires the seller to fill out a disclosure form, giving the history of the house. In other cases, brokers—who have also been held liable when the seller lies about defects—are requiring sellers to fill out disclosure forms.

Some cities have passed Truth-in-Housing ordinances requiring licensed inspectors to inspect the property prior to the sale and to complete a detailed disclosure form, which the seller must present to the buyer.

In other areas, new, specific disclosures are required.

For many years, most homes have been subject to termite inspections. In some locations, homes are also now required to undergo environmental inspections for radon, asbestos, or other conditions.

> After homes slid off their foundations in the Loma Prieta earthquake of 1989, California passed a law requiring sellers of wood-frame homes built before 1960 to disclose earthquake hazards to purchasers.

In addition, the seller must permit the prospective buyer to undertake appropriate inspections—for example, an asbestos inspection, even when it is not required by law.

If the buyer wants inspections that are not required by law, the seller can negotiate them as part of the contract to purchase. The seller can reject a buyer insisting on unreasonable terms before the contract is signed. A seller who signs a contract but refuses the buyer the right to make a reasonable inspection could be held liable later for defects on the property. At the same time, the seller needs protection from the nervous buyer who, in the middle of the purchase, has a change of mind and begins demanding inspections that are unreasonable as a way of getting out of the deal.

Since lawsuits against sellers are on the rise, and courts have been inclined to protect buyers, some states have moved to safeguard sellers in certain circumstances. For example, in 1991, Tennessee and New Mexico passed laws that protect sellers who fail to disclose that a prior occupant of the property was suffering from AIDS or an HIV infection, or that the property was the site of a suicide, murder, or other felony.

Disclosure law differs from state to state. A seller must be prepared to tell the truth about the house and all material aspects of its condition. The test for full disclosure is not merely what the seller knows about the property, but what a seller should know. The seller has an obligation to be familiar with the property and, in some cases, to inspect it or have an inspection done. The legally dangerous route is to highlight the positive, while failing to mention the negatives.

The seller has the option of selling the property as is, which is likely to bring a lower sales price. Or the seller can correct defects prior to the sale or agree to correct them as part of the negotiated contract with the buyer. If a defect is to be corrected, that must be noted in the contract for purchase.

Similarly, if a defect is to go unrepaired, its condition should be specifically and explicitly stated in the contract: "The property is being sold subject to the following conditions of which the buyer has been made aware: a broken toilet in the basement, five missing shingles, and cracks on the west wall of the exterior foundation." In this way, the buyer cannot later deny knowledge of the problem.

What's Included in the Sale: Fixtures

When a house is sold, the sale includes the property, the house, and all fixtures. Fixtures are items attached to the property. A ceiling light is a fixture; an unattached floor lamp is personal property and is not a fixture. The seller is free to remove all nonfixtures.

> *When a house is sold, the sale includes the property, the house, and all fixtures.*

Defining what is a fixture is not always easy. Appliances—dishwashers, refrigerators, freezers, stoves, washers, dryers, air conditioners, and humidifiers—can be viewed as either fixtures attached to the property or nonfixtures that the seller can remove. Is the outdoor grill a fixture? What about the bird feeder? The tetherball pole? The jungle gym? The aboveground pool? Extended wall stereo speakers? Recessed bookcases? Drapes?

In some cases, an item is clearly a fixture, but the seller plans to remove it. To do so, the seller must specify that intention to the prospective buyer.

Prior to placing the property for sale, the seller should make an inventory of everything in the house:

- All items the seller considers fixtures
- All items the seller does not consider to be fixtures
- All fixtures the seller plans to remove

The seller should specify these items by name and location on the property and include this information in the offering and the contract for purchase.

If the seller is not sure whether something is a fixture, it should be excluded from the sale. Once included, it is difficult—psychologically as well as legally—to remove an item. If a fixture is removed without the buyer's agreement, the buyer can take legal action for breach of contract.

The seller can sell nonfixtures to the buyer. They should be the subject of a separate personal property sales contract. In some locations, the seller must collect and pay sales tax on nonfixtures sold as part of a real estate sale.

If there are nonfixtures that neither the seller nor the buyer wants—the old Coke machine that has been a curio on the back porch—the seller is responsible for removal.

BROKERS

Unless they decide to sell the property by themselves, most sellers deal with a broker.

Brokers have different types of arrangements and commissions. The average commission is 5 percent to 7 percent of the sale price—a hefty amount. The seller needs to understand what arrangements are possible, what the broker will offer, what the broker will charge, and get it all in writing. Prior to signing with a broker, the seller should ask questions and comparison shop.

- Is the broker licensed? A local broker? Part of a national chain?
- Will the listing be exclusive? Or is the seller allowed to sell the property personally and avoid paying a broker's fee?
- Will the house be listed on a multiple listing that alerts other real estate brokers of the sale?
- Will the broker handle the property personally or will sub-agents handle it?
- Will there be open houses?
- What ideas does the broker have for a marketing strategy?
- Does the broker have any conflicts, for example, in representing buyers or owning an escrow company?
- Will there be advertisements and in what types of publications?
- What will the asking price be and how was it determined?
- Will buyers be prequalified?
- Will the broker seek a reasonable three-month contract or one that is longer?
- Will there be any costs or fees to the broker that are not included in the commission?
- How will disputes between the seller and the broker be resolved? Is there a mediation or arbitration clause?

All of the details should be spelled out in the contract with the broker. If the seller has questions, a real estate lawyer can be asked to review the contract.

Brokers are licensed by state and local boards. Complaints about the handling of the property, as well as ethics of or contract with the broker, can be made to the appropriate licensing agency.

A broker can commit malpractice and may be liable for damages caused to the seller by (1) making misrepresentations to a buyer, who later sues; (2) having hidden agreements with an inspector, bank, condominium sponsor, or other person, which result in a loss or damage to the seller; (3) engaging in unethical activities; (4) failing to lock and secure the property, resulting in damages; and (5) otherwise breaching the contract with the seller, resulting in a financial loss.

The seller can sue the broker. Some contracts between the broker and seller call for arbitration of disputes. A broker normally has insurance that covers liabilities arising from customer disputes.

Homeowners who decide to market the house without a broker should consult with a lawyer before putting the house up for sale.

Lawn Advertising

In some communities, zoning laws and the rules of neighborhood, condo, and co-op associations prevent owners from placing a For Sale sign on the lawn or in a window.

In some cases, owners may be able to put up a sign, but there is a limit on the number of signs and their size.

Fair Housing Laws

In selling a home, homeowners are prohibited by federal law from discriminating against any purchaser because of race, religion, ethnicity, color, sex, disability, or age. In addition, some local laws prohibit discrimination against people because of their sexual orientation or because they are students, unmarried couples, or recipients of government subsidies.

No references to the preferred type of buyer may be made in

an advertisement. Purchasers cannot be screened or cued in ways that elicit any prohibited classification.

Prospective buyers coming to the property also cannot be encouraged or discouraged by any statements intended to limit the sale to a preferred group. If a prospective buyer asks questions that might lead the homeowner to describe the neighborhood in racial, religious, or other prohibited ways, the homeowner should answer in neutral terms and defer.

Violation of fair housing laws can subject the seller to a complaint before a human rights commission, a lawsuit, or a fine.

THE CONTRACT FOR PURCHASE

A sale of property is only valid if it is in writing. No oral agreement—no matter how firm the handshake—is binding. Oral side agreements between the buyer and seller of real property don't count at all, with the exception that the seller can be liable for oral misrepresentations if they amount to fraud or deception.

> *A sale of property is only valid if it is in writing. No oral agreement—no matter how firm the handshake—is binding.*

The signed contract for purchase is a binding agreement. Prior to signing the contract, the buyer and seller usually engage in negotiations in which the buyer makes an offer backed by a deposit or earnest money check. The seller can accept the offer or make a counteroffer. If a counteroffer is made, there is no agreement unless the buyer accepts the counteroffer.

Once an agreement is reached, the buyer and seller enter into a preliminary agreement, or the binder, in which the parties agree to negotiate in good faith. The contract for purchase is the agreement with all specifics—price, closing date, fixtures, settlement costs, and any contingencies. Even when the sale is finalized with a transfer of title, the terms in the contract for purchase are still binding on the buyer and seller. The seller must make certain that all important conditions are included in the contract. A lawyer can review it.

Contingency clauses in the contract state that the deal doesn't become final unless some other event happens—for example, unless the buyer gets financing, is able to sell another piece of property, or can have the property inspected. The seller wants to limit the number and extent of contingencies, providing at a minimum specific deadlines by which the contingencies end. Otherwise, the seller can be left dangling indefinitely while the buyer procrastinates. If the contingency clause is limited, the seller can always enter into a new contract to extend it. But if it isn't limited, the seller may have to live with it.

The seller should also take note of how selling costs are being divided. There is no set division on some costs—bank points, for example, can be negotiated. Local practice may prevail.

Finally, if the seller is in any way agreeing to join in the buyer's financing, either through the assignment of the seller's mortgage to the buyer or the seller's offer of financing through a second mortgage or other finance tools, the contract for purchase must not be signed without having a lawyer and an accountant review the conditions.

TITLE INSURANCE AND HOME WARRANTIES

Traditionally, title insurance is purchased by the buyer or seller when property is transferred. The title insurance is the seller's protection against an error in the title—if, for example, the boundaries are misstated or a formal easement on the property was not recorded.

Recently introduced in real estate, home warranties guarantee the condition of the major components of the home. Most cover plumbing, electrical, central heating, air-conditioning, and major systems in the house. Structural conditions—such as the foundation or the land itself—are not covered. The cost of the home warranty can be paid for by the seller or the buyer. Premiums run about one-tenth of 1 percent of the home's purchase price, or a few hundred dollars in an average home sale. If the buyer discovers a flaw in a major house system within the warranty period— one to three years—the warranty insurance covers the costs of repair. Most policies also have a deductible of several hundred dollars. Home warranties, when used, can insulate the seller from unanticipated defects in the house.

OTHER COSTS AND FEES

The sale of a home can involve a transfer tax, state capital gains tax, costs for a new survey, a recorder's fee, a fee to a condo or co-op board, attorney's fees, escrow costs, and other miscellaneous charges.

Prior to putting the home on the market, the homeowner should get a complete list of costs. A local real estate association or local bar association may have free information.

SALE OF COOPERATIVE UNIT

Typically, a co-op board has the right to approve a prospective buyer. So long as the board does not discriminate under fair housing or human rights laws, any factors can be taken into consideration in making a decision.

The board can consider financial requirements, personal background, occupation, and hobbies. In nearly all cases, boards are given wide latitude to reject prospective purchasers (see chapter 17).

In order to smooth the path, the owner should get the board's requirements in advance, along with the timetable for approval. In some co-ops, a fee must be paid to the board for the review process. Talking favorably about the buyer to board members can't hurt. Also, the seller should prepare a list of questions the board might ask, and show it to the prospective buyer. In some cases, brokers are willing to lead the buyer through the process, as well.

INCOME TAXES

The sale of a home figures significantly in federal income tax reporting. Unlike other sales of property, homeowners potentially can avoid some or all income tax on the sale of a home if (1) they reinvest the money in a new home within two years, or (2) they are over 55 and claim a once-in-a-lifetime exclusion of $125,000 on gain from the sale of a home (see chapter 11). Money made on a sale that does not fall into those exclusions is reportable income.

What is actually taxable is the gain on the home. Gain is based on the tax basis of the original home. In simple terms, gain is the original purchase price plus the value of any improvements and minus sales costs. If a seller ends up making money on the deal, it must be reported as a capital gain, unless a homeowner's exclusion or other deduction is available.

All home sales must be reported on Form 2119, Sale of Your Home. Taxable gain must be reported on Schedule D, Capital Gains and Losses. (Information is available in IRS Publications 523, *Tax Information on Selling Your Home,* and 530, *Tax Information for Homeowners.*)

SALES COSTS

The seller receives a break on federal income taxes in being permitted to deduct the cost of the sales process from any gain realized on the home. Selling expenses include commissions to a real estate broker, advertising, legal fees, and loan charges, as well as certain costs for fixing up the property.

REPAIRS PRIOR TO SALE

Some repairs made prior to selling the home can be used to adjust the gain on the sale, although there are strict limitations on such expenses. According to IRS rules, the costs must be only for repairs, not major improvements. Painting, fixing gutters, and planting flowers are repairs.

The expenses must have been incurred in the 90-day period prior to signing a contract with a buyer and must be paid within 30 days after the sale is complete.

The expenses also cannot be deductible in arriving at taxable income or be capital improvements. Fix-up costs can be considered only on gain that is taxed in the year of the sale.

SELLER BEWARE

The changing nature of home sales means that the seller has greater responsibilities than in the past. Failure to disclose the true condition of the property could make the seller liable for the costs of repairs and could cause a cancellation or recision of the deal. In addition, the seller must recognize the legal ramifications that can arise from the sales process—in advertisements, statements made to the buyer, and the exact language used in the contract for sale.

21

The Legal Process and the Homeowner

When a homeowner confronts a legal matter, it will, with rare exceptions, fall in the category of a civil law case. Each state has a slightly different system for handling lawsuits, but there are many similarities as well. Process is as important as content in legal disputes, and the homeowner with a legal problem should be familiar with the legal procedures involved.

At its essence, a legal dispute is any disagreement in which two parties interpret their rights and responsibilities differently. Homeowners can be the initiating party, or they may be responding to claims of others. Not all legal disputes end up in court. The vast majority are resolved before they get to court. Even after a lawsuit is initiated, less than 10 percent are decided in court.

Most problems are ultimately settled by agreement between the parties or their attorneys, or by mediation, arbitration, or other negotiations. In many cases, attorneys file a lawsuit to state or protect a claim, fully expecting the matter to settle well before the case comes to court.

COURTS THAT HEAR CIVIL CASES

Both state and federal court systems can hear civil cases. Most matters involving a homeowner take place in a state court.

State court systems have different levels of courts with varying jurisdiction, or authority to hear particular types of cases. State court systems include:

Small Claims Courts   Judges without juries are empowered to hear cases involving small amounts of money and with simplified procedures.

The amount of money that can be involved in small claims court cases generally ranges from $1,500 to $5,000, depending on the state, although the amounts can be higher or lower.

There are limits on the types of cases that can go to small claims court. A government agency probably cannot be sued there. In addition, if you don't want to recover monetary damage, but want something done—the boundary lines changed on the title, your neighbor to stop drilling in the driveway at midnight—you cannot use small claims court.

In almost all cases, even if a small amount of money is involved, you also can use a municipal or district court, although small claims court cases are usually processed more quickly. Cases can be appealed, although not always easily. The courts in many cities, as well as local bar associations, often have books that can help people with small claims cases.

Municipal Courts   Usually located in cities, these courts can accept cases with a higher dollar limit on damages than small claims courts. Municipal courts can use juries and follow formalized procedures of law. Some may hear appeals from small claims court, and in many states are used to process the collection on judgments, even if the case started in small claims court.

District Courts   With general civil court jurisdiction, district courts can hear any civil case, with no maximum dollar limit on damages (although there is a minimum in some instances). Procedures are formalized. District courts are also empowered to issue orders that don't involve money, and they often hear appeals from municipal or small claims court. Liens and other collection procedures—such as attachment of a bank account or garnishment of a paycheck—often go through a district court, as well as matters such as foreclosure.

Specialized Courts These courts have limited jurisdiction to hear particular types of cases, such as divorce, probate, and rental housing.

Administrative Courts As part of government agencies' responsibility to provide citizens with due process, many have an internal process by which government decisions can be appealed. Administrative courts cover matters of tax, welfare, building code decisions, zoning, water permits, and others, depending on the state.

Administrative court decisions can be appealed, usually to a district court. However, courts uphold the decision of the administrative agency, unless the person appealing can show not only that the decision was wrong, but that the agency acted improperly. This is a difficult standard to meet. Only in a few limited areas will a court review the full scope of an administrative decision.

An administrative hearing—even if it seems informal—must be approached with the utmost seriousness. In some cases, an attorney is needed.

Appeals Courts District appellate courts, courts of appeal, and courts of final resort hear appeals on civil cases that have been decided by a state lower court. After a case has worked its way through the appeals process in a state, in extremely rare circumstances when a question of the interpretation of the U.S. Constitution is involved, an appeal can be made to the United States Supreme Court. Because of the technical complexities of appeals, an attorney is generally necessary.

Federal courts are more specialized than state courts, and a homeowner is less likely to have a case filed there. The jurisdictions of federal courts include:

Federal District Court This is the lowest federal court, which hears disputes in limited areas—for example, cases between a person and a company (or person) in another state when the

amount in question is over $10,000; class actions that involve
companies or people from different states; cases that raise issues
under the U.S. Constitution, including some environmental cases
or claims that a local government has violated federal law; cases
arising under certain federal laws that give specific jurisdiction,
such as Fair Housing and Truth-in-Lending.

In some cases, an individual has a choice of filing a case in state
or federal court. The procedures in federal district court normally require the assistance of an attorney. Juries can be used in
a civil case filed in a federal district court.

Bankruptcy Court All bankruptcy filings in the country are
filed in federal bankruptcy courts. These courts apply federal
bankruptcy law, but rely on state laws for certain interpretations
of the role between a creditor and a debtor, such as the level and
type of homestead protection.

Tax Court This court hears appeals of tax cases that have proceeded through the several layers of Internal Revenue Service
administrative process (see chapter 11).

Administrative Courts The appeals from the decisions of certain federal administrative agencies are heard in administrative
courts. Under the principles of administrative law, these decisions can be appealed, but as with state agencies and courts, the
courts are likely to exercise limited review.

Circuit Courts of Appeals and U.S. Supreme Court Circuit
courts of appeals hear appeals from federal district courts, after
which some cases can be appealed to the U.S. Supreme Court.
The U.S. Supreme Court hears only a very small number of cases.

PREVENTING LEGAL PROBLEMS

Preventing a legal dispute can involve legal steps, such as writing
a good contract. But it is just as likely to involve practical matters
that seem far removed from the law—good judgment, caution,
and common sense.

Some legal problems can be prevented by clear communication. In other instances, a formal agreement or contract that

spells out the duties and obligations of each party prevents a serious legal dispute from arising. Contracts are, in fact, part of clear communication. An agreement between neighbors as to who will care for a tree on the boundary can prevent later disputes. The contract with a builder can set out mutual rights and responsibilities.

Personal injury lawsuits can sometimes be prevented by warning people about dangers on the property (see chapter 7). Even better, eliminate the dangers.

Some problems are not preventable under any standard. An unreasonable appraisal by a taxing authority is beyond the homeowner's control. In the end the role of the legal system is to resolve problems that already exist.

RECORD KEEPING

When a problem first arises, the homeowner should recognize that it could develop into a legal dispute. To protect the homeowner's rights, any owner should begin to exercise precaution by solid record keeping and information tracking.

Copies should be kept of all papers and communication related to the situation. The problem can be documented by taking photographs, where appropriate, and recording on a calendar or diary the times and dates that matters arise and the names, addresses, and phone numbers of any people involved.

If a lawsuit or any type of hearing becomes necessary, this information may be vital.

INFORMAL RESOLUTION

With informal resolution of a problem, a homeowner can avoid the hassle and expense of a lawsuit or even of mediation or arbitration. Informal resolution occurs when one party contacts the other and they find a mutually satisfactory solution.

> *With informal resolution of a problem, a homeowner can avoid the hassle and expense of a lawsuit or even of mediation or arbitration.*

Four factors are important when pursuing an informal resolution of a legal problem.

Filing Deadline   Parties should take care not to hurt their legal claim by missing deadlines. Under the law, a person can bring suit on particular situations only within the statute of limitations, a designated time limit. The statute of limitations varies depending on the type of case and the state in which the proceeding takes place. Commonly, in civil matters the statute of limitations is from one to six years. The deadline is met by filing legal documents in court and completing the process of legal service on the other party. If someone misses the deadline, the case can be thrown out of court.

Even if both parties hope to resolve a problem informally, they should not allow the deadline to slip by. If the problem isn't settled and the deadline passes, a person can be stranded without recourse. In addition, the sad truth is that as serious as the threat of a lawsuit may be, often it is the only incentive to settle—missing the filing deadline eliminates that possibility.

Defending Against a Claim   When allegations are made against a homeowner by someone who is already proceeding in court, they must be answered in the proper legal fashion and without delay, whether or not the homeowner hopes to resolve the matter informally.

Even after a claim is brought, an informal resolution is possible. But if a summons and complaint or other formal document is received, the homeowner who does not answer in the legally appropriate manner can lose by default.

In addition, when responding to a problem or a formal complaint, a homeowner should be careful about making damaging statements. The homeowner can agree to pay for injuries suffered by a neighbor child without admitting that Fido wasn't tied up. An attorney can assist.

In Writing   Whenever possible, parties should document a settlement agreement. Legal stationery stores have forms for settlement agreements. The homeowner and the other party write, sign, and date a statement, describing the problem, when the problem occurred, the resolution, and that the settlement is voluntary. It is wise for the parties to sign in front of a notary public.

Before presenting a check, the homeowner should specify that the money is payment in full for the occurrence and cross-reference to the dated settlement agreement. The homeowner should contact an attorney for a review.

Other Parties at Interest The homeowner should remember that there are other parties with a stake in the property—the bank that holds the mortgage, the insurance company, or a spouse. Although the homeowner may agree to a settlement, in some cases other parties have to be notified or consent. If a person is injured on the property, the insurance company may need to be involved. If boundaries are readjusted by an informal agreement or if an easement or license is signed, a bank holding the mortgage may have to consent.

ACTION LETTER

When a problem arises, the homeowner should approach it calmly and reasonably by first writing a letter to the person who is directly responsible for causing the problem, such as the neighbor who owns the barking dog or the contractor who failed to install the hardware on the cupboards. If a company or corporation is involved, the homeowner can write to the president or other top executive.

The letter should be a straightforward explanation of the problem. The tone should be direct and firm, but pleasant. A letter is better than a phone call, because it documents the communication and allows more control. The writer should avoid rhetoric, name-calling, or angry charges. The goal is to get the problem solved.

Sample letter to a neighbor:

Dear Marty:
I am writing to you in hope of resolving a problem that involves your property.

Water flows from the drainpipe near your roof. The pipe is pouring water onto my new deck, and the deck is beginning to show damage. I'm also worried about someone slipping because pools of water form even after a light rain.

I hope you will correct this problem as soon as possible, but before the spring rains begin at the end of next month. As your neighbor, I am, of course, interested in resolving this problem in an amicable fashion. If you have any thoughts or questions, please feel free to get back to me.

Cordially,
Kim Clarke

Sample letter to a corporation:

Dear President Watt:
I am writing to you about a serious problem that your corporation is causing to my property at 1440 Bounty Road.

The Watt Supply Company discharges acidic water into a pipe that flows directly onto my land. The water is toxic to greenery, animals, and people. This fact was recently verified by an engineer I hired to test the soil and water. A copy of the engineer's report is enclosed.

This water has turned the grass in that area a sickly orange color. Last week, my dog, Atlas, wandered into that part of the yard and became extremely ill. Atlas had to be rushed to the animal hospital to have her stomach pumped. Fortunately, Atlas seems to have recovered.

At this point, I am seeking from you an immediate cessation of the drainage onto my property, as well as compensation for damages that have already occurred.

At my latest calculation, I will incur $950 in direct costs, and I feel that you should reimburse me for that amount. To date, these damages include $290 for an engineer to test the ground and trace the pollution source, $160 for veterinary costs, and $500 to have that portion of my property resodded and landscaped. I enclose photocopies of the bills from the engineer and the veterinarian, as well as an estimate from a gardener.

I understand that other neighbors may have problems with drainage from the Watt Company, as well. At this point, I am seeking compensation only on my own behalf.

If I do not hear from you within the next 30 days, I will pursue my options elsewhere.

I am hopeful of resolving this matter amicably. I look forward to hearing from you.

> *Sincerely,*
> *Pat Bennett*

FOLLOW-UP LETTER

If there is no response from the first letter, the homeowner should send a second one that makes note of the fact that no response has been received to the first letter and that further action may be necessary.

Sample second letter:

Dear President Watt:
Five weeks ago, I wrote to you about a problem on my property at 1440 Bounty Road. The draining of acidic water onto my property is caused by a pipe flowing from the Watt Supply Company.

At that time, I requested that you cease draining this pipe onto my property. I also sought the sum of $950 for damages that I had suffered at that time, including relandscaping, injuries to my pet, and the cost of an engineer's analysis. I enclosed copies of the engineer's report and bills that I have incurred.

Since that time, Watt Supply has taken no action to stop the pipe from damaging my property. In addition, I have received no compensation from Watt or, for that matter, any response at all.

If I do not receive a response in the next seven days, I will assume that you are not interested in resolving this matter amicably and I will take further action. Since we have been neighbors for eight years, I hope that step can be avoided.

Please contact me at once. Thank you for your interest in this matter.

> *Sincerely,*
> *Pat Bennett*

RESOLUTION THROUGH CONSUMER AGENCIES

Consider what organization or individual might be able to provide assistance. Consumer organizations, government agencies, the state attorney general's office, or a trade association may be able to apply pressure to resolve a problem. In addition, the Better Business Bureau sometimes intervenes on an individual's behalf, as will media programs that have consumer hot lines. If the home is a condo or co-op, or located in a subdivision governed by a homeowner's association, that organization may be able to help (see chapter 17).

Consumer organizations are best contacted in writing. The homeowner should specify the type of problem, the name of the other party, the amount of money involved, the type of resolution the homeowner is seeking, and include backup information. *Consumer's Resource Handbook,* a listing of federal and state agencies, is available from Consumer Information Center, Pueblo, CO 81009.

Sample letter:

To the State Banking Authority:
I am writing to you about a problem that I am having with a bank.

Seven years ago, I took out a mortgage with The More Interest Bank, 101 West Commerce Street, in Luap. The mortgage is for my home at 821 Lane, also in Luap.

Every month, I have been sending along with my mortgage check a $20 prepayment on the mortgage principal. Yet on my statements from the bank, the prepayments were not credited. Three months ago, I wrote to the bank, asking for an accounting on my prepayments and mortgage. Last week, I received a letter from A. Smith at the bank, who says that the bank is not obligated to give me any accounting.

I think I am entitled to know if my prepayments have been credited to the principal, and I am very upset by the bank's response. I would appreciate any assistance that you can offer. I would also like to know if there is any formal complaint that I can file against the bank. I look forward to hearing from you.

Sincerely,
C. Rudner

FORMAL RESOLUTION THROUGH
MEDIATION OR ARBITRATION

Instead of going to court, other mechanisms for resolving disputes may be available in some circumstances, such as mediation or arbitration. These methods of alternative dispute resolution can spare a person the cost of a lawsuit, but they should not be undertaken lightly. Not all programs of alternative dispute resolution are alike, and benefits and drawbacks of each must be weighed carefully. A copy of the rules of the arbitration or mediation must be obtained and reviewed prior to entering into a proceeding.

Alternative dispute resolution is likely to work best when

- A quick resolution is necessary.
- The parties have an ongoing relationship—neighbors or a contracting job in progress.
- The parties are equal in bargaining power, such as a solo contractor and a homeowner, as opposed to a major corporation and a homeowner.
- The matter is technically complicated and a person with expertise in the area can make a decision as well as or better than a judge.

Mediation occurs when the parties agree to meet with someone who will try to find a consensus or voluntary agreement. The mediator is much like a counselor and can come from any background—attorney, social worker, businessperson. The mediator tries to find areas for common solution. For example, if two neighbors have a disagreement about noise, the mediator might try to come to a voluntary agreement that no loud music will be played after 11 P.M. at night on weekdays, and 1 A.M. on weekends.

If an agreement is reached, the two parties sign it. The agreement is voluntary, but once signed, it can become an enforceable contract. A person should know what the enforcement mechanism is before signing an agreement. Homeowners should not sign an agreement that they do not like or doubt.

Mediation can be conducted by community organizations, and some communities have neighborhood dispute resolution organizations. Mediators can also be hired privately.

Arbitration is not much different from small claims court, except that it is conducted in a private office. Some contracts call for automatic arbitration of disputes, often through the American Arbitration Association.

Arbitration is suited to matters involving contract rights and responsibilities. Arbitration is most often used between companies. When the case involves individuals, arbitration can pose certain drawbacks. Arbitration may involve fees and costs that are as great as or greater than going to court. Sometimes rules of evidence apply, and the average individual may be handicapped against a company if the rules are unfamiliar. Often, arbitration is final and there is no appeal. If the homeowner is unhappy with the decision, there is nothing that can be done.

The Better Business Bureau offers arbitration of consumer complaints. In addition, many trade associations make arbitration available to members with homeowner disputes.

Prior to entering mediation or arbitration, the homeowner will want to know

- Who will conduct the arbitration or mediation?
- How is this person selected? What experience and background does the person have? Do the parties have input in the selection?
- If the parties have input—for example, by proposing three names—how can they find out about the background of the arbitrators or mediators who are part of the program?
- What will the proceeding cost?
- Who will pay the costs?
- How will the proceeding be handled?
- Is an attorney permitted, necessary, or desirable?
- Can the decision be appealed?
- Does the sponsoring organization have any bias toward mediators or arbitrators with particular backgrounds—for example, are only former contractors used in a homeowner-contractor dispute?
- Is testimony sworn?
- Do the parties exchange information in advance?
- What type of evidence will be used?
- How will a decision be enforced?
- Will the proceeding require the homeowner to take time off work or incur other unanticipated expenses?

If homeowners decide to participate in arbitration or mediation, they should prepare the case as if it were going to small claims court (see following). The homeowner should state the problem in one sentence and state in another sentence the desired outcome; type a chronology of events leading to the problem; have available all receipts, letters, bills, estimates, and other documentation of the problem; have available photographs or drawings; write out what the other party is likely to say and prepare a one-sentence response to it.

In other words, although arbitration or even mediation may seem more informal than court, the wise homeowner does not treat it as such.

FORMAL LEGAL RESOLUTION: DECIDING HOW STRONG THE CLAIM IS

Analyzing whether or not there is a valid claim in the law—and how strong that claim is—is an important step to take when a problem arises. It's the first thing an attorney does, too.

The fact is that the law is constantly changing, recognizing new problems and new solutions. Not all problems have legal solutions—or at least not yet. If a case is arguable, an individual can certainly proceed, but in the end, the cost may be greater than the headaches. The challenge is to make an educated guess about how strong the case is and whether it is worth pursuing.

An attorney presented with a homeowner's claim will initially research the legal standing of the case in light of the facts at hand: Is the law clear on this issue or in flux? The attorney then will analyze what facts and evidence are needed to prove the claim: Can the claims be proven? How? What evidence is available? What other materials can be gathered? Finally, the attorney will look at what type of damages the homeowner has suffered: Is the ownership to the property at stake? Is a financial claim being made? Was someone injured and what will be the lifetime impact of the injury? Do the people who are responsible for the injury have any money or assets to pay for it?

The attorney then makes a recommendation. The attorney might find that there is a great legal case, but no facts to back it up. Or that there are plenty of facts, but the likely defendant is broke, bankrupt, or out of the country, and a victory would be a hollow one. Most often, the case comes down to a balancing: Given the solidness (or weakness) of the case, is it worth the cost to pursue it? The homeowner might want to pursue the case only to a point, then reevaluate the costs and work involved in carrying on.

. With or without an attorney, the homeowner's task is to evaluate whether there is a good enough legal case to go ahead with a lawsuit. A list of pros, cons, outcomes, and options will help. Pros might include preserving the value of the property, quality-of-life, or getting money back. Cons might include the annoyance, attorney's fees, or that certain evidence isn't available. Outcomes might include preventing a blot on the title, recovering future costs, getting a nuisance abated, or losing. Options might include pursuing the case to the maximum, pursuing the case only through informal steps—letter-writing, negotiations—or putting the matter aside as a bad experience never to be repeated.

Of course, in some instances, a homeowner may feel strongly about a situation. The goal at the outset is to examine and analyze the case closely and to make considered decisions about it.

BASES FOR THE LAW

Although the law is referred to in one fell swoop, there are several different bases for legal matters:

The U.S. Constitution, which has the basic premises of American law.

Federal laws, which are passed by Congress and apply to people in all states.

Federal regulations, which are enacted by federal government agencies (such as the Internal Revenue Service or the Department of Housing and Urban Development)

State constitutions, which contain the rights of state residents, some of which are greater than those granted under the U.S. Constitution

State laws, which are passed by state legislatures and apply to the citizens and activities in that state

State regulations, which are enacted by state agencies, such as a banking commission

Municipal ordinances, which are passed by local governments, such as a city council or county executive board

Local regulations, which are rules adopted by certain local administrative bodies empowered to enforce local ordinances, such as a zoning board.

Court decisions, which provide interpretations of problems raised in prior legal cases and, as case law, serve as criterion or precedent for similar cases that follow; decisions of the highest courts have the most precedential value

Common law, which are commonly accepted practices that have existed over long periods of time, even if not written.

DAMAGES AND OTHER RELIEF

The concept of damages is a key part of American law because lawsuits are meant to restore a loss or make whole a person who has been treated wrongly or has been injured.

Lawsuits deal with problems that have arisen, rather than speculate on problems that might arise. A homeowner could sue for the costs of re-repair after a contractor breached a contract. But the owner could not go to court because a contractor was threatening to breach a contract—no damage has yet occurred. The legal system discourages lawsuits to enforce merely technical violations that cause no injury.

In order to succeed in court, a person must demonstrate what damages have been incurred.

In order to succeed in court, a person must demonstrate what damages have been incurred. Every lawsuit ends with a statement about what the plaintiff is seeking in damages.

Damages can be of several types:

Direct Damages The costs to repair a broken item or to pay an injured person's medical expenses are direct damages.

Some direct damages are less concrete. The loss of value to property can be a direct damage, but depends on proving the value of the property and how it declined. Direct damages can be calculated in different ways—for example, replacement value of property, or the market value if it were sold.

Consequential Damages   Indirect damages that result from the act complained of can be consequential damages. If a contractor's error results in a roof caving in, and a homeowner has to stay in a hotel, these out-of-pocket expenses are consequential damages.

Pain and Suffering   Some acts are so disturbing that an individual suffers emotional turmoil—an inability to sleep, for example. In some cases, monetary payment for these harms can be recovered. In personal injury cases in which an individual has been physically injured, damages for pain and suffering can be recovered.

Nominal Damages   In some cases, a person is entitled to very small—or nominal—damages, simply because a property right is invaded. A trespass that causes no injury may result in nominal damages because property rights were disregarded. The request for nominal damages can be used as a means to settle the underlying property claim—for example, when a trespasser uses a path that threatens to create an easement by adverse possession.

Punitive Damages   In limited situations, a defendant has acted so wrongly that a plaintiff is entitled to recover a punitive amount. A manufacturer who knowingly distributes a product that has been shown to be unsafe can be ordered to pay punitive damages.

As a deterrent, some laws permit a plaintiff to seek double or triple damages because of the wrongful act of a defendant. A homeowner who locks out a tenant could be forced to pay double damages under such a law.

Equitable Relief   Sometimes an individual is seeking an order of the court to resolve a problem that cannot be quantified in dollar damages, or equitable relief. In such cases, the harm that will be caused is irreplaceable—for example, the wrongful cutting of timber. Or an ongoing action may cause harm every day that it occurs—for example, the continuous pollution of a stream. An individual seeks to stop the damage by an order of the court, or an injunction.

The appropriate relief in some cases might be to order a rescind or cancel an agreement. For example, when a purchaser finds that the seller lied about major defects on the property, the purchaser may want to get out of the deal by requesting that the contract be voided and the money refunded.

WHAT'S INVOLVED IN A CIVIL LAWSUIT

When a problem moves to the lawsuit stage, legal procedure becomes a central concern. The steps of procedure for a lawsuit are

1. *Summons and complaint.* The person with a grievance, the plaintiff, sues the party claimed to be at fault, the defendant. The defendant can be a person, a company, or a government agency. The plaintiff must know the exact name and address of the defendant. A lawsuit can be brought in the state in which the defendant lives or in which the harmful activity occurred.

The plaintiff's case is stated in the complaint, a legal document that is in most cases delivered by hand, or served, on the other defendant with a summons. The summons, complaint, and a certificate of service are filed in the appropriate court with a filing fee. (In some localities, the documents are not filed until the matter is ready to be heard in court.)

2. *Answer.* The summons literally calls on the defendant to respond to the complaint, usually within 20 or 30 days. The answer or response is sent to the plaintiff and is also filed in court. In small claims court, usually little more takes place on the case until a court hearing is set.

3. *Default.* If an answer is not made, the plaintiff can win by default, since the defendant is presumed to agree with the statements in the complaint. The defendant doesn't have to be notified about any further proceedings.

4. *Counterclaim and response.* If the defendant has independent claims against the plaintiff, they are stated in a counterclaim. The plaintiff might state in a complaint that the defendant contractor didn't do the job properly. In the answer, the contractor

might deny that the job wasn't done properly and state affirmatively in a counterclaim that the plaintiff owes the contractor money. The plaintiff can formally answer the counterclaim in a response. The plaintiff homeowner might state in a response that the contractor was paid in full.

5. *Cross claim or third-party complaint.* If the defendant feels that third parties were responsible for the problem, a cross claim or third-party complaint can be made against them. The plaintiff homeowner sues the contractor because a newly installed air-conditioning system has exploded. The contractor doesn't disagree that the air-conditioning system exploded, but believes that the manufacturer is responsible, and so brings a third-party complaint against the manufacturer. The contractor asserts that if plaintiff wins, then the manufacturer should pay. If the homeowner had sued the manufacturer and the contractor, the contractor would bring a cross claim, stating that only the manufacturer is responsible.

6. *Discovery: interrogatories, requests for documents, and depositions.* During the period after a lawsuit is filed, attorneys engage in discovery, to learn the other party's view of the case. The idea is for the parties to gather as much information as possible about the case so that the issues can be streamlined before going to court.

In discovery, the attorney can request information from the other party, and the other party is largely obligated to reply. The information can be in the form of written questions, or interrogatories; requests for documents; sworn testimony in the presence of a court reporter, or a deposition, which is then typed into a verbatim transcript; a formal request asking the other party to admit or deny certain facts in requests for admissions. In cases in which one party claims to have suffered physical injuries, an examination by a doctor can be required.

7. *Witnesses, experts, evaluations, and research.* Prior to the trial, the attorney seeks to gather evidence to support the case and conduct legal and factual research. Witnesses are interviewed and evaluated.

One frequent element in a civil lawsuit—and one that can become costly—is finding experts who can verify the party's version of the problem and the amount of damage that has been suffered. Appraisers or other evaluators are commonly involved in homeowner problems, as well as engineers, accountants, contractors, and, in some cases, doctors. The opposing party may also want to take interrogatories or depositions of the experts.

8. *Motions.* Prior to a trial, attorneys or the parties might need to go to court to settle a particular legal point, which is made in a pretrial motion. The motion is presented in writing, along with a legal argument to support it in a brief. The defendant's attorney might claim that the plaintiff is trying to harass the defendant by requesting documents that are not relevant to the case. The facts are presented in an affidavit, or a sworn written statement signed in the presence of a notary public. In a hearing on the motion, the attorneys make their case to a judge, who rules on the motion.

9. *Negotiations.* During the pretrial period, parties also enter into negotiations. Negotiation is a fundamental part of the process of a lawsuit. Since a trial can go either way and one person can win or lose, negotiations allow the parties to find solutions that are less drastic and more comfortable for all. In many civil cases, parties are not allowed to go to trial unless they can prove that they have engaged in serious negotiations.

> **In many civil cases, parties are not allowed to go to trial unless they can prove that they have engaged in serious negotiations.**

10. *Settlement.* In a settlement, both parties sign an agreement by which the lawsuit is ended and other conditions are met—for example, the defendant agrees to pay the plaintiff damages or to repair the problem.

11. *Certification for trial.* When both parties have completed all pretrial matters—a process that can take months, if not years—the case can be certified as ready to go to trial. It is then placed on the court calendar.

12. *Referees and bench negotiations.* In an effort to avoid the cost of a trial, some states have mini hearings in civil cases with referees who are lawyers appointed to make decisions. In almost all cases, a judge—even on the day the trial is scheduled to commence—will try to get the parties to settle by working directly with them.

13. *Trial.* The trial is fairly familiar on the American land-

scape. Civil trials can be before a judge alone, or before a jury, often of six people.

The plaintiff presents the case first. Witnesses are called and asked questions in direct examination and can be cross-examined by the defendant. Written or visual evidence is introduced.

Then the defendant presents witnesses or evidence by direct testimony, which the plaintiff can cross-examine. After the defendant closes, the plaintiff may have an opportunity to present a rebuttal to the evidence presented by the defendant.

After the evidence is complete, the attorneys (or the parties if they have no attorney) sum up their view of the evidence in a closing argument. The plaintiff has the burden of proof and must convince the judge or jury by a preponderance of the evidence.

14. *Judgment.* If a jury is used, the jury will receive instructions from the judge and then deliberate in private and return a verdict. If a judge is hearing the case without a jury, the decision can be issued immediately or can be decided in the following weeks or months, and sent out by mail.

15. *Appeals.* If a legal basis exists, an appeal of the decision can be made by the losing party or a party who did not receive a satisfactory verdict. A legal basis for appeal arises because of a misapplication of the law by the judge or jury or a mistake in the proceedings, such as the exclusion of proper evidence. An appeal is not available simply because a party is unhappy with the decision. In some cases, post-trial motions are made to the judge who heard the case, as well—for example, arguing that the amount of money awarded by a jury is not supported by the facts.

16. *Collecting the judgment.* If a plaintiff wins, the judgment must still be collected. Courts do not automatically make a losing party pay. This is true in small claims courts, as well as in municipal and district courts.

Further legal proceedings may be necessary to locate assets belonging to the defendant. The winning party may have to find a defendant's bank account and attach it, garnish wages, or place a lien on property. If the party who was sued has no money or other assets, all may have been for nothing. In other instances, a losing party tries to hide assets. It is not uncommon for a settlement to be entered even after the judgment in order to avoid the collection process.

CLASS ACTIONS

Sometimes several homeowners are in exactly the same situation. For example, all the purchasers of Double A Brand Insulation may suffer from the same types of lung problems. In such cases, individuals can come together in a class action.

A class action can benefit individuals because the costs of pressing the case are shared. Indeed, in some cases—particularly with environmental problems—an individual rarely can afford the costs of litigation. But in a class action an individual does not have the same control and the case will proceed more slowly because of the large number of people involved.

SELF-REPRESENTATION

The risk of representing oneself is that a nonlawyer may miss some details that an attorney might grasp. Self-representation, or serving as an attorney pro se (for oneself), takes caution, a willingness to do the work, and emotional distance. On the other hand, a sense of empowerment can be achieved that doesn't occur when an attorney is handling the case.

In small claims cases, in arbitration or mediation proceedings, and before regulatory or administrative boards, people often represent themselves. But if a lien is involved or the very ownership of the property is at stake, a homeowner would be foolish not to engage an attorney.

Preparation will be the key to doing a good job in self-representation. The homeowner should take several steps, as follow:

1. Find out the exact procedures for the hearing, sitting in on a hearing on someone else's case, if possible.

2. Write a one-sentence statement of exactly what the problem is: The countertop collapsed after contractor installed a washing machine.

3. Write a one-sentence statement of exactly what the damages are: Entire counter needs to be replaced at a cost of $1,200; falling debris broke cat's toe, at a vet cost of $150.

4. Write a statement of whom the homeowner believes is responsible and why: The contractor is responsible for failing to follow directions in installing the dishwasher.

5. Consider how each phrase of the statements in 2, 3, and 4

can be proven, and find the evidence to prove them. What proof is there that the counter collapsed—are there photos? Witnesses? Letters written at the time? Admissions by the contractor?

In order to be successful, the homeowner must prove that the problem exists; the other party is responsible for causing the damage; and what relief is sought, such as the cost of fixing the problem, and how much that will be. If any element is missing, the case will be lost.

6. Write in one sentence what the other party is likely to say—for example: The counter was already broken, and kids jumping on the counter were the real cause of collapse.

7. Write in one sentence how other party's claim (or defense) can be disproved: The counter was brand new, and the only kids around belonged to the contractor.

8. Gather evidence to disprove the defense in 6 and verify the statements in 7. Is there a copy of the receipt for the new counter? Do condo documents prohibit children from living on the property?

9. Try to find out about the law and decisions in prior similar cases. If the problem involves a regulatory agency, a copy of its rules and regulations should be obtained. If the problem involves a contract or breach of agreement, the homeowner should analyze how serious the breach is—that is, if it goes to the heart of the agreement. For legal background information, try a bar association hot line, the public library, or a bookstore. Look up similar cases in the court's index and read the files on them. If necessary, seek help conducting legal research in a law library.

10. Write a full chronology of everything that has led to the problem and all efforts to resolve it.

11. Gather all documents, bills, and receipts. Without writing on them, the owner should make a list of them, the dates, and what they are. They should be organized in a logical fashion so that they can be pulled out quickly, and extra copies should be made.

12. Gather other evidence. If the problem is visible on the scene, take photographs. Have someone else go along when the photographs are taken, so, if necessary, that person can sign a

written statement that the photographs were not altered in any way. If the problem is noise, a tape recording could be made, marking the date, time, and place of the recording. Ask a third party to verify it.

13.   Talk to witnesses. If the rules of the proceeding will allow witnesses to testify, arrange for them to appear. The rules might allow a written statement by a witness. The witness could sign an affidavit and swear to it before a notary public. If witnesses can be required to testify by a court order, consider subpoenaing them and prepare necessary documents.

14.   Figure out what experts will be needed. If the house has lost its value because of a nuisance in the neighborhood, a real estate expert or appraiser will be necessary. Make certain that experts have real training or experience in the area in which they are giving an opinion.

15.   Organize the information in a logical way and cut out all extraneous information or emotional reactions. Try to aim for crisp facts and make an outline or chart, listing each fact that needs to be proved, the law that applies, and the information or documents that are relevant to that point.

16.   Prepare a short opening statement that will explain the problem to the judge or arbitrator and also prepare a brief closing statement.

17.   In the hearing, speak in an even tone without becoming agitated. Be polite and courteous to everyone, including the other party. If the other party makes statements that are not true, do not interrupt, but make a note of the statement. After the other party is done, the homeowner should tell the judge or the referee that there are some points that need clarification.

18.   Before ending, ask the judge or arbitrator if there is any other relevant information that has been neglected. If the judge wants information that is not on hand, ask if this can be provided the next day or if it is possible to be granted a continuance.

Using a Lawyer

Some cases are too technical, complicated, or risky for the average homeowner to handle alone. The homeowner should engage a lawyer

- If the other party has a lawyer
- If the amount in question is large
- If there is any threat to the ownership of the property, such as a lien
- If someone has been seriously injured
- If the matter presents technicalities
- If the homeowner is experiencing anxiety or emotional strain because of the problem

If homeowner's insurance covers the problem, the insurance company may take up the legal representation. For example, if a neighbor's child falls through a glass door, the insurance company should cover the damages and may also wish to contest the matter in court. The homeowner cannot control the insurance company's decision.

Hiring a lawyer is no different from engaging any professional. To get recommendations of lawyers, people should ask friends whose judgment they trust, other lawyers, even an accountant or real estate broker. A local bar association can also provide the names of lawyers in the area who handle homeowner disputes. Before going to see a lawyer for the first time, the homeowner should find out if there will be any costs involved in the first visit.

Prior to talking to the lawyer, a homeowner should organize all the information, including the legal description of the property, the name and address of the party with whom there is a problem, and a clear written chronology of the problem. This will simplify the first visit a great deal. Either at or before the first visit, find out about the lawyer's background and general type of practice, and whether this problem is the type that the lawyer would ordinarily handle. Be prepared to ask the lawyer for an evaluation of the case—although it is not uncommon for the lawyer to want to do some research and to call or write with a response later.

Be certain to ask about the lawyer's fees. Lawyers have three ways of charging: hourly fee, contingency fee, and flat fee.

Lawyers usually charge by the hour. The homeowner should find out what the hourly fee is, who in the office will be involved in the case, the plan of action, and the estimated amount of time involved. Expenses such as depositions, court filing fee, document checking, or expert witnesses are all added to the fee. Clients should ask about these costs as well. A limit can be placed on the number of hours that the attorney spends on the case, after which the client can reevaluate the matter. Most of the problems that face a homeowner are likely to be billed by an hourly fee.

A homeowner should not count on getting the fees back, even if the case is successful. The award of attorney's fees and costs is not automatic.

In a contingency fee arrangement, the lawyer collects a fee only if successful in securing a money judgment for the client. Then the lawyer takes a percentage of the amount recovered.

Only the plaintiff is likely to be taken on as a client on a contingency basis, and usually in personal injury cases. In homeowner cases, contingency fees will be most common when the homeowner or family member is injured by a dangerous product, by a defect in the property, or by a hazard in a new home. In some cases, attorneys will take clients who have been victims of discrimination or who have property tax appeals or eminent domain appraisal cases on a contingency basis.

A flat fee is used by lawyers in cases involving routine matters such as a closing, a landlord-tenant dispute, a tax appeal, a title correction, or contract drafting or review.

Getting the most out of an attorney ultimately means communication. The homeowner should be clear with the attorney, honest about what is going on, and should quickly get all of the information the attorney needs. The client should also ask that the attorney keep in regular and frequent contact about the progress of the case (progress is usually a lot slower than the client would like).

People with limited incomes or who are elderly or disabled may be eligible for free or low-cost legal services. Most communities have a local legal aid or legal services organization. Unfortunately, many of these programs are overwhelmed by the number of clients, and a client may have difficulty getting an appointment. If the matter is one in which the homeowner could lose the home or face some other emergency, an appeal for immediate help should be made to the legal services office.

Senior centers and other organizations, such as veterans' programs, affordable-housing organizations (or landlord-tenant groups), women's centers, and programs for the disabled may also have legal services.

In addition, some private lawyers volunteer a certain amount of time to helping people with legal problems. These programs are generally operated by a local bar association with a central number and referral system. Some local bar associations even have legal telephone services or community legal clinics.

Finally, low-cost legal services can sometimes be obtained through local law schools, which put students to work under the supervision of attorneys. The people who are eligible for these services often get an eager—if inexperienced—representative at little or no cost.

Some individuals belong to prepaid legal service programs through their employer, union, or participation in a private plan. A homeowner's case is a perfect one to take to such a program.

If a homeowner has a serious complaint about the actions of an attorney, the client should not hesitate to raise the issue directly with the attorney. If satisfaction is not forthcoming, the homeowner should remember that the attorney was hired by the homeowner, not the other way around. The client can discharge the attorney, although the client may still be responsible for fees owed on work already done.

Serious complaints about an attorney can be made to a state attorney disciplinary organization or to a local bar association. These bodies generally are not empowered to review the attorney's fees—although some may arrange to mediate a fee dispute—and they also do not undertake to correct the attorney's errors. What they do is review attorney licenses and determine whether the individual is fit to practice law.

Finally, a client can initiate a lawsuit against the attorney for damages owing to malpractice, which will probably mean finding another attorney to handle the case.

AFFECTING CHANGE

Homeowners can help themselves by getting the law changed. This is sometimes the most successful way to prevent (and occasionally, to resolve) a difficult legal problem.

Changing the law means contacting legislators, especially on the state or local level, to lobby for new legislation. Certain citizens' groups and community homeowner's associations regularly keep people informed about the law and its status. Legislators are very responsive to homeowners.

Homeowners might want laws that require banks to permit homeowners to prepay the principal, or change the date of the appraisal of fair market value for property tax purposes. Or homeowners might see a need for neighborhood dispute resolution centers, new laws establishing noise levels, or ordinances that protect trees from being removed when developments are approved. Zoning laws, adopted by local planning boards, are of great importance because they can change the character of an entire community. Laws on smokestack emissions, discharges into waterways, or utility thoroughfares all affect the homeowner.

Every state considers dozens of these bills each year. Homeowners should not underestimate their power to have an impact on legislation.

KNOWING LEGAL RIGHTS AND REMEDIES

Most of what happens in a civil case does not happen in a court; it happens in legal documents and papers. Having a grip on the legal process ranks on an equal plane with having familiarity with the subject matter. With that dual perspective, a homeowner can intelligently evaluate the best course to follow when faced with any legal situation.

INDEX

Abatements, 164–80
Absolute liability, 136
Abstract of title, 8, 47
Acceleration, 186, 188
Access, right of, 125, 235
Action letter, 313–15
Activities, liability from, 108–109
Adjustable-rate mortgage loan, 204
Administrative courts, 309, 310
Administrative law, 136–37
Adverse claims, 47, 60
Adverse possession, 46, 56, 130, 134, 157; trespass and, 147–48
Advertising, 296, 301, 302
Affadavit, 325, 329
Agreements, 128, 307; *see also* Negotiated settlement
Air, 116–38
Airplanes, 130–31, 147, 149, 151, 234
Air pollution, indoor, 226–32
Air rights, 55, 130, 141, 235
Airspace, 130–32, 137; ownership of, 47, 155
Animals, 109–10, 145–46, 151; *see also* Pets
Appeals, 326; tax decisions, 179–80
Appeals courts, 309
Appliances, 33, 299
Appliance warranties, 12
Application fees, 204, 206, 207
Appraisal, 9, 204, 239, 244; and compensation, 238
Appraisers, 14, 17, 31, 324–25
Appropriation system (water), 119–20
Arbitration, 88, 94, 101–102, 301, 307, 311, 317–19, 327
Architectural restrictions, 259–60
Asbestos, 11, 24, 227, 230, 231, 297, 298
Assessment reports, 12

Assessments, special: condos, co-ops, 256, 257, 266
Assessment (taxes), 164, 165, 166, 170, 173, 177; rental units, 292–93
Assessment (valuation), 165, 167–68; appealing, 168–70
Asset forfeiture, 244–45
Assets, 182, 326
Attorney(s): complaints about, 332; consumer-oriented, 211; fees, 331; in lawsuits, 324, 325, 326, 327, 330–32; specialists, 239, 244; validity of claim, 319–20
Attorney, when needed, 4, 8, 21, 22, 33, 44, 48, 73, 90, 99, 102, 128, 193, 245, 289, 313: bankruptcy, 201, 202; in court, 310; divorce, 221; personal injury cases, 114
Attractive nuisance (doctrine); 15, 107, 112, 145

Bailment laws, 292
Balloon payment(s), 11, 183
Bank errors, 209, 210
Bank escrow, 11: taxes, 170–71; *see also* Escrow accounts
Bankruptcy, 181, 190, 198–201, 202; and foreclosure, 200–201
Bankruptcy court, 310
Banks, 8–9, 14, 333: challenging, 210; and prepayment, 207, 208, 209
Below ground ownership, 47
Bid bond, 95
Binder agreement, 6, 302
"Black book," 12
Bonds, contractor, 94–95
Boundaries, 3, 6, 9, 32, 45–60: of easements, 52; fixing, 47; legal questions about, 46–60; legal

restrictions on, 55; trees as, 57; uncertain, 48–49; water, 49–50
Boundary disputes, 58–59
Boundary errors, 46, 47–48
Boundary fences, 58
Bounds, 6
Breach, 105: duty of care, 105, 106, 109
Breach of contract, 100
Breach of duty, 135
Breach of warranty, 38, 40, 101, 231
Breaches of implied warranty, 36, 37, 100–101
Brokers, 134, 296, 300–301
Builders, 34, 35, 230, 231: liability for negligence, 38–39; standards for, 39; and warranties, 36–37, 40, 41
Building codes, 28, 44, 77, 80, 81–82, 230: and rental property, 277, 278–79
Building permits, 78, 80–81, 167
Building restrictions, 83–84

Capital gain, 79, 164, 176–77, 305
Carbon monoxide, 229
Casualty insurance, 14, 16–20; policy types, 18–20
Caveat emptor, 25
CC&Rs: *see* Covenants, conditions, and restrictions (CC&Rs)
Certificate of title, 8
Children: injury to, 104–105, 107, 113; and trespass, 145
Citizens' groups, 126, 133, 137, 162, 247, 333
City income tax, 178
City laws: rights/responsibilities of landlords and tenants, 280
Civil action, for trespass, 139, 140
Civil court, 154, 163, 268
Civil law, 151, 307
Civil lawsuits, 162, 307, 309, 333: courts hearing, 308–10; in enforcement of mechanic's lien, 98; nuisance, 154, 163; private nuisance claims, 153, 160; steps of procedures in, 323–26; in trespass, 149, 151
Claims, 8, 14, 319–20: against contractors, 100–101; defending against, 312; on homeowner's insurance, 21–22; personal injury, 114; for product defects and failure, 40–42
Class action, 42, 243–44, 310, 327
Cohabitation, 13, 214, 215, 222–24
Collateral, 100, 182, 206–207

Commercial zoning, 66
Common law, 127, 321
Common-law marriages, 221
Community health, welfare, safety, morals, 2, 63, 71, 77, 81
Community property, 215, 216–17, 218, 220
Compensation, 32, 134–35: with eminent domain, 233, 234, 235–36, 238, 239, 241, 242, 244, 245
Complaint(s), 323: against banks, 210, 211–13; rental property, 286–87
Compliance with laws (defense), 157
Con artists, 89
Concealment, 29–30
Condemnation, 233, 234, 236–38, 242, 244, 245
Condemnation proceeding, 238–39
Conditional uses, 70–71
Condominium associations, 246, 254–55, 266
Condominium building, 255
Condominium default, 197
Condominium insurance, 19
Condominium rider, 10
Condominiums, 3–4, 112, 129, 161, 227, 230, 316: architectural restrictions, 260; building restrictions, 83–84; and home business, 270; homeowner associations, 268; and incidental rights, 136; and joint ownership, 254–55; land-use controls, 62; rental units, 279–80; responsibility for repairs, 262–63; rules and restrictions, 11–12; taxes, 173, 176
Construction, 78–84
Consumer agencies/organizations, 87, 211, 213, 232, 316
Consumer protection, 2, 25–26; laws regarding, 27, 90
Contract(s), 296, 310–11, 318: boundaries in, 45, 46, 47; with contractor, 85, 89–94, 97, 100, 101–102; fixtures in, 33–34; indoor air pollution, 230; language of, 30–31; in nontraditional ownership, 222–24; remodeling, 37
Contract cancellation, 94
Contract claim, 39
Contract for deed, 183–84, 195
Contract for nonfixture purchases, 12
Contract for purchase, 6, 302–303
Contract waivers, 89
Contractors, 14, 15, 80, 81, 84, 108, 128: bonds, 94–95; dealing with, 102; final payment, 92–93; financing

Contractors (*cont'd.*)
with, 100; hiring, 85–102;
homeowner claims against, 100–101;
insurance, 99–100; licensed, 86–87,
96, 102; payment schedule, 91–92;
pitfalls in hiring, 88–89; screening
and evaluating, 87–88; searching for
good, 86; warranty programs, 96
Control over property, 151–52
Cooperative boards, 9, 51, 246, 256,
266
Cooperative default, 196–97, 202
Cooperative owners, 10
Cooperatives, 3–4, 112, 129, 161, 198,
227, 230, 316: approval of
purchaser, 262; architectural
restrictions, 260; building
restrictions, 83–84; and divorce,
222; foreclosures on, 193; and home
business, 270; homeowner's
associations, 268; and incidental
rights, 136; land-use controls, 61–
62; and refinancing, 205; rental
units, 279–80; responsibility for
repairs, 262–63; rules and
restrictions, 11–12; sale of, 304;
share loans, 184–85; and share
ownership, 255–56; taxes, 171–72,
173, 176; transfer of, 219
Co-ownership, 214–25
Correlative rights, 123
Cosigner, 182, 191
County recorder's office, 6, 13, 47, 48,
50, 54, 55
Court appeal(s), 64, 170; *see also*
Appeals
Courts, 308–10
Covenants, 7–8, 12, 46, 47, 50–51, 59,
78, 125, 129, 131, 248: architectural
restrictions in, 260; building
restrictions in, 83–84; and
homeowner's associations, 252–53;
illegal, 51, 253; and incidental rights,
136; subdivisions, 58; trees, 57
Covenants, conditions, and restrictions
(CC&Rs), 4, 7, 51, 62, 161, 252–53
Criminal law, 150–51, 154

Damages, 59: consequential, 38; from
defect, 32, 33, 42; earth support,
129–30; in excavation, 126–28;
lawsuits over, 321–23; in private
nuisance, 158; types of, 321–22
Dangerous conditions, 28, 103–104,
107, 108, 111–12, 115; and duty to
warn, 105–106
Death, 214, 216, 217–19
Debt(s), 181, 182, 199

Declaration of condominium, 248, 254
Deductible (insurance), 15, 20, 21
Deductions, deductibility (taxes), 32,
169, 172, 173–75, 178, 205
Deductions, special, 177–78
Deed, 6–7, 8, 32, 54, 55, 248:
boundaries in, 45, 46, 47, 48;
building restrictions in, 83–84;
homeowner associations established
by covenants in, 252–53; type of
ownership in, 215
Deed in Lieu of Foreclosure, 186, 189
Deeds of trust, 184, 190
Default, 9, 10, 11, 182, 183, 186, 187–
88, 200, 205, 207: condominium/
subdivision, 197; cooperative, 196–
97, 202; curing, 188, 195;
installment contract, 195–96; in
lawsuit, 323
Defects, 298, 303: discovered after
purchase, 24–44, 47; latent, 28–29,
31; law regarding, 44; recovery for,
25–26; rental unit, 285; seriousness
of, 27–28; undisclosed, 230–31
Defendant, 323, 325, 326
Defending against a claim, 312
Defenses: to foreclosure, 189, 190–91,
202; tenant, in eviction, 289–90
Deficiency, 182, 187, 194
Depreciation, 175, 274, 275, 293
Developers, 34, 134, 197, 252; and
homeowner's association, 257–58
Direct damages, 321–22
Disclosure: of pollutants, 227, 228,
230; required, 2, 11; rules/
regulations, 27, 296; in sale of home,
296, 297–98
Discovery, 324
Discrimination, 296, 301–302
Dispute resolution, 40: through
consumer agencies, 316; with
contractor, 94, 101–102; formal,
317–20; informal, 311–13
District court, 59, 308–309, 326
Divorce, 214, 219–22
Documentation (property claims), 21
Documents, 5–23, 248, 324
Due process, 189–90, 264
Dumping, dumps, 67, 125, 132, 133
Duty: of care, 135; to children, 107; of
homeowner, 104–105; to tenants,
107; to warn, 105–106, 109, 111

Earth support, 116–38
Earthquakes, 16, 20–21
Easements, 8, 32–33, 45–60, 141, 235:
airspace, 130, 131, 132; formal/
informal, 51–53; granting/getting,

54–55; homeowner's associations,
259; incidental rights, 137; party
walls as, 129; pollution, 134;
regarding trees, 57
Emergency, 3, 142, 160
Eminent domain, 52, 118, 136, 233–
35, 236, 237, 238, 239, 241, 245;
elements of, 235–38
Encroachments, 3, 45–60: of airspace,
130, 137; trespass and, 147–48, 151,
152; trees as, 56–57
Encumbrances, 8, 31, 47, 48, 194
Endorsements, 9, 19
Environmental considerations, 116–17,
134
Environmental contaminants, inside
the home, 226–32
Environmental inspections, 11, 24, 297
Environmental laws, 76–77, 81, 132–
33, 157, 162, 194
Environmental regulations, 50, 61, 66,
234, 240–41
Equitable defense, 290
Equity of redemption, 186, 191, 195
Equity value, 199–200, 205
Escrow accounts, 291, 293; contractor
payments, 92, 96
Esthetic zoning, 68
Eviction, 192–93, 198, 288–90
Evidence, 326, 328, 329
Excavation, 82, 126–28, 136
Excavation clause, 91
Excess condemnation, 237
Exempt property, 198, 199–200
Exemptions (tax), 166, 168
Experts, 42, 324–25, 329
Express warranties, 34–35, 39, 40

Fair housing laws, 283–84, 310; and
sale of home, 301–304
Fair market value, 79, 205, 209, 221,
238, 239, 244
Family relations, 260–61
Federal courts, 133, 308, 309–10
Federal district court, 309–10
Federal income taxes, 100, 164, 173,
179–80, 205: deductions for home
business, 272–73; effects of sale of
home with business use on, 274–75,
276; failure to pay, 178; and rental
property, 277; sale of house and,
304–305
Federal laws, 40, 44, 320; pollution,
132, 137
Fee simple town house condominium,
255
Fences, 2, 3, 19, 55, 58, 145
Filing deadline, 312

Fill, 128
Financial difficulties, 181–202; in
divorce, 221, 222
Financial institutions: government
regulation of, 203, 210, 211–12;
legal responses to, 210–11
Financing, 100, 303
Fire codes, 81, 278–79
Fixtures, 33–34, 299–300
Floaters, riders, 18
Floating zones, 70–71
Flood insurance, 20–21, 120
Flooding, 16, 117, 120–21
Foreclosed homeowner, 192–93
Foreclosed property, 197–98
Foreclosure, 9, 96, 99, 100, 172, 178,
183, 184, 188, 207, 309: bankruptcy
and, 200–201; condominiums, 197;
cooperatives, 185, 196–97; defenses
to, 189, 190–91; FHA, 193; rules
regarding, 181–82; types of, 185–87
Foreclosure sale, 191–92, 195, 201
Forfeiture, 195, 196, 244–45
Formal resolution: legal, 319–21;
mediation/arbitration, 317–19
Formaldehyde, 228–29, 230, 231

Government officers, and trespass,
143–44
Grading, 128
"Green River" ordinances, 150
Ground support, 126–30, 155; rights
to, 235
Groundwater contamination, 123–24
Group residences, 67

Habitability standard, 36; rental
property, 279, 284–85, 286; *see also*
Implied warranty of habitability
Harm, 127, 322–23 in nuisance claims,
156, 163; in takings, 241, 243
Hazardous waste dumping, 132, 133
Health codes, 77, 81, 278–79
High-crime-area insurance, 19, 20–21
Historical districts, 76, 80
Home: leasing portion of, 277–95; loss
of, 181; *see also* New homes; Sale of
home
Home business, 68, 174–75, 269–76
Home equity loans, 100, 183, 204–
205, 206–207
Home improvement loans, 174
Homeowner(s): duty of, in injuries,
103–108; foreclosed, 192–93; and
legal process, 307–33; rights/
responsibilities, 1–4, 137–38
Homeowner's associations, 4, 59, 62,
84, 160, 246–53, 316, 333:

Homeowner's associations (cont'd.)
challenges to, 264–66; co-ops and,
256; covenants, 51; creation of, 248;
dealing with, 267–68; defining, 247–
48; established by covenants in deed,
252–53; fiscal concerns, 266–67;
legal attitudes toward, 249–50; legal
strategies in disputes with, 267;
power and responsibilities of, 250–
52, 268; role of, 249; rules and
regulations, 136, 258–64, 270
Homeowner reinvestment on sale,
175–76
Homeowner's insurance, 13, 14–22,
57, 78–79, 100, 108, 330: costs of,
19; exclusions, 16, 18; and injuries,
106, 113–14
Home Owners Warranty Corporation,
87, 96
Home Owners Warranty (H.O.W.)
program, 39–40, 94, 96
Homestead protection, 194, 198
Homestead exemption, 13, 199–200,
202; effect of, in bankruptcy, 200
Home warranties, 11, 26, 27, 32
Home warranty insurance, 11, 25
Household workers, 15, 178–79
Housing codes, 78

Implied right of habitability, 284
Implied warranties, 26–27, 32, 39, 40,
41: claiming breach of, 37, 39; new
homes, 35–36
Implied warranty of fitness, 26–27
Implied warranty of habitability, 26,
35, 36, 37, 100–101, 231
Implied warranty of workmanship, 35,.
36–37, 100–101
Improvement(s), 79–80, 167, 205;
upon sale, 176–77
Incidental rights, 116–17, 138, 155,
236: legal strategies, 134–37;
pollution and, 132–34
Indemnity clauses, 25
Independent contractors, 99–100, 108
Indirect takings, 240–41
Indoor air pollution, 229–30
Industrial zoning, 66
Informal resolution, 311–13
Information, 5, 13–14: and insurance,
22–23; for lawsuit, 329–30
Injunction(s), 52, 54, 56, 59, 76, 135,
323: in nuisance claims, 154, 158,
163; in trespass, 140, 150, 151
Injured person(s), 105, 106, 110
Injuries, 3, 15, 78–79, 232: claims for
product failure causing, 41–42;
home business, 272; intentional,

106; legal action in, 114; liability in,
231; negligence in, 38, 39; in
nuisance claims, 154; personal, 2, 32,
102; preventing, 111–12; rental
property, 285–86; in trespass, 145
Injuries (third party), 103–15; duty of
homeowner, 104–108
Injury to property, 101
Inspections, 2, 24, 144, 204, 296, 297–
98
Inspectors, 14, 24, 31, 81, 88, 93
Installment contract default, 195–96
Installment sales contracts, 183–84
Insurance: broker, 301; contractors,
99–100; covering injuries, 103; and
defects, 33; home business, 271–72;
rental units, 292; and repairs, 263;
see also Homeowner's insurance;
Liability insurance
Intention, 141, 156
Intentional harm, 106
Interest: 173–74, 207–208
Interference, 155–56, 158, 159, 161,
163, 235, 240, 241
Internal Revenue Service (IRS), 175,
176, 177, 179–80, 207, 275, 305,
310
Intestacy laws, 217, 218
Intruders, 2, 139–52
Inverse condemnation, 121, 234, 240,
242, 244, 245; public use and, 241–
42; tests in, 242–43

Joint nonmarried owners, 214, 222–24
Joint ownership, 217, 218;
condominiums and, 254–55
Joint tenancy with right of
survivorship, 214, 215–16, 222
Judicial sale (foreclosure), 185–87,
189–90, 191, 196, 202
Just compensation, 238, 239, 241, 244,
245

Lakes, 49, 117, 118, 132, 136; private,
124–25
Landlords, 143, 278, 293
Landmark designation/preservation,
61, 76, 81, 240
Landscaping, 17, 63
Land use regulations, 2, 61–77
Late penalty clause, 93
Latent defects, 28–29, 31
Lateral support, right to, 126, 128–29,
137–38
Law(s), 1, 2, 4: affecting homeowner
use, 77; bases for, 320–21; changing,
331; on defects, 33, 44;
environmental, 76–77, 81, 132–33,

157, 162; fair housing, 283–84, 301–304, 310; federal, 310; forfeiture, 244–45; homeowner's association and, 246, 267–68; home ownership, 296; indoor air pollution, 229–30; mechanic's lien, 87, 98–99; nuisance, 77, 163; product defects, 40, 42; product warranty/liability, 34, 43–44; property, 225; purchaser expectations and, 26–27; recreational use, 108; rental property, 277, 278, 280; search and seizure, 144; tax, 180; valid claim in, 319–20; zoning, 62, 63, 72–73, 81, 83; *see also* State laws; Zoning laws

Lawn chemicals, 229, 230, 231

Lawsuit(s), 1, 8, 31, 307, 311, 312: boundary disputes, 59; damages, 321–23; against financial institutions, 210–11; nuisance claim, 161, 163; pollution, 133–34; product warranties, 40; against sellers, 298; self-representation, 327–30; regarding trespass, 140, 147; zoning violations and, 73, 76; *see also* Civil lawsuits

Lead, 227

Lead paint, 227, 230

Lease(s), 281–83, 287, 288

Lease clauses, 277, 286, 287

Leash laws, 146, 151

Leasing portion of home, 277–95

Legal description of property, 6

Legal disputes: information needed in, 5, 6–14; *see also* Dispute resolution

Legal issues, 2, 4

Legal problems, preventing, 310–11

Legal procedure, 323–26

Legal process, 307–33

Legal recourse: for defects, 25–26, 27, 28, 29, 32–33; in flooding, 121

Legal resolution, strength of claim in, 319–20

Legal rights and remedies, 333

Legal strategies: boundary disputes, 58–59; with financial institutions, 210–11; homeowner's association disputes, 267; incidental rights, 134–37; indoor air pollution, 230–32; new home purchasers, 42–43; in takings cases, 243–44

Legislators, 232, 333; and banking complaints, 210, 211, 213

Liability: from activity, 108–109; for defects discovered after purchase, 30, 31; for injuries, 106, 107, 108, 109–10, 112–13, 146, 151; for negligence, 38–39; product defects,

40; and trespassing individual, 144–45, 149; *see also* Premises liability

Liability claims, 114, 115

Liability insurance, 14, 15, 99, 108, 113–14, 115, 272

Licensed care, 68, 272, 273–74

Licenses, 8, 46, 50, 55, 56, 59: airspace, 130; home business, 271

Lien(s), 8, 96–99, 172, 178, 179, 191, 194–95, 198, 247, 264, 308–309, 327

Lien paper/claim, 98

Lien releases, 8, 89, 93, 95, 97

Lien waiver, 95, 97, 98

Light, 116, 131–32, 136, 137

Living trust, 217, 219

Loans, 9, 10, 11, 205; sold, transferred, 189, 193, 212

Local government, and public nuisance, 161, 162

Local ordinances: air rights, 130, 131; excavation, 127; incidental rights, 136; mobile homes, 44

Local regulations, 321

Lockstep payment plan, 88, 92, 102

Look-alike ordinances, 68

Maintenance, 46: as legal protection, 78–79; rental property, 285–86, 293

Manufacturers: liability, 231; warranties, 40, 41, 42, 101

Market value, 19, 167–68; test of, 239–40

Marriage, 214, 219–22

Material defects, 27–28, 297

Materialman's lien, 96–97

Mechanic lien laws, 87, 98–99

Mechanic's lien, 8, 88–89, 96–99, 189, 194; protection against, 97–98

Mediation, 59, 94, 160, 307, 311, 317–19, 327

Medicare taxes, 178–79

Metes, 6

Misrepresentation, 22, 26, 88, 131, 302: of boundaries, 47; by seller, 29–30, 31

Mobile (manufactured) homes, 43–44, 229, 231

Modular homes, 44

Mortgage(s), 9–10, 54, 182; rules covering, 212

Mortgage brokers, 14, 206

Mortgage instruments, 205–206

Mortgage insurance, 10

Mortgage life insurance, 10

Mortgage loans, 9, 181: "due-on-sale" clause, 184, 187; prepayments, 174; *see also* Default

Mortgage points, 174, 204, 205
Mortgage principal prepayment, 207–209
Mortgagee/mortgagor, 182
Municipal courts, 308, 326
Municipal ordinances, 321
Municipal waste, 121
Municipalities: easements, 51, 52; restrictions on cases against, 121

Natural resources, 138
Navigable water, 117–18, 124
Negligence, 141, 146, 156: contractor, 101, 102; in excavation, 127; and incidental rights, 135; indoor air pollution, 231–32; and injury, 105; standards of, 105, 109
Negotiated settlement, landlord/ tenant, 290–91
Negotiated solution (foreclosure), 186, 188
Negotiation, 135, 325
Neighborhood associations, 2, 11
Neighborhood counseling center, 94
Neighborhood dispute resolution center, 58, 59, 160, 333
Neighborhood restrictions on working at home, 269–70
Net value, 221
New homes, 40, 44: implied warranties, 26; legal strategies, 42–43; liability for negligence by builders of, 38–39; special protection for, 34–36; warranties, 26, 27
Noise, 2, 3, 77
Nonconforming uses, 69
Nondisruption, rule of, 258
Nonfixtures, 12, 34, 299–300
Not in my backyard (NIMBY); questions, 67
Not responsible (defense), 157
Notice of deficiency, 179
Notice of protest, 169
Nuisance, 132, 134, 135, 147, 241: air pollution as, 231; excavation as, 127; home business as, 271; private and public, 153–63; trespass and, 142
Nuisance actions/claims, 153, 154–55: competing rights in, 155–56; defenses to, 156–57; types of, 159–60
Nuisance law, 77, 163

Oceanfront property, 125–26
Oceans, 49–50, 118, 125–26, 132
Older citizen's exclusion, 275
Older homes, 19, 26

Out-of-court foreclosure, 185, 187, 189, 191, 192
Over-55 seller, 176, 304
Ownership, 214, 215–17: of airspace, 47; of land, 129; of land below ground, 47; of land underwater, 49–50; types of, 222
Ownership rights, 116–38
Ownership status of home, personal relations and, 214–15

Pain and suffering (damages), 322
Palimony cases, 221
Parties at interest, 313
Party wall, 128–29, 136
Payment bond, 95
Performance bond, 88, 95
Perils, 18, 19
Permission to be on a property, 141–42
Permits, 128: building, 78, 80–81, 176; home business, 271
Personal injury cases, 144, 311, 322
Personal injury law, 38, 104, 105
Personal injury lawyers, 42, 114
Personal relations, 214–25
Pest inspection report, 11
Pets, 15, 66, 77, 142, 258: homeowner's association and, 261; injuries caused by, 109–10, 146; and trespass, 148
Plaintiff, 323, 325, 326
Planned communities, 51, 61–62, 125, 131, 268
Planned unit developments (PUDs), 3–4, 83, 136, 161
Plat, 6, 47
Pollutants, 227–29
Pollution, 2, 3, 116–17, 151, 152: air, 132; from neighboring property, 132–34; water, 119, 126; see also Indoor air pollution
Post-sale buy-back (foreclosure), 192
Power of sale, 184, 185
Premises liability, 104–105, 115
Prenuptial agreement, 13, 220–21
Prepayment, 203, 207–209
Presale buy-back period, 191
Presale notice (foreclosure), 186, 189–90
Prescription as defense, 157
Prescriptive right(s), 151, 162; to pollute, 134
Preservation commission, 76
Priority (defense), 156–57
Privacy (tenants), 277, 284
Private nuisance, 57, 58, 135, 154–61, 231, 259: CC&Rs, 161; damages,

158; defenses to, 156–57; determination of, 155–56; taking action, 160–61; test of, 159
Private nuisance laws, 57
Private right of action, 133: on public nuisance, 154, 162, 163
Privileged entries (private property), 142–43, 144, 146
Procedural failure, 265–66, 268
Procedural fairness, zoning and, 71–72
Product defect/failure, 101; claims for, 40–42
Product information, 84
Product liability/warranty, 113, 231, 258; laws of, 34, 43–44
Property claims, 21–22
Property damage, 18
Property disclosure statements, 12
Property interest, 235–36
Property rights, 2, 56, 59–60. *See also* Interference
Property tax assessments, 3
Property tax reports, 12
Property taxes, 164, 165–67: authorization for, 166; deductibility, 172, 173; delinquency/failure to pay, 172; remodeling and, 79
Property use: laws affecting, 77; nonpermitted, 53–54; right to, 8, 154, 161
Property value, 16
Property warranties, 12
Proprietary lease, 10, 11–12
Protecting the investment, 23
Proximate causation, 105, 109
Public claims adjuster, 22
Public health, safety, morals, 161, 163
Public nuisance, 153–63
Public use: and condemnation, 236–38; and inverse condemnation, 241–42; taking private property for, 233–45
Punitive damages, 321
Purchase money contract, 10
Purchaser, homeowner's association approval of, 262, 304
Purchaser expectations, 26–27

Quality-of-life issues, 255, 256, 259
Quiet title (action), 48, 49, 51, 59, 137
Quitclaim deed, 7, 48–49

Radon, 11, 24, 227–28, 230, 232, 297
Real estate brokers, 14, 31, 34, 230
"Reasonable care under the circumstances" standard, 104–105, 106, 115

Reasonable force, 146, 148–49, 160
Reasonableness standard, 261, 265, 268
Reasonable-use doctrine, 118–19
Record keeping, 5, 84: home business, 275; home improvement, 79; insurance, 22–23; and legal process, 311; prepayment, 209; rental property, 294–95; taxes, 164
Recovery for defects, 25–26, 32, 34
Recreational use laws, 108
Refinancing, 100, 174, 203–206, 213
Reinvestment rule, 274
Regulatory takings, 240; tests in, 242–43
Release of claim, 114
Remodeling, 40, 78, 85, 100, 248, 260: contracts for, 37; legal aspects of, 102; and taxes, 79–80
Remodeling warranties, 12
Rent, right to, 261–62
Rent increases, 287
Rental, 175: oral agreement in, 281; termination, 287–88
Rental property, 277
Renter's insurance, 19
Repairs, 78–84, 286: prior to sale, 305; responsibility for, 262–63, 286
Replacement cost, 16–17
Replacement value, 17, 18, 19, 238, 239
Rescinding the contract, 32
Residential zoning, 66
Restraining order(s), 150
Restrictions, 11–12, 136
Retaining wall, 128
Revenue-annuity mortgage (RAM), 209–10
Review of sale (foreclosure), 191–92
Rezoning, 62, 71, 74
Riders, 10, 19
Rights: competing, 155–56; ownership, 225; protection of, 137–38, 151; under tax laws, 180; use and enjoyment of property, 8, 154, 161
Rights of others, 50–55
Riparian rights, 117, 119
Rivers, 117, 118
Rules and regulations, 11–12, 248: building restrictions, 83–84; condos, co-ops, 255, 256; homeowner's associations, 249–50, 258–64, 268, 270

Sale of home, 296–306: with business use, 274–75; capital gains and improvements, 176–77; contract for

Sale of home (*cont'd.*)
  purchase, 302–303; costs and fees,
  304, 305; documents in, 5–13;
  homeowner reinvestment, 175–76;
  repairs prior to, 305
Sanitation codes, 77
Search warrant, 143–44
Second mortgage loans, 10, 100, 174,
  183, 189, 204–205, 206–207, 303
Secondary loan instruments, 10
Security, 19, 149–50
Security deposits, 291–92
Security/safety devices, 19
Self-representation (lawsuit), 327–30
Seller, 34: misrepresentation or
  concealment by, 29–30, 31;
  responsibility of, 296, 297, 298,
  305–306
Service contracts, 12
Servitude, 117
Settlement (lawsuit), 325
Settlement agreements, 312–13, 317
Severance damages, 239
Sewage, 121, 126
Share certificates, 10
Share loan(s), 10, 184–85, 190, 196,
  202, 205
Share ownership, 255–56
Small claims court, 57, 58, 59, 160,
  211, 231, 308, 319, 326, 327
Smells, 2, 3, 154, 155
Social Security taxes, 178–79
Social utility (defense), 157
Solar panels, 131–32
Sole ownership, 214, 215, 217
Sounds, 2, 3, 77, 154, 155
Sovereign immunity (doctrine), 121
Special uses, 70–71
Specialized courts, 309
Spite fence, 58
Sponsors, 257–58
State attorney general's office, 87, 89,
  90, 133, 137, 211–12, 213, 258, 267
State courts, 308–309, 310
State income tax, 178
State laws, 320: consumer protection,
  27; contracts in, 30; express
  warranties, 39; foreclosure, 182;
  indoor air pollution, 229–30;
  pollution, 132, 137; property
  ownership, 214; public nuisance,
  162; recovery, 25–26; rights/
  responsibilities of landlords and
  tenants, 280; tenant property
  storage, 292; warranties, 37, 40, 43
States, 117; and property tax, 116; and
  zoning, 63–64

Statute of limitations, 37, 134, 312
Statutory redemption, 186, 192, 197–
  98
Storm drainage, 121
Streams, 117, 122, 138: flooding, 120–
  21; permits to use, 119–20;
  pollution, 132, 133; reasonable use,
  118–19; underground, 123
Strict liability (theory), 38, 135–36
Structural conditions, 40, 303; condos,
  co-ops, 262, 263
Subcontractors, 86, 88, 93, 95, 96, 97–
  98, 108
Subdivision default, 197
Subdivisions, 3–4, 47–48, 51, 131,
  146, 240, 259, 316: covenants, 58;
  and home business, 270;
  homeowner's associations, 246, 252–
  53, 254–55, 268; and incidental
  rights, 136; land-use controls, 61–
  62; nuisance in, 161; rental units,
  279–80
Subjacent support, 129–30, 136
Sublet, right to, 261–62
Suppliers, 92, 93, 96, 97–98
Surety, 95
Surface water, 121–22
Surveys, 9, 47
Swimming pool, 15, 107, 108;
  problems related to, 112–13

Taking(s) (private property), 160–61,
  235, 236, 245: partial, 239, 240;
  raised by homeowners, 240–41
Taking/just compensation clause, 233–
  34
Takings cases, 243–44
Takings implication assessment (TIA),
  243
Tax court, 310
Tax decisions, appeals, 179–80
Tax implications of rental property,
  292–94
Tax laws, 180
Tax liens, 8, 194, 198
Tax provisions, special, 177–78
Tax rate, 165, 166–67
Tax transfer, 12
Taxes, 2, 164–80: constitutional
  challenges, 172; deductibility, 172,
  173–75, 207; in homeowner
  reinvestment sale, 175–76; for
  household workers, 178–79; record
  keeping, 84; remodeling and, 79–80;
  see also Federal income tax; Property
  taxes
Tenancy, 215

Tenancy at will, 281
Tenancy by the entireties, 215, 217, 218
Tenancy in common, 214, 215, 216, 218, 222
Tenants: and injury, 107; privacy, 277, 284; property storage, 292; rights of, 280
Termite inspection, 11, 24, 204, 297
Termiticides, 229, 232
Testamentary trust, 217, 219
Timeliness, 31
Time-share condos, 255, 263
Title insurance, 7, 8–9, 32–33, 47, 204, 303
Title insurance claims, 59
Title(s), 7, 46, 215, 296; foreclosed property, 198
Title search, 7, 8, 24–25, 47, 49
Title search company, 31, 134
Tort claim, 39
Trees, 3, 56–57, 77
Trespass, 3, 56, 129, 132, 134, 135, 154, 241: nature of, 140; by objects/substances, 147; place of, 141; preventing, 152
Trespass claim(s), 140, 147–48, 155
Trespassers, 139–52; injury to, 103, 106
Trial, 244, 325–26
Trusts, 215, 217, 218–19
Truth-in-lending, 11, 100, 190

Umbrella policy(ies), 15, 99, 108
Underground water, 117, 122–23; right to, 55
Underinsurance, 16, 17, 18
Uniform Settlement Statement, 10–11
U.S. Constitution, 309, 310, 320: Fourth Amendment, 143; Fifth Amendment, 233
U.S. Supreme Court, 66, 234, 237, 240, 309, 310
Unlawful detainer, 288
Unreasonable search, 143
Urban renewal, 234, 237
Use and enjoyment of property, 8, 135, 154, 161, 163, 246
Use zoning, 65–66

Vacation home, 3–4, 19, 136, 173, 176
Value (compensation), 238, 245
Variances, 69–70, 71, 72, 73, 270: objecting to, 75–76; standards in granting, 74–75
Vehicles, 261
View, 116, 131–32, 137
Visitors, unwanted, 139–52
Voluntary associations, 256–57

Warning (trespassers), 140, 152
Warranties, 2, 11, 12, 34–36, 296: new homes, 34–36; product, 40–41; in sale of home, 303; *see also* Breach of warranty; Express warranties; Implied warranties
Warranty deed, 6–7, 47
Warranty of merchantability, 41, 44
Warranty programs: contractors, 96; private, 39–40
Water, 116–38
Water permits, 119–20, 136
Water rights, 49, 117–26, 137, 155, 235
Waterfront property, 49–50
Wetlands, 125–26, 240
Witnesses, 42, 324–25, 326, 329
Work stoppage clause, 93
Worker's compensation insurance, 99, 107–108
Workers on the property: injury to, 107–108; insurance coverage for, 15
Working at home, 269–76

Zoning, 64–65, 240, 243–44: agencies of, 64; and air rights, 130, 131; and building alterations, 83; effect on property owners, 62–63; esthetic, 68; existing uses, 69; and incidental rights, 136; and procedural fairness, 71–72; seeking modification in, 73–74; spot, 69, 70, 71, 236; use, 65–66; and working at home, 269–70
Zoning issues, 67–68, 259
Zoning laws, 2, 44, 55, 62, 63, 72–73, 81, 301, 333
Zoning regulations, 61–77, 78, 157, 162, 234; and rental property, 277, 278